The Rice Economies

For Sandy

The Rice Economies

*Technology and Development
in Asian Societies*

FRANCESCA BRAY

Basil Blackwell

© Francesca Bray 1986

First published 1986
Basil Blackwell Ltd
108 Cowley Road, Oxford OX4 1JF, UK

First published in the USA 1986
Basil Blackwell Inc.
432 Park Avenue South, Suite 1503,
New York, NY 10016, USA

British Library Cataloguing in Publication Data

Bray, Francesca
The rice economies.
1. Rice trade — East Asia.
2. Rice trade — Asia, South eastern.
I. Title
338.1'7318'095   HD9066.E18

ISBN 0–631–14877–9

Library of Congress Cataloging in Publication Data

Bray, Francesca
The rice economies.
Bibliography: p.
Includes index.
1. Rice trade — Asia.
2 Asia — Economic conditions — 1945–
3. Agriculture — Economic aspects — Asia.
I. Title.
HD9066.A7B73 1986   338.1'7318'095   85–30819

ISBN 0–631–14877–9

Typeset by Oxford Publishing Services, Oxford
Printed in Great Britain by T.J. Press Ltd, Padstow

Contents

Figures and tables

Figures

Tables

Chinese dynasties

Zhou:	1066–221 BC
Spring and Autumn period:	722–481 BC
Warring States:	*c.*403–221 BC
Qin:	221–206 BC
Han:	206 BC–AD 220
Three Kingdoms:	220–80
Six Dynasties:	222–589
Northern and Southern Dynasties:	317–589
Sui:	581–618
Tang:	618–907
Five Dynasties:	907–60
Northern Song:	960–1127
Southern Song:	1127–1279
Yuan:	1279–1368
Ming:	1368–1644
Qing:	1644–1911
Republic of China:	1911–49

Japanese eras

(There is little agreement as to the exact nomenclature and dates of the periods of Japanese history; the following is a rough guide.)

Jōmon:	To *c*.200 BC
Yayoi:	200 BC–AD 250
Kofun:	250–552
Yamato:	300–710
Asuka:	552–645
Nara:	645–794
Heian:	794–1185
Kamakura:	1185–1392
Muromachi:	1473–1568
Momoyama:	1568–1600
Tokugawa:	1600–1868
Modern:	1868 to date
Meiji:	1868–1912
Taisho:	1912–26
Shōwa	1926–

Preface

While the social and economic history of Europe undergoes continual refinement, that of Asia often remains at a level one can at best call primitive, for lack not so much of information (though this excuse is often given) as of appropriate methods of analysis.

Most Asian states were traditionally agrarian and remain so today; it is thus crucial to understand the process of agricultural change if we are to make sense either of their historical development or of such contemporary problems as the differential impact of the 'Green Revolution'.

Such features of a society as the ratio between land and population, or the technical methods employed in different occupations, are hardly matters of chance, as the difficulties encountered by the proponents of 'intermediate' or 'appropriate technology' indicate. But although a number of studies have been devoted to investigating technology transfer and diffusion in agriculture, and to examining how social and economic factors may affect attitudes to technological change, the nature of the existing technology itself, its roots in material culture, the inherent constraints and dynamics which shape the development of a particular system – these are relatively unknown. Yet very basic facts, such as a particular crop's fertiliser requirements or the size or number of grains produced by each plant, what one might perhaps call the basic conditions of production, may have far-reaching effects on economic development as a whole. Indeed, they have shaped the course of agricultural development in the West no less than in Asia.

While working on the history of Chinese agriculture as part of Joseph Needham's series *Science and Civilisation in China* (Bray 1984), I became increasingly aware of the importance of understanding the evolution of China's agrarian base if one wished to investigate the 'Needham question'. This, put simply, runs: why, since until about 1500 China was ahead of Europe in many branches of science and technology, was there no scientific revolution or rise of capitalism in China? Although China's agrarian economy was unlikely to provide a complete answer, it seemed to me that it would certainly furnish crucial elements of any satisfactory explanation of China's failure to develop capitalism. And since rice had been the most important crop in China since about AD 800, perhaps a closer examination of rice cultivation systems would provide some clues.

I was encouraged to pursue this path after noticing that in North China, where dry cereals were the staple crops, a pattern of development of technology and of relations of production rather similar to that of Northwest Europe had started to emerge in the early centuries AD, typified by the formation of large estates, centrally managed and heavily dependent upon economies of scale such as the use of animal-powered machinery (Bray 1980). Nomadic invasions and civil unrest then pushed the political centre south to China's rice regions, and although large-scale ownership of land persisted throughout China's history, large-scale management became a thing of the past. The Chinese government, whether through benevolence or self-interest, traditionally supported the rights of the individual peasant against aristocratic or gentry landowners, but this was a position easier to sustain when rice cultivation was the mainstay of the economy, because even though land-ownership might be concentrated, farms were predominantly small family farms. Peasant farmers were easier to tax than gentry, and the persistence of peasant farming must surely be a factor in the longevity of the Chinese empire. But what was it that allowed peasant farming to survive in the teeth of gentry ambitions? That government encouragement was not sufficient was demonstrated by what happened during the early dynasties in North China. Unlike Gourou (1984: 8), who denies any determining influence of rice cultivation on the societies in which it is practised, I felt sure that the reason must lie in the conditions of rice production.

It was a period of fieldwork in Malaysia which first brought home to me how inappropriate it was to apply the eurocentric model to Asian rice cultivation. One instance: the introduction of new technology (the Green Revolution 'package' of irrigation, high-yielding rice varieties, chemical fertilisers, tractors, etc.) and the commercialisation of Malaysian rice production was bound, according to many social scientists, to result in the differentiation of the peasantry and the emergence of capitalist farming, as similar innovations had done earlier in the West. There are, of course, several ways in which 'capitalist farming' can be defined, but it seemed to me then, as it still does a decade later, that none of them could be aptly applied to what was happening in Malaysia, or indeed in the other rice-growing areas which I had studied. What seemed to me to be the most striking and significant feature common to rice economies, as described both in historical documents and in contemporary literature, was that although the ownership of land tended to become concentrated when methods were improved and production increased, economies of scale did not apply as in Europe, and the basic unit of management remained the small family farm.

One question I was anxious to address was that of historical change. Asian societies have most often been considered static. The concepts of the Asiatic Mode of Production, of hydraulic societies and of Asian feudalism all presume that an essentially unchanging rural world was for centuries systematically drained of its riches by a political elite, thus discouraging any tendencies towards development. Yet as Perkins (1969) demonstrates, Chinese agriculture developed and expanded sufficiently rapidly to maintain (and sometimes improve) overall living standards at least until 1800. Was this growth without historical change, or was it perhaps historical change of a different type from that with which we are familiar?

It has frequently been suggested that the key to understanding Asian societies and their history lies in their dependence upon irrigation. But apart from any other objections one might have, such concepts as 'hydraulic society', 'oriental despotism', or even the more general idea of an Asiatic Mode of Production, seem to obscure rather than to clarify; they can hardly be used to explicate history since they imply inherent stagnation and the quasi-impossibility of endogenous historical change. Of course the presence of irrigation works does affect technical and social organisation, as we shall see in chapter 3, though it may do so in a variety of ways. But as the case of contemporary India suggests, the presence *per se* of irrigation works is not sufficient to explain many of the features characteristic of Asian societies. More significant is the association of irrigation with labour-intensive methods of cultivation and, more particularly, with the labour-intensive cultivation of rice.

What follows, then, is an essay on the historical development of a technology and its relations to social and economic change. 'History' is taken to be a continuum, not ending at some arbitrary date like 1700 or 1949, and contemporary events are just as vital elements in my argument as purely historical data. But although I do not make a break between past, present and future, the conclusions can only be at the level of implications and lay no claim to the status of predictions. Some strategies may seem, in the light of historical experience, more appropriate than others to the problems of rural Asia today: that is as much as one can say.

The book is thus a historical argument deriving from the idea of the specificity of wet-rice cultivation, perhaps the most labour-and land-intensive cultivation system in the world. The technical specificity of rice cultivation has for some years been a fundamental concept among Japanese scholars (e.g. Kanazawa 1971; Ishikawa 1967), but they have not used it to explore long-term historical change. Here I have tried to use evidence, historical, economic and anthropological, from a wide range of Asian societies to construct an argument of general rather than national validity. It may be objected that I have not dealt fully with Asia, having largely omitted the nations of the subcontinent as well as contemporary Burma and North Korea, on which information is very hard to come by. I have chosen to concentrate on East and Southeast Asia because I know them best, but also because rice is indisputably the most important food grain in all their economies.

In a study of this nature one cannot hope to do everything. This is not a comprehensive account of the range of rice cultivation techniques, nor does it provide a detailed account of the history of rice in each Asian country. It does not contain a comprehensive analysis of the costs and benefits of the introduction of the New Technology, nor do the references cited provide a complete bibliography, which in itself would stretch to several hundred pages.

In defence of this undertaking I should say that for me the implications of such a study reach beyond the rice economies of Asia. The contrast between a 'Western model' of agricultural development and the 'model' which can be abstracted from Asia's rice economies suggests a spectrum of agricultural systems, each using land, labour and capital with a different degree of intensity which in some measure determines its dynamic of evolution and its pattern of adaptation to such phenomena as modern capitalism.

I am grateful to the British Academy and the Royal Society for financing a field-trip to Malaysia in 1976–7, to the British Council and to the Universities' China Committee for supporting a study-tour to China in 1980, and to the Leverhulme Trust for providing a most generous two-year fellowship in 1982–4, which enabled me to spend several months in Asia. The British Academy helped me again in 1982 with a Wolfson Fellowship which allowed me to spend several months in Paris working on archival material. Dr Joseph Needham and the East Asian History of Science Library, or Needham Research Institute as it is now, have given me unfailing support throughout.

It would be impossible to thank by name all those who have given me help and advice on this project. The villagers of Bunut Susu, and especially their *imam*, Encik Abdul Rahman bin Haji Suleiman, were its inspiration; it was through the kindness of the Kemubu Agricultural

Development Authority staff and their economist, Puan Rohaini Zakaria, that I made their acquaintance. In Singapore I received generous help from the staff of the Institute for Southeast Asian Studies, in Kuala Lumpur from Wan Ahmad Radzi and from Puan Fadillah Ibrahim and their families, in Kota Baru from Datuk Haji Yussuf Bangs, Encik Johan Arif and Robert and Pauline Whyte. In Penang the staff of the Centre for Policies Research kindly allowed me access to their invaluable collection. In Hong Kong I have been given help and encouragement by, among others, Peter and Ei-Yoke Lisowski, Mr and Mrs P. L. Lam and George Hicks, who has been most generous in providing material from his collection on the economies of Southeast Asia. In 1977 a visit to Taiwan was made fruitful through the good offices of the Joint Committee for Rural Reconstruction, and Professor T. T. Chang of the International Rice Research Institute gave me valuable assistance in the Philippines. A study-tour of China in 1980 was arranged through the kindness of Academia Sinica; to that organisation, and to all the distinguished scholars of agricultural development and history who kindly spared time to discuss their work with an undistinguished foreigner, I am most grateful. In Japan I must mention Professors Hayashi Takeshi, Kojima Reiitsu and Tada Hirokazu and their colleagues at the Institute of Developing Economies, Professors Ichimura Shinichi, Ishii Yoneo and Tsubouchi Yoshihiro of the Institute of Southeast Asian Studies, Kyōto, as well as Professors Katō Yuzo and Nakaoka Tetsurō and Drs Fujimoto Akimi and Christian Daniels, all of whom were kind enough to discuss my work with me.

I have been fortunate in the encouragement of my directors at the CNRS, M. Lucien Bernot and M. Jacques Gernet, and of Ben Farmer and Sir Joseph Hutchinson in Cambridge. My colleagues at the Needham Research Institute, Gregory Blue and Timothy Brook, were kind enough to read and comment on parts of the manuscript. Sean Magee of Basil Blackwell has renewed my faith in editors. Without Sandy Robertson this book would never have been written, and my gratitude goes beyond words.

Centre National de la Recherche Scientifique
Paris, October 1985

Acknowledgements

The author and the publishers would like to thank the following for permission to use figures and tables from, or base figures and tables on, their own copyright material. Dr T. T. Chang, International Rice Research Institute, Manila, for figure 1.1, redrawn from his article 'The origin, evolution, dissemination and diversification of African and Asian Rices', *Euphytica* 1976; Routledge and Kegan Paul, London, for figure 2.3, from Hsiao-T'ung Fei, *Peasant Life in China: A Field Study of Country Life in the Yangtze Valley*; Professor Keiji Nagahara, Department of Economics, Hitotsubashi University, for figure 2.5, from Hideo Kuroda, 'Chūsei nōgyō jutsu no yōsō', in Nagahara and Yamaguchi (eds), *Nōgyō, nōsankoko* (Nihon Hyoronsha, Tokyo, 1983); International Rice Research Institute, Manila, for figure 2.7, from R. Barker, 'Yield and fertiliser input', *IRRI*, 1978; Professor Shigeru Ishikawa, Aoyama University, Tokyo, for figure 3.1, from Ishikawa, *Economic Development in Asian Perspective* (Tokyo, 1967); Professor Yoneo Ishii, Centre for South East Asian Studies, Kyoto University, for figure 3.6, from Yoshiro Kaida, 'Irrigation and drainage: present and future', in Ishii (ed.), *Thailand: A Rice-Growing Society* (Hawaii UP, 1978); University of Malaya, Kuala Lumpur, Malaysia, for figure 4.2, from J. T. Purcal, *Rice Economy: Employment and Income in Malaysia* (East-West Center Press, Honolulu, 1972); Board of Trustees, Stanford University Press, for figure 5.1, from Thomas C. Smith, *The Agrarian Origins of Modern Japan* (Stanford UP, 1959); Dr Janice Stargardt, Cambridge Project on Ancient Civilization in South East Asia, for table 3.1, based on table 21 from Stargardt, *Satingpra I: The Environmental and Economic Archaeology of South Thailand* (Oxford and Singapore, 1983).

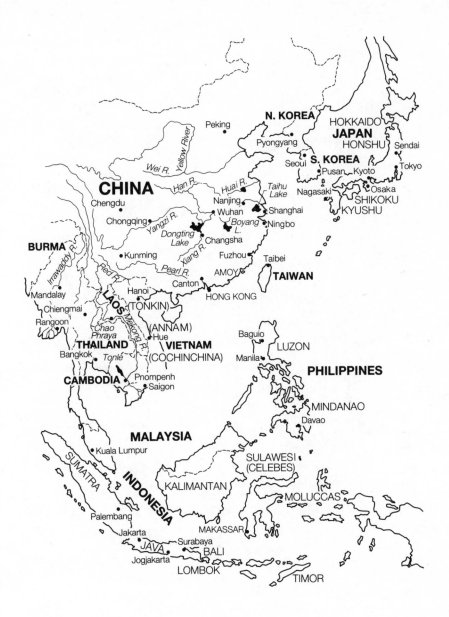

Map 1   East and Southeast Asia

Map 2　Central provinces of China

Map 3 States of peninsular Malaysia (showing Muda and Kemubu regions)

Introduction

Eurocentric models of historical change

European historical methodology has understandably been profoundly marked by the growth of capitalism, but it is doubtful to what extent models derived from Europe's highly specific experience are applicable to other parts of the world. Historians attempting to interpret Asian history find themselves wrestling with such intractable categories as 'feudalism' or 'peasants' which, despite their reassuring vagueness, rarely seem to fit the case exactly. Evading the issue entirely, one long-standing Western tradition recognises the essential 'otherness' of Asian societies by attributing to them a timelessness and unchanging quality encapsulated in the concept of the Asian Mode of Production. Others, recognising that all societies change eventually, and faced with the necessity of accounting for such awkward facts as the development of commerce and commodity production in pre-modern India and China, or industrialisation and the emergence of capitalism in Meiji Japan, have preferred to think of Asia as following basically the same path as Europe, but less successfully and less rapidly. Thus Marxist historians in China and Japan categorise a vast span of Chinese history (from about 200 BC to 1911 or 1949) as feudal, with 'sprouts of capitalism' emerging intermittently during the past four or five centuries but withering before they bore fruit (see Grove and Esherick 1980; Brook 1981). Non-Marxist historians too, especially when explaining the failure to develop capitalism (or the contrary in the case of Japan), usually measure off Asian societies point for point against a European model of development, to see where they are lacking (Elvin 1973; Tang 1979; Yamamura 1979; Jones 1981).

Both of these methods are essentially negative, the one denying the occurrence of any significant change, the other obscuring the specificity of non-European societies. If we look only for what is typical of Europe, the significant features of a less familiar society may simply escape our notice. Over the last four centuries European society has been completely transformed, and advanced capitalism has accustomed us to a breakneck pace of change. By comparison it is not surprising that Asian societies seem to have stood still. Yet where adequate documents exist it is not difficult to show that in Asian societies too the forces of production were expanded and relations of production transformed – though not always in the way one might expect. The difficulty lies in accounting for the nature of such changes: if the dynamics of change differ from those we have identified as operating in European history, then it is not surprising that our traditional models fail adequately to interpret change in non-European societies, or even to acknowledge its existence.

While it is easy to appreciate that eurocentric models will generally prove inadequate to explain the evolution of non-European societies, it is not so easy to construct appropriate alternatives. One important obstacle is our failure (in the main) to recognise the relativity of our conception of technological progress. Changes in technology are clearly one key to explicating economic history, though of course there is considerable debate as to the exact degree to which technological development determines, affects, or is simply an expression of changes in the social formation. But what exactly constitutes technological development? Here all our doubts seem to evaporate. Philosophers like Gehlen (1965) and Habermas (1971) have pointed out the immanent connection between the contemporary evaluation of technology and the 'rationality' (in the Weberian sense) that prevails in capitalist society. To be more specific, in a society where relatively scarce and expensive wage-labour is the basis of production, technical progress is largely evaluated in terms of efficiency in replacing labour. Yet this highly specific model of technological advance is generally presumed to be universal in its application. Although one can easily envisage situations in which different criteria might apply, little attempt has been made to hypothesise alternative paths of technological development or to examine the social and economic implications of such differences.

If we consider the case of agriculture, we find that technological progress is generally construed as a sequence from primitive tools like digging-sticks or hoes to more complex instruments like ploughs or harrows, culminating in the mechanical sophistication of tractors, combine-harvesters and crop-spraying aeroplanes. To this one would add the application of scientific methods to such agricultural procedures as crop selection, nutrition and weeding, resulting in the laboratory breeding of new crop strains with desirable characteristics, and the industrial production of chemical fertilisers, herbicides and pesticides. 'Progress' seems to lie chiefly in the increasingly efficient substitution of alternative forms of energy for human labour. Now labour-saving changes in agriculture have three possible effects: first, they may enable the same number of workers to bring larger areas of land under cultivation; secondly, they may enable the same area to be cultivated by fewer workers, thus liberating the surplus labour for some other employment; and thirdly, they may allow the same area of land to be more intensively cultivated without increasing the number of workers.

The first type of change is of particular importance where land is plentiful and labour scarce, as it has been in much of the New World; it is not surprising, for example, that it was in underpopulated Australia and the United States, as the world market for wheat expanded in the later nineteenth century, that the reaper-binder and the combine-harvester were developed (Jones 1979). The second type of change is important where labour is in high demand, scarce and expensive, as was the case in Europe in the early stages of the development of capitalism. As Boserup (1981: 99) says: 'There was usually keen competition for scarce labour [between agriculture and manufactures], and most often agriculture lost in this competition. Nothing could be more inappropriate than to characterise the European economy in this period as a labour surplus economy. On the contrary, one of the most serious problems in the period of pre-industrial urbanisation in Western and Central Europe was insufficiency of food production, due not to shortage of land, but to shortage of labour.' In fact in the early stages of the 'Agricultural Revolution' demands for labour generally grew, as cropping frequency increased and as techniques became more intensive in response to the greater demand for agricultural produce (Chambers 1967). At first the greater demand for agricultural labour could be accommodated by population increase, but as industrialisation advanced and the competition for labour grew, it became both necessary and (given advances in engineering and design) possible to develop labour-saving agricultural machinery such as the multiple-furrow plough, patent seed-drills, threshers and so on.

Changes of the third type are particularly valuable where land is in short supply; they do not necessarily displace labour but may increase its effectiveness by eliminating bottlenecks or performing tasks more thoroughly. The substitution for hoeing of deep ploughing with horses in nineteenth-century Japan, and the twentieth-century introduction of hand-tillers and transplanting machines are instances of this (see chapter 2).

But in similar situations of land shortage and abundant labour – such as are characteristic of most regions where rice is intensively farmed – a fourth type of technical change is equally important, namely changes which increase both land productivity and labour demands. In areas such as the Yangzi Delta or Java, the introduction of high-yielding and quick-ripening crop varieties was extremely valuable because it not only increased the yields of a single crop but also permitted multi-cropping; by the same token it increased the number of operations and the quantity of labour required (which does not necessarily mean that the productivity of labour was reduced). Where rural populations are dense and opportunities for alternative employment few, technical changes which absorb labour and reduce agricultural underemployment are preferable to those which increase output at the cost of reducing the labour force. Advances of this fourth type, while frequently dependent upon highly skilled labour, do not necessarily require mechanical sophistication; indeed it is not unusual for agricultural implements to become simpler as cultivation techniques become more sophisticated and productivity rises (Boserup 1965).

Certain economists (Hayami and Ruttan 1979: 6) have characterised technological changes which produce the first or second effects just described as *labour-substitutes*, while those of the third and fourth type are essentially *land-substitutes*.

It is clear, then, that the development of agricultural techniques may take more than one direction, and that this will probably be significantly influenced by such factors as population density, demands for labour in other sectors, tenurial relations, or cropping patterns, to mention but a few. If technological changes are introduced rather than developing spontaneously, then it is crucial to ensure that they are of the appropriate type. Introducing labour-saving machinery in a poor country which is heavily overpopulated is bound to lead to economic problems and social upheavals, as the literature on contemporary development makes abundantly plain. Nevertheless, just as international banks and Third World governments alike have been dogged in their conviction that the development of heavy industry is an essential prerequisite for more general economic development (a belief which Lenin was perhaps justified in holding but which hardly applies to most nations today [Dumont 1983–4: passim]), so the majority of agricultural ministries and development agencies working in Asia have aimed at the 'modernisation' of local agriculture along lines with which, it is true, we are familiar from the experience of Western Europe and the New World, but which in many respects seem incompatible with prevailing conditions in East Asia and elsewhere.

An alternative model?

A significant difference between the technical development of Western grain-farming (described in appendix A) and Asian rice cultivation, which has important implications for socio-economic change, is that while wet-rice agriculture has enormous potential for increasing land productivity, most improvements are either scale-neutral and relatively cheap, or else they involve increasing not capital inputs but inputs of manual labour (see chapter 5). It has often been assumed that this implies a corresponding reduction in the productivity of labour, but this is not necessarily true. Where a transition from broadcast sowing to transplanting, or from single-to double-cropping is made, the increases in yield will certainly outstrip concomitant rises in labour inputs. The additional labour requirements are spread out over the year, and for most tasks household labour suffices to run a wet-rice smallholding. But even small farms will usually have to exchange or hire labour to cope with the bottlenecks of transplanting and harvesting, and farmers within a community will often agree to stagger planting and harvesting so that effective rotas for labour exchange or hire can be established; like the demands of irrigation, this is an important factor in creating a spirit of communality within rice communities (Liefrinck 1886; Embree 1946; Takahashi 1970; Bray and Robertson 1980) – which is not to say that individualism and conflict are absent, as we shall see in chapter 6.

The inconspicuous, low-cost nature of many improvements to wet-rice cultivation, and the association of highly productive techniques with a form of tenurial relations, namely smallholding, regarded by many as backward, have contributed to the image of Asian economies as historically stagnating and resistant to change. Yet there is an abundance of evidence to show that great progress has been made over the centuries in increasing the productivity of rice-land. Furthermore, the development of rice agriculture has often been accompanied by the growth of commercial cropping, trade and manufacture, as well as by significant changes in the relations of production.

The significance of a model of development for rice economies

There is good historical evidence to suggest that the dynamic underlying the development of the forces of production in wet-rice societies is very different from that manifest in the European transition from feudalism to capitalism. The model of technological and economic progress accepted as generally valid is directly derived from the Western experience (see appendix A): it postulates the superior efficiency of large units of production, culminating in the rationality of modern capitalism. But in Asian agriculture the historical trend was towards not larger but smaller units of production – are we then to conclude that Asian agriculture stagnated or became increasingly inefficient as time went by? If we take as our yardstick the isolated examples of late nineteenth-century China or contemporary Java, with their dense and impoverished populations and cripplingly subdivided landholdings, we might perhaps be justified in such a conclusion. But a broader historical perspective forbids such a view. How would such an interpretation account for medieval China or eighteenth-century Japan, where changes in farming techniques did reduce the size of holdings but were accompanied by spectacular increases in agricultural productivity and in commercial and manufacturing activity? And how would we explain contemporary events in East and Southeast Asia, where the incursions of advanced capitalist technology have failed to modify basic patterns of land tenure and rural production?

The universal pretensions of our Western model of technological and economic progress have been strengthened by various scholars' claims to find 'feudal relations', 'sprouts of capitalism', or other elements of European social formations in non-European societies. But the recognition of these superficial resemblances often serves to obscure more fundamental and determinant differences. Reams of paper have been covered in the attempt to explain Song China's failure to develop capitalism, because historians have identified in Song society certain features believed to have contributed to the development of capitalism in Europe. If such phenomena as the high level of scientific and technical knowledge, the existence of a free market in land, or the advanced development of commercial institutions are taken in isolation from the relations of production, then the problem seems valid enough. But if we situate them in the context of Song China's economic base and the general dynamic of expansion of the forces of production, then we see that 'China's failure to develop capitalism' is simply a red herring, distracting us from a more thorough and fruitful examination of the specific characteristics of China's economic evolution. An obsession with classifying India as 'feudal' or 'non-feudal' has, as Mukhia (1981) shows, similarly diverted attention from India's specific path of historical development. Political scientists have identified Japan as the single nation in Asia to conform to the Western model of transition from feudalism to industrial capitalism, yet profound dissimilarities between Japanese and Western capitalism continue to puzzle them. Such mysteries are unlikely to be solved until it is recognised that the superficial similarities between Japan and Europe mask differences deeply rooted in the productive forces.

Clearly the role of the technological base in determining overall social change must not be overestimated. A model based on technical dynamics alone cannot account for the political, institutional and external factors which have played such a crucial role in shaping the Asian nations. Yet despite their many cultural and political differences, I hope to show that societies which depend for their subsistence on wet-rice cultivation have in common a basic dynamic of technical evolution, which differs from the model of progress derived from the Western experience, and which imposes very different constraints upon social and economic development. A basic model of this nature serves an important purpose: it not only focuses our attention upon specific characteristics of non-Western societies but situates them in an evolutionary rather than a static framework. It should thus enable us to supersede the image of Asia as unchanging, as a Europe *manquée*, and help us to explicate the history of Asian societies in their own terms. Last but not least, it should provide fresh and perhaps constructive insights into contemporary processes of change in Asia.

The first three chapters of the book are an investigation of the technical means by which rice cultivation has been intensified and levels of land- and labour-productivity raised. The first chapter considers the potential of the rice-plant itself; the second looks at ways in which land use is developed by rice-farmers and the scope for rationalisation and mechanisation; the third is a study of water control, an essential feature of any developed rice technology. The fourth chapter makes a distinction between 'mechanical' technologies, like that of European agriculture, and 'skill-oriented' technologies such as rice cultivation; from this perspective it looks at rice cultivation as a basis for more general economic development and diversification, with particular reference to its links with petty commodity production and rural industrialisation. The fifth chapter considers the issues involved in the planned development of rice economies, taking as its point of departure a historical evaluation of the relative efficacy of capital and labour inputs in improving rice technology. Rice societies are a paradoxical combination of individualism and communalism, and the sixth chapter looks at how technological development affects relations of production; is a socialist reorganisation of rice production beneficial and stable, and to what extent has the impact of capitalism resulted in a shift towards capitalist farming and the differentiation of the peasantry?

1

The rice-plant: diversity and intensification

Rice is the staple food of almost half the population of the world, second only to wheat in its importance. The annual world rice harvest in 1981–2 came to over 400 million tonnes, from a cultivated area of about 145 million hectares (Swaminathan 1984: 65), while in 1978–9 world production of wheat was 450 million tonnes from 230 hectares (Fischer 1981: 249). Over the centuries rice has become an increasingly popular food not only in Asia but throughout the world, replacing tubers, millets and other food grains as the staple food in island Southeast Asia and parts of Europe, Africa and Latin America; it has become an increasingly important export crop in the USA and Australia. But the bulk of the world's rice crop is produced in monsoon Asia, the zone where it was first domesticated: 90% in monsoon Asia as a whole, and 64% in East and Southeast Asia alone (Swaminathan 1984: 65).[1] Despite a recent preference for bread and other wheat products among the wealthier classes, rice is by far the most widely consumed and cultivated crop in the Far East.[2]

This chapter will describe briefly the historical advance of rice cultivation through East and Southeast Asia, showing how the natural characteristics of the plant, its flexibility and enormous potential for breeding varieties suitable to almost any ecological or economic circumstance, permitted the increasingly intensive use of land and encouraged an ever greater number of both subsistence and commercial farmers to rely on it as their staple food.

The origins of Asian rice

The origins of domesticated Asian rice are still undetermined, but the distribution of wild rices (figure 1.1) suggests a centre, or centres, of

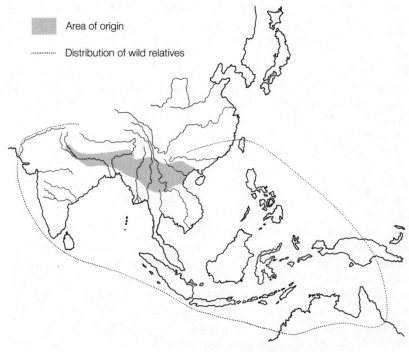

□ Area of origin

··········· Distribution of wild relatives

Figure 1.1   Area of origin of domesticated rice
(from Chang 1976a)

domestication somewhere in the piedmont zone of Assam, Upper Burma and Thailand, Southwest China and North Vietnam.[3] There is linguistic and ethnographic evidence to suggest that the earliest staple foods grown in monsoon Asia were tuber crops and millets, which were later superseded by rice (Kano 1946). The earliest archeological finds of domesticated rice to date come from China, from the site of Hemudu in Zhejiang province (near Ningbo in the Yangzi Delta). Excavations began in 1976 and are still continuing. The earliest stratum of Hemudu village, which is situated at the edge of a marsh, has been carbon-dated to about 5000 BC; the sheer volume of rice remains shows that the villagers were not proto-farmers but relied heavily on cultivated rice as a food supply even at that early date (Zhejiang CPAM 1976, 1978; Zhejiang Prov. Mus. 1978; You 1979).

A great number of Central and Southern Chinese neolithic sites of slightly later date contain remains of domesticated rice, among them several fourth millennium sites in the Yangzi Delta and further upstream, and a couple of sites in Guangdong which may date back to

2000 or 3000 BC (Yang 1978). There are also two early sites in North Thailand, Non Nok Tha and Ban Chiang (dated to about 5000 and 4500 BC respectively), which 'strongly suggest the presence of rice-farming in the northeastern Thai plateau prior to 4500 BC' (Gorman 1977: 433).[4] Gorman suggests that the domestication of rice began in naturally marshy areas in upland Southeast Asia about 9,000 years ago and that, as their skills improved, early rice-farmers were able to occupy non-marshy sites such as Ban Chiang and Non Nok Tha. Such a hypothesis seems consistent with the evidence from China and Thailand, and from Vietnam, where wet-rice cultivation was established in the Red River Delta by the mid-third millennium BC or perhaps earlier (Higham 1984). There is also linguistic evidence for a domestication of rice in the extended piedmont zone of Southeast Asia.[5]

India was for long believed to be the original centre of rice domestication, not only because of the varietal diversity of Indian rices (Vavilov 1949: 29), but also because until recently the supposed remains of rice from sites of the great Harappan civilisation were, at 1800 BC, the earliest known in the world (Vishnu-Mittre 1974). The Harappan 'rice' remains proved to be a misidentification however (Reed 1977: 918), and with the earliest Indian evidence now dated to about 1500 BC (Vishnu-Mittre 1977: 585), there is a clear case for giving preference to the Southeast Asian piedmont zone as the original home of domesticated rice.

Rice cultivation was probably a rather late introduction to Japan. The earliest evidence comes from sites in the southern island of Kyūshū which can be dated back to about 300–400 BC,[6] and from Kyūshū it spread gradually northwards, reaching the northern tip of Honshū before the Yayoi period ended in the mid-third century AD (Sahara, forthcoming; Tamaki and Hatade 1974: 58). Japanese rices are assumed to have originated in the Yangzi Delta, and there are three possible routes by which they might have reached Japan: overland through North China to Korea and then by sea; by sea from the Yangzi Delta to Korea and thence to Japan; or by sea from the Yangzi Delta directly to Kyūshū. The second hypothesis is currently favoured on the basis of associated tool typologies (Gina Barnes, pers. comm. 1984).

As we have seen, rice was cultivated from very early times on the mainland of Southeast Asia, but tuber crops or millets remained the staple crops of much of the Malay peninsula and Indonesian archipelago until rather late. The magnificent carvings of Borobudur (*c.*ninth century AD) depict millet but not rice, and rice seems to have been introduced to Java, not by land through Siam and then Malaya, but by sea from India during the later period of Hindu influence. Irrigated rice appears to have been introduced to Java in medieval times (perhaps before the establishment of the kingdom of Majapahit in the thirteenth century), whence it spread gradually to the scattered communities of the Southern Malay peninsula, though dates for this are generally uncertain (Hill 1977: 20–7; van Setten 1979: 1–9). However the northern kingdoms of Malaya, Kedah and Kelantan, seem to have adopted wet-rice cultivation somewhat earlier, deriving their skills from the mainland Southeast Asian tradition (unlike the other Malay and Indonesian regions, which refer to wet-rice fields as *sawah*, the Northern Malays use the term *bendang*). Furthermore in early medieval times a sophisticated system of wet-rice cultivation flourished on the Songkla peninsula in Southern Thailand, an area which probably had close trade relations with the Cambodian state of Funan (Stargardt 1983).

Although rice was a relative late-comer to the outer fringes of the Far Eastern world, it always arrived to stay. Once people became accustomed to eating rice they were loath to change back to other foods, and once they had built rice-fields on their land they were understandably reluctant to abandon them. The adaptability of the rice-plant meant that its cultivation was not confined to well-watered river valleys or deltas: it could be grown on steep slopes cleared of virgin forest in Borneo, along deeply flooded river-banks in Burma and Bangladesh, or on salt-marshes won back from the sea along the China coast. Under such difficult conditions as these crops might be small, but where conditions were slightly more favourable rich harvests could be had, and most of the great civilisations of the Far East, the Chinese dynasties, the kingdoms of South India and Ceylon, the Angkorian empire, Srivijaya and many more, were founded on the wealth of their rice-fields. Let us look at the natural characteristics of the rice-plant which account for its historical popularity and success.

Natural characteristics of rice

Rice is by nature a swamp plant, and by far the greatest number of varieties are grown in standing water, but there are also dry rices which are grown on steeply sloping hillside fields (Freeman 1970; Geddes 1976; Hill 1977). Generally speaking, dry or hill rice varieties will not grow in wet fields, nor can wet rices be grown in upland fields, but some interchangeable varieties do exist. It has been suggested that dry-rice cultivation developed earlier than wet, on the grounds that the techniques involved are less complex (see Watabe 1977: 16), but most botanists reject this on morphological grounds (Grist 1975: 27). Hill rice can only be grown by systems of shifting cultivation and does not, therefore, provide a suitable base for the development of complex technical systems or of the related social and economic organisations, and so our discussion will be confined to wet-rice systems.

Rice is an extremely adaptable plant, with an efficient system of air passages connecting the roots and the shoot which enables it to grow in dry upland soils, in irrigated fields, or along flooded river-beds. It is largely self-pollinated, but cross-pollination does occur in degrees varying between less than 1% and as much as 30% (Grist 1975: 72), and a very large number of wild varieties exists.[7] The range of variation in rice is so great that no internationally recognised system of classification has yet been developed, although repeated attempts have been made ever since the Rice Congress at Valencia in 1914 urged 'the formation of a real botanical classification of the varieties of cultivated rice'.[8]

Among the Asian domesticated rices, *Oryza sativa*, two sub-species are commonly distinguished, *indica* and *japonica*, both of which include glutinous and non-glutinous varieties. A list of the most important differences beween the sub-species is given by Grist (1975: 94). The contrasts which most immediately strike the non-specialist are that *indica* rices have longer, more slender grains which usually remain separate when cooked, while *japonicas* have shorter, rounder and more translucent grains which quickly become slightly sticky. The *indica/japonica* distinction was first drawn in the late 1920s by a group of Japanese botanists, on the basis of morphology, hybrid sterility and geographic distribution. But some Asian rices, notably those of Indonesia, do not seem to conform to either category, and in 1958 a third sub-group named *javanica* was proposed to designate the *bulu* and *gundil* varieties of Indonesia (Grist 1975: 93).

In China both *indica* and *japonica* varieties have been cultivated since neolithic times (Bray 1984: 484). The earliest Chinese dictionary, the *Shuowen jiezi* of AD 100, was the first work to contain the terms *geng* and *xian* which have been used to designate *japonica* and *indica* rices in Chinese ever since (ibid.: 487). Not surprisingly, the majority of rice varieties grown in India are *indicas* and in Japan *japonicas*. Most rices grown in the tropical zones belong to the *indica* and *javanica* groups, which tend to have a fixed growth period. *Japonica* rices are highly sensitive to photoperiod, or day-length, and do poorly in the short-day tropics. They are, however, widely grown in North China, Korea and Japan. Altitude is also an important factor: a study of cultivated rices in Yunnan province in the Chinese foothills of the Himalayas showed that *indica* varieties predominated up to 1,750 m and *japonica* varieties over 2,000 m, while in the zone between 1,750 and 2,000 m intermediate varieties were found (Ding 1964).[9]

Rice (figure 1.2) has a number of advantages compared with many other food crops. First, it is very palatable, and is the only cereal which can simply be boiled and eaten without disintegrating into mush. Perhaps because of its flavour it has frequently been considered a luxury food: in medieval Japan peasants paid their dues to their lords in rice grown specially for this purpose, though they could afford to eat only millets themselves, and similarly in many parts of India today poor farmers sell their rice crops to the cities and buy cheaper grains for their own consumption.

The nutritional value of rice varies considerably according to type, environment and method of preparation, but generally speaking it is highly digestible and nutritious. Unmilled rice compares favourably with wheat and other cereals in its protein, fat, vitamin and mineral content, but unmilled or 'brown' rice has little sale outside the health-food stores of the West. It takes a long time to cook and is difficult to chew, and most rice-eaters prefer their rice to be not only hulled (removing the husk), but also milled and polished (removing all the coloured pericarp as bran). This leaves the grain white and shining. In polishing rice loses much of its nutritional value: highly polished rice contains only 7% protein, whereas rice that has simply been husked still contains nearly 10%.[10] Washing and cooking methods often deplete the nutrients further, and deficiency diseases such as beri-beri are not uncommon among consumers of rice too poor to supplement their diets with alternative sources of protein and vitamins. But just as Europeans traditionally regarded white bread as a luxury more desirable than brown, so most Asians wish their rice to be as highly polished as possible. The problem of nutritional deficiency has been exacerbated by the recent spread of efficient mechanised mills, for now almost all rice is highly polished, even in villages. Traditionally the Asian poor used their own hand-mills or bought inexpensive rice that was poorly polished and so they were, despite themselves, protected in some measure against deficiency diseases. They also garnished their rice with soy products, fish sauces and vegetables, which combined to make an impressively healthy diet compared with that consumed by the proletarians of urban or rural Europe (Fortune 1857: 42). So although modern analyses of the nutritional value of rice show it to be poorer in many respects than wheat, in fact many traditional Asian rice-based diets are nutritionally more than adequate.[11]

Rice is a relatively high-yielding crop even under adverse conditions. Provided the water supply is adequate, nitrogen-fixing organisms which occur naturally in the paddy-fields enable farmers to harvest up to 2 tonnes/hectare without applying any mineral fertilisers (Swaminathan

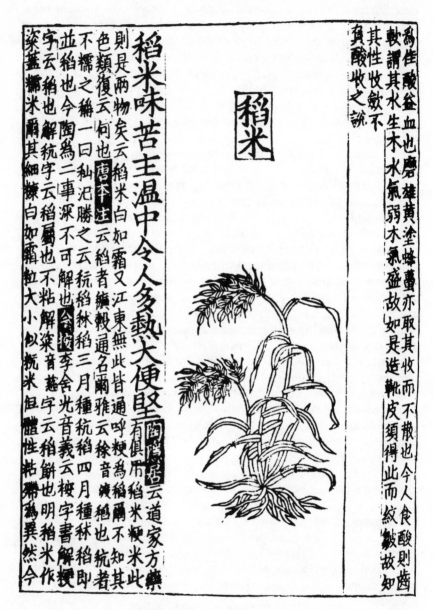

Figure 1.2   The rice-plant
(from a twelfth-century Chinese botanical work, the *Zhenglei bencao*, 1468 edn)

1984: 69). A very rough idea of the productivity of rice is given by the world production figures cited earlier, from which one can derive average annual yields of 1.95 t/ha for wheat and 2.75 t/ha for rice.[12] And this is not just a recent contrast. A map of one of the Gufukuji Temple's holdings in Kagawa prefecture, Japan, dating to 753, shows that dry fields were only one-quarter to one-third as productive as neighbouring rice-fields; even poor quality rice-fields yielded about one-third more grain than a dry field (Farris 1985: 107).

Of course yields may be much higher or much lower than those just mentioned. The highest rice yields in the world are in fact obtained in Australia (Grist 1975: 485), where as much as 7 t/ha may be had on fields which are sown with rice once every six or seven years, being used as pastures in the interim. In contrast, in parts of Malaysia where there is no irrigation and modern varieties and inputs cannot be used, subsistence farmers may get as little as 1.5 t/ha (pers. obs.).

But of special interest to farmers living on the margins of subsistence is that rice has a high yield to seed ratio. Wheat, barley and rye, the staple cereals of Northern Europe, bear heads with relatively few grains, say between 20 and 90; each plant will normally develop four or five tillers, giving a possible maximum of 400 or so grains per plant in all (Leonard and Martin 1963: 291). Theoretically, then, each seed-grain could produce 400 offspring. In reality, given the physiology of the plant and inefficient sowing techniques like broadcasting, in Europe up to the seventeenth or eighteenth century the ratio of crop to seed-grain averaged no more than 4 : 1 or 3 : 1, of which of course a high proportion had to be set aside as seed for the next crop (Slicher van Bath 1963: 382). A single panicle of rice may contain up to 500 grains, though 75 to 150 is more usual, and a well-watered plant on fertile soil can produce up to 50 tillers (Leonard and Martin 1963: 615); the number of grains produced from a single seed could thus easily average 2,000 in transplanted rice. Yield to seed ratios of 100 : 1 can be obtained even using such simple cultivation techniques as those practised in parts of Malaysia which have not seen the benefits of the 'Green Revolution' (pers. obs.; Hill 1977: 134). Setting aside one-fiftieth or one-hundredth of the rice harvest for seed-grain is much less of a hardship and a risk for subsistence farmers, then, than keeping enough wheat for sowing.

One reason why rice gives high annual yields is that it is often possible to grow two or even three crops a year in the same field. This does not mean that the annual yield is thereby doubled or tripled, but it will certainly be increased significantly. Alternatively, overall output can be increased by draining the rice-fields after the harvest and planting crops such as wheat, vegetables or tobacco. Since a crop of transplanted rice

may occupy the field for as little as two to three months, there is more
scope for multi-cropping than when directly sown cereals like wheat,
millet or maize are the main crop.

The possibilities of multi-cropping and the high yields of wet rice are
consistent with very high land productivity, though this does depend on
heavy inputs of labour. As a wet-rice farming system becomes more
intensive the land's population-carrying capacity increases sharply, as do
labour requirements. The intensification of rice-farming both permits
and requires demographic increase. It is no coincidence that the most
densely populated agricultural regions of the world, Java, the Tonkin
Delta and the Lower Yangzi provinces of China, all have a centuries-
long tradition of intensive wet-rice farming. No wheat-growing areas can
sustain such numerous populations.

Rice-fields planted with a second crop generally give higher yields
each season than those which are only single-cropped, thanks to the
additional ploughing and manuring, and also to the beneficial effects of
drying out the soil (Grist 1975: 44; Watabe 1967: 103). This fact is
clearly appreciated by landowners in Northern Thailand, for example,
who will often lend their rice-fields free to landless peasants in the dry
season to grow soybeans or groundnuts (Bruneau 1980: 386). If the field
is continuously planted with wet rice its fertility, unlike that of dry fields,
will not diminish over time even if few or no fertilisers are used, for the
nutrient content of the irrigation water, together with the nitrogenising
power of the naturally occurring algae, are sufficient to maintain regular
returns from traditional rice varieties. This is obviously an important
consideration for a subsistence farmer.

So rice will allow poor farmers to produce reasonable yields from their
land, at the cost, it is true, of heavy investments of labour, but without
necessitating such capital outlays as the purchase of fertilisers. Another
important consideration for subsistence farmers is the risks involved in
production. If one may reap a hundredfold in a good year but three years
out of four are bad, one's hold on life is bound to be precarious. Here
again, rice offers significant advantages.

A very important risk-reducing factor in rice-growing is the enormous
range of varieties available to farmers even in isolated areas. The number
of cultivated varieties of *Triticum aestivum* (by far the most important of
the six types of domesticated wheat) totals some 20,000 throughout the
world (Feldman and Sears 1981: 98). There are about 120,000
cultivated varieties of Asian rice (Swaminathan 1984: 66). The great
range of rice varieties derives in part from its natural propensity to
diversify, but this propensity has been encouraged and channelled by the
conscious intervention of rice farmers through the ages.

Rice-farmers usually grow several different varieties of rice in any one season, partly to provide for different requirements and partly as a means of minimising their risks. Different fields will suit different varieties depending on the soil, exposure or water supply. Late rains will mean that quick-ripening varieties must be planted instead of better-yielding slow-maturing rices. It is often desirable to rotate varieties to reduce the incidence of disease. Small quantities of special rice are required for ceremonies, while less desirable but sturdier varieties are grown for sale. Another very important factor which rice-farmers must take into account is timing: labour is in peak demand at transplanting and harvesting, water (also a limited commodity) at ploughing and just after transplanting. If a number of different varieties are planted, then the requirements of water and labour will be spread over a more manageable period. Thus an Iban family would commonly plant 15 or more varieties of rice (Freeman 1970: 188); Lüe farmers in Northern Thailand grow various types of glutinous rice for their own consumption and of non-glutinous rice for sale according to carefully calculated harvesting schedules (Moerman 1968: 150); and in eleventh-century Anhui (Central China) poor farmers grew large-grained *japonica* rices to pay their taxes, and *indicas* for their own consumption (Bray 1984: 491).

Rice-farmers, then, have traditionally used a wide range of varieties both as a policy to ensure subsistence and as a strategy to increase their income. Where rice is the main commodity, as in the Northern Thai village of Ban Ping, or in San-lin village in Central Taiwan, farmers wish to maximise their rice yields; indeed even today they will often make their financial calculations in terms not of cash – whose value to such farmers in a fluctuating market or inflationary economy appears highly unstable – but of rice (Moerman 1968: 153; Huang 1981: 44). Where other sources of income predominate, farmers wish to plant rice varieties which free the rice-fields sufficiently early for them to plant commercial crops such as tobacco, vegetables or sugar-cane, or varieties whose peak labour requirements will not clash with other activities such as the cultivation of cash crops in dry fields (e.g. Bruneau 1980: 407).

Since their requirements are so specific and varied, it is not surprising that rice-farmers have always devoted considerable attention to the development and maintenance of desirable strains according to a number of criteria such as yield, habitat, flavour, growth period and season, resistance to flood, drought and disease, glutinous or non-glutinous endosperm, and fragrance. There are black and red rices as well as white. 'Rouge-red rice is soft, fragrant and sweet, and when it is cooked it turns a uniform red in colour. It is one of the best of the late rices. One variety tolerates saline conditions and is ideal for brackish fields by lakes

or near river mouths', says the *Qun fang pu*, a seventeenth-century
Chinese botanical work (Bray 1984: 494). Rices such as these were used
to reclaim the swamp-lands of Hong Kong by migrant Chinese fleeing
from the Mongols in the thirteenth and fourteenth centuries (Watson
1975: 30).

The 'glutinous' characteristic is one that has been much valued by
Asian rice-farmers. 'Glutinous' varieties in fact contain no gluten; the
stickiness of the cooked grain is generally assumed to result from the
presence of dextrin and a little maltose as well as starch in the endosperm
(Grist 1975: 100). Glutinous rice is highly valued as a ceremonial food
and as the chief ingredient in rice 'wines' or beers. Cakes made of
glutinous rice are exchanged at weddings and religious festivals all over
Asia. In Malaya a large cake of glutinous rice, coloured brilliant red,
yellow or purple and decorated with eggs and flowers, is offered to the
bride as a symbol of fertility. In South China cakes of glutinous rice,
wrapped in broad bamboo leaves and steamed, are exchanged on the day
of the Dragon Boat Festival. Most Asians eat ordinary rice as their staple,
but some mountain-dwellers prefer the glutinous kind, regarding it as
more nutritious – if inclined to make the brain sluggish. In Northern
Thailand this dietary distinction is seen by the local peasants as a mark of
both ethnic and political identity: only effete southerners, soldiers or
government officials, eat non-glutinous rice, and though local farmers
grow the higher-yielding non-glutinous varieties for sale, they always
take care to plant enough glutinous rice for their own consumption
(Moerman 1968).

From the point of view of the cultivator, one of the most important
differences between rice varieties is the ripening period, which may vary
between 90 and 260 days. *Japonica* rices take a fixed period to ripen
regardless of the date at which they are planted, but most *indicas* are
photosensitive and will always flower at a particular date (Grist 1975: 84).
It is therefore easier to breed quick-ripening varieties of *indica* than of
japonica. Quick-ripening varieties are especially useful where the water
supply is uncertain or insufficient. They also make multi-cropping
possible, but they usually yield significantly less than medium-or
long-term rices. The great exceptions, of course, are the recently
developed 'high-yielding varieties' (HYVs) which have come to play such
an important part in Asian rice production since the 1960s. These are
derived from semi-dwarf mutants of *indica* rices; they are mostly
quick-ripening, permitting double-or even triple-cropping, and they
respond very positively to chemical fertilisers, often yielding more than
half as much again as traditional varieties.

Where deep flooding rather than inadequate water is the problem, in deltas or lakelands for example, the introduction of floating rices has sometimes proved effective. Floating rices are most extensively grown in the deltaic plains of Burma and Bangladesh; in Bangladesh they constitute almost one-quarter of the total rice crop (Oka 1975b: 279), and about 25 varieties are known (Grist 1975: 140). They are also important in the other flood-plains of Southeast Asia, and the introduction of floating rices to the Burma Delta at the end of the nineteenth century was one of the major agricultural innovations of the colonial period (Adas 1974: 130). And in pre-revolutionary Cambodia, although floating rice occupied only a small area (some 85,000 out of over 1 million hectares under rice), it had great economic significance, for unlike ordinary rices it was grown almost exclusively for sale. The crop was supposed to be very ancient in the Plaine des Lacs, but was only introduced to the south of Cambodia by French officials in the late nineteenth century (Delvert 1961: 329).

Yields of floating rice in Cochinchina generally were quite high: 2 t/ha as opposed to 1.8 t/ha in single-cropped and 2.6 t/ha in double-cropped fields (Henry and de Visme 1928: 52). In parts of Thailand floating rices will yield up to 5 t/ha if transplanted, even though no fertilisers are used; average yields in areas prone to flood are likely to be much lower, but at 2 t/ha still higher than non-floating rices in the same vicinity, which yield only 1.45 t/ha (Oka 1975b: 282). So far little attention has been devoted to breeding improved varieties of floating rice, despite their great potential importance, but work in this field is now in progress (ibid.: 284 ff).

Selection techniques

Since rice-farmers' requirements are so specific and vary so widely, it is not surprising that they have always devoted considerable attention to the development and maintenance of desirable strains. As cross-pollination does occur in varying degrees, and since wild rices are common in many of the areas where rice is cultivated, in the natural course of events one would expect rice cultivars to evolve and change continuously. Human selection has thus been crucial in maintaining desirable strains and selecting new cultivars. The techniques of rice-farming lend themselves particularly well to selection.

One of the simplest methods of improvement is to pick out the best panicles at harvest time and set them aside for seed-grain. This process was probably facilitated from very early times by the use of the reaping-knife. A small, flat knife with a curved blade, the reaping-knife is

held in the palm of the hand and the heads of grain are cut off just below
the ear, one by one, by drawing the stem across the blade with the index
finger (figure 1.3). Stone, shell and pottery reaping-knives are common
in neolithic sites throughout China and Japan, and knives with small
metal blades were used to harvest rice throughout much of Southeast
Asia until very recently. Ethnographers have frequently linked this knife
specifically with the cultivation of rice, for its use is often accorded ritual
significance by rice-growers: Malay farmers, for instance, believed that
since it was hidden in the palm of the hand, unlike the naked blade of the
sickle it would not frighten away the 'rice soul', *semangat padi*, without
which the seed-grain could not grow (Hill 1951: 70). But the
reaping-knife is also used by Asian farmers growing foxtail and
broomcorn millets (Fogg 1983; *Wang Zhen nongshu* 1313: 14/6b), the
cultivation of which preceded that of rice in many parts of East and
Southeast Asia. However, all the early domesticated cereals of the Far
East, including rice, have large seed-heads or panicles, are naturally
free-tillering and tend to ripen unevenly. In such circumstances it is not
desirable to reap all the heads from a single plant simultaneously: it is
better to gather the heads individually as they ripen, for which purpose a
small knife is preferable to a sickle. And if each panicle is cut individually
in this way, then it is easy for the farmer to pick out specially fine heads,
or to select seed-grain from a plant which has ripened earlier than the
rest and may thus produce quick-ripening offspring.

Transplanting is another stage of rice cultivation at which the farmer
has a chance, not so much to select the best plants, as to eliminate sickly
plants or mutants, and so maintain reasonably pure strains.

A third stage of possible control in traditional rice-farming occurs just
before sowing, when the seed-grain, which has usually been stored in the
ear as a protection against insects and mildew, is taken out and husked. It
is then common practice to soak the seed briefly in order to separate out
empty or rotten kernels and weed-seed. Sometimes clear water is used;
in early and medieval China it was commonly believed that water
obtained from melted snow was especially beneficial: 'It will immediately
dissolve the hot properties of the grain so that the young shoots will be
unusually handsome' (Song 1966: 11). Later on a brine solution was
often used to test the seed:

First construct a bucket of 2 gallon capacity. (Separately prepare a fine-meshed
bamboo basket slightly smaller than the bucket.) Put in 1 gallon of water and add
salt. For ordinary rice use 120 ounces of salt, for glutinous rice use 100. Stir with
a bamboo brush for five or six minutes until the salt has dissolved, then insert the
basket into the bucket and gradually pour in 4 or 5 pints of seed, not too much at
once. Skim off the empty kernels that float to the surface with a bamboo strainer.

Figure 1.3   Harvesting-knife, ketaman, *used in Kelantan*
(photo courtesy A. F. Robertson)

Repeat several times until no floating seeds remain, then draw out the basket, put it into another vat of water and rinse away the salt. (Zeng 1902: 1/18b)

In Malaya the strength of the brine was tested by floating a duck-egg in the water, and in post-revolutionary China a hen's egg was used to test a thin suspension of clay. Modern agronomists recommend specific concentrations of salt, ammonium sulphate or lime as more accurate than the folk methods just described (Bray 1984: 246). Even though the grain has already been selected at harvest the process of soaking is not superfluous, for there may be significant differences in speed of germination and in flowering time even between grains taken from the same ear, and the heavier grains can be relied upon to flower and set more quickly (Ding 1961: 310). This is of particular importance where quick-maturing varieties are being grown.

In the past it was usually peasant farmers who selected and developed new strains of rice and passed them from hand to hand. Specially successful varieties might sometimes travel great distances in this fashion: for example in seventeenth-century China a variety known as 'Henan early' was recorded as far away as South Fujian, perhaps 750 miles away (Ho 1959: 173).

An interesting example of the development of quick-ripening varieties is provided by the so-called 'Champa' rices. Champa was an Indochinese state to the south of Annam, known to the Chinese as early as the first century AD for having rices so precocious they could be cropped twice in one year (Bray 1984: 492). There is also archeological evidence that double-cropping was practised even earlier, in the Dong S'on period (Higham 1984: 105). By the sixth century the Annamese apparently possessed such a wide range of wet and dry, early and late varieties that they could grow rice all the year round, but the quick-ripening varieties gave very low yields while requiring just as much labour as the other sorts (Amano 1979: 193). They did, however, have very moderate water requirements: they would grow in poorly watered fields, did well as dry crops when grown in hilly regions and were generally highly resistant to drought. Many farmers must have grown them, if not as their main crop, at least as a form of insurance.

The Champa rices had spread northwards as far as South China by the medieval period, passing from farm to farm, for when the Song emperor Zhenzong decided to encourage their cultivation in the Lower Yangzi region he sent not to Annam but to Fujian province for 30,000 bushels of Champa seed; this was in AD 1012. The Champa rices, unlike those most popular in much of China at that time, were *indicas*, and at first they gave consistently lower yields than most traditional

Chinese varieties. But peasants quickly selected and developed higher-yielding varieties to grow in the well-watered lowland fields. By the end of the Song dynasty, some 250 years after their official introduction, later-ripening and more prolific Champa rices had been bred and soon the range was as wide as for any other type of rice.

Although it was the Song government which first introduced the Champa rices to the Yangzi Delta, it was through the efforts of individual peasant farmers that the best varieties of Champa rices were developed. In recent times, however, the breeding and even the choice of rice varieties has become increasingly a matter for officialdom.

The Japanese set up agricultural research stations where the best 'native' varieties were crossed to produce 'improved' varieties as early as the 1870s (Dore 1969: 98); these improved rices were distributed to local farmers, together with detailed instructions as to their cultivation, through the recently founded Agricultural Associations. In the early 1920s the Japanese authorities introduced high-yielding *japonica* rices to Taiwan to replace the local *indicas*, which they considered insipid (Huang 1981: 59). Many Taiwanese farmers adopted the new *japonica* rices enthusiastically, for as they were mostly exported to Japan they commanded almost double the price of local rices (Wang and Apthorpe 1974: 163), but Taiwanese consumers continued to prefer the *indicas*, which offered farmers the additional advantage of requiring fewer fertilisers. When the Japanese first occupied Taiwan in 1895, 1,365 varieties of rice, all *indicas*, were grown on the island. Today many farmers grow *japonicas* in the main season and *indicas* in the off-season, and a 1969 report stated that only 86 *indicas* and 53 *japonicas* were then grown on Taiwan (Huang 1981: 48). Seed of the *japonicas* is these days distributed through the Farmers' Associations; the villagers do not keep the *japonica* seed themselves as they say it will deteriorate. However they refuse to use the *indica* seed bred at the Agricultural Research Station. Instead they select their own, sharing out seed from high-yielding fields; they say that, like the native fowls, the original native rices will never degenerate (Wang and Apthorpe 1974: 163).

In China, in contrast to Japan and its colonies, the emphasis was on improving *indica* strains. Breeding programmes were first set up in the universities in Canton and Nanking in 1925, and in 1934 a national breeding programme and distribution service was set up by the National Agricultural Research Bureau (Shen 1951: 199). Traditional *indicas*, in China as elsewhere, are tall and have a tendency to lodge (that is, to fall over if wind or rain are too strong). The Chinese breeders concentrated on producing new varieties from semi-dwarf mutants, and had developed high-yielding types by the early 1960s, a few years before similar 'miracle rices' were developed by the International Rice Research Institute (IRRI) in the Philippines (Harlan 1980: 307).

The Chinese and Japanese policy had been to select the best varieties available locally and to improve them through pure-line selection. IRRI, founded by the Ford and Rockefeller Foundations in 1960, was able to draw on the best available strains from many nations for its breeding programmes. The chief characteristics of the new heavy-yielding varieties (HYVs) are their short growing period, their pronounced response to chemical fertilisers and of course their high yields. The early HYVs had a number of shortcomings, chief among them being their lack of flavour, their inadaptability to local conditions and their vulnerability to disease. Since they were often grown as part of a 'technological package' which imposed virtual monoculture of a single variety over large areas (we shall discuss this further in chapter 4), such shortcomings were sometimes exacerbated to the point where yields were hardly greater or more reliable than those of the traditional varieties. But more careful attention to local testing and adjustment, and to breeding for reliability as well as simply high yields, has brought about enormous improvements:

IR36, a variety now grown on more than 10 million hectares of the world's rice land, is a result of this strategy. It resists four major rice diseases and four serious plant pests, including brown planthopper biotypes 1 and 2. It grows well in a variety of cultural environments, tolerates several adverse soil conditions, has grain of good quality and matures in 110 days, which enables farmers to harvest as many as three crops in one year on irrigated paddies. IR36 is the progeny of 13 different varieties from six nations. (Swaminathan 1984: 70)

Both insect pests and disease organisms show remarkable rapidity in adapting themselves to attack resistant varieties. It is often wild or primitive crop varieties which exhibit the greatest capacity for long-term resistance to pests and diseases, and a continuous supply of genetic material is necessary to ensure successful and sustained breeding programmes (Chang 1976b). Most Asian rice-growing nations started national collections of rice varieties in the 1930s, but these collections tended to concentrate on commercial varieties and to neglect the wild and primitive strains whose germ plasm is the most useful for breeding purposes. Only in the 1960s did IRRI's germ plasm centre start systematically collecting and classifying wild and cultivated rices from all over the world; by 1983 their collection included '63,000 Asian cultivars, 2,575 African rices, 1,100 wild rices and 680 varieties maintained to test genetic traits. Thousands of breeding lines with one or more desirable traits are also preserved' (Swaminathan 1984: 67).

IRRI has provided the world with many of its most successful rice varieties in recent years, but research at national level is also producing interesting results. Most rice-breeding programmes are based on the technique of crossing selected parents to achieve a new variety which combines their desirable characteristics and which will, in principle, breed true. But since 1970 Chinese scientists, using male-sterile plants, have overcome the difficulties inherent in working with this mainly self-pollinated crop and have managed to produce hybrid rices (Harlan 1980: 302). These may eventually produce results as spectacular as those achieved with other hybrid crops like maize.

The drawback of hybrids is that while the first generation is more vigorous than either of its parents, subsequent generations quickly lose the desired characteristics. This means that the hybrid seed must be produced in laboratories, and that farmers must buy new supplies every year. In any case it is becoming generally true that rice-farmers no longer have any direct part in selection or breeding. If the improved variety they choose to grow is particularly stable, then they may be able to produce their own seed-grain at least for a few years; otherwise they have to purchase their seed from a Farmers' Association (Harriss 1977: 147). But many poorer farmers cannot afford this, and pleas have been made for the professional breeders to develop more stable varieties, as well as to consult more carefully with local farmers to take their requirements into account (Chambers 1977: 405). Plant-breeders today have at their disposal enormous resources which should enable them to produce the right variety for every situation, but given the time and expense involved it is possible they may choose to serve the peasant farmers' interests less well than their own. In any case it is clear that the number of rice varieties of which a late-twentieth-century rice-farmer disposes is far less than it would have been even thirty years ago. But the new varieties often combine the advantages of several traditional varieties, so in a sense the farmer's choice has not been reduced, but has become less direct.

In conclusion, we see that rice offers several significant advantages to the peasant farmer. Although we shall see in subsequent chapters that it is hard work to grow, generally requiring more labour than other crops, it is also the highest yielding of all cereals after maize, but has superior nutritional value (Huang 1981: 49). It is highly adaptable, can be grown under almost any conditions, does not necessarily require fertilisers (although it does respond well to their use) and will produce as many as three crops a year if there is sufficient water, without exhausting the fertility of the paddy field. The techniques of rice cultivation are such that farmers themselves have been able to select for desirable traits through the centuries, and so a very wide range of cultivars has been developed. By keeping a range of varieties in stock the farmer can protect himself in fair measure against the risk of drought or flood, and can also increase his income, either by producing more rice, or by combining rice cultivation with more profitable activities like cash-cropping.

The distinctive feature of wet-rice cultivation is the degree of intensity with which land can be used. If quick-ripening varieties are used, as many as three crops of rice a year can be grown even by farmers who do not have access to chemical fertilisers, for the water supply provides nutrients naturally. This means that once rice cultivation is established in a region it will sustain population growth almost indefinitely. No other crop has such a great population-carrying capacity, and this is one of the factors to which we can attribute the success and popularity of rice. Although it is possible to increase yields even with traditional inputs alone, as we shall see in the next chapter the techniques of rice-farming are such that intensification is achieved, not through high levels of capital investment, but rather through using increased amounts of labour.

2

Paths of technical development

As societies develop and their populations grow, so too their agriculture expands and develops to produce more food, and eventually to support the growth of commerce, manufactures and industry. Increases in agricultural production may be achieved through expanding the area under cultivation or through improving the productivity of existing farm-land. Where land is freely available, where agricultural labour is scarce, or where more attractive employment than farming beckons, innovations in farming practice will tend to improve the productivity of labour. But if land is scarce and labour plentiful, then farmers will usually consider the productivity of land more important.

Asian rice cultivation is generally considered labour-intensive and technologically primitive compared to the advanced farming systems of the West today. It is certainly true that the historical development of Asian rice cultivation techniques has followed a very different pattern from that of European wheat cultivation (outlined in appendix A). In both cases, however, the long-term trend was the same: more grain was produced. But in Europe many of the most striking advances increased the productivity of human labour by substituting animals or machines, taking advantage of the essentially extensive nature of the farming system to introduce economies of scale. As we shall see in this chapter, by their nature the wet-rice systems of Asia respond positively to increases in the application of labour, but are not as susceptible as Western farming systems to capital-intensive economies of scale. Instead, highly sophisticated management skills were developed which brought about enormous improvements in rice yields.

This chapter explores the dynamics of wet-rice systems: the technical means by which increases in rice production may be achieved, and the inherent trend towards intensification of land-use and small-scale management.

Building new fields

Wet-rice fields have a great advantage over dry fields in that they tend to gain rather than lose fertility over the years. Swidden fields cut from the jungle will often produce very high yields of dry rice (and other crops) during the first year of cultivation, but their great fertility comes from the forest humus and the ashes of the felled trees, which are quickly washed away. During the second year much of the fertility is lost, and unless in exceptional circumstances it is unusual for farmers to cultivate their swidden fields for more than three years before moving on to clear new land. Of course most permanent dry fields retain some natural fertility over a much longer period, but manuring and fertilising are really crucial for growing cereals without irrigation, which is one reason why livestock play such an important role in most dry-grain farming systems.

Wet-rice yields are affected by the natural fertility of the soil to some extent, as well as by the soil structure. Heavy, alluvial soils with only slight acidity are most suitable for rice, while sandy soils give satisfactory yields only if they are heavily treated with organic matter (e.g. Grist 1975: 21). But in fact soil type is much less important than the water supply. 'Whether the land be good or poor, if the water is clear then the rice will be good', says the sixth-century Chinese agricultural treatise *Qimin yaoshu* (Bray 1984: 498). 'Water is the most important factor in rice-growing, the water-soil relationship largely determining the ability of the soil to develop its full potentiality for rice production' (Grist 1975: 20). The distinctive feature of wet-rice fields is that, whatever their original fertility, several years' continuous cultivation brings it up to a higher level which is then maintained almost indefinitely. This is because water seepage alters the chemical composition and structure of the different soil layers in a process known as *pozdolisation*.

The podzolisation of soils is caused by the influence of percolating water in conjunction with various organic acids. The latter help to dissolve some of the mineral compounds and to deflocculate the clay particles so that they may be carried down to the subsoil in colloidal suspension. The cultivation of rice requires that the land be kept under water during much of the year, and this irrigation water slowly but continually seeps from the surface horizons to the subsoils, carrying with it more or less colloidal clay and some compounds in solution. The addition of more or less organic manures, including a considerable amount of night-soil [the author is describing the Chinese case], helps to increase the podzolisation effect. Occasional liming of the soil tends to offset the leaching effect since lime helps to coagulate the clays and prevents their forming colloidal suspensions in the water.

Wherever it is possible to obtain water for irrigation, practically all the soils of the important groups of South China are planted to rice. After formerly well-drained upland soils have been used in this way for a period of several years, their characteristics are changed, much of the red iron compounds are dissolved and removed from the surface to the subsoil or into the river waters, and the soils fade in colour until, after a long time, they are predominantly grey like the rice lands of the alluvial plains . . . Practically every bit of land in South China which will hold water and which can be irrigated is planted to rice for at least a part of the time. The soils are worked and cultivated and fertilised until they become well adapted to rice culture, regardless of their original characteristics. (Thorp 1937: 155)

This transformation requires years of hard work, in return for decades if not centuries of stable yields. It is not surprising, then, that rice-farmers often prefer to work existing fields more intensively rather than opening up of new fields which, at least for the first few years, will produce less than long-established ones (see Geertz 1963: 32).

But even a well-established paddy-field may eventually be overtaxed. When quick-ripening new HYVs were introduced to Lombok (an island off Bali) in the 1970s, three crops were grown annually instead of two, and two of them were often rice. 'However, it seems that this intensification of land use has meant that the limits for the stability of the flooded field ecosystem have been transgressed: in the 1940s, one hectare could yield four to five tons of rice in one harvest, in the 1970s only three tons' (Gerdin 1982: 66).

Well before such limits are reached, overpopulation, inequality of land distribution, or the dissemination of new techniques may lead rice-farmers to overcome their aversion to opening up new fields. Perhaps 'build' is a more appropriate term than 'open up', when one considers the engineering skills which are often required. Rice-fields come in an astonishing and ingenious variety, from dizzying flights of terraces perched high up on mountainsides, to dyked fields reclaimed from marshes or the shores of the sea.

The rice-farmers of most ancient times grew their crops in natural swamps. Several neolithic sites have been found in or near marshes (see chapter 1). In pre-Indian Java rice was grown only in swamps (van Setten 1979: 33), as indeed it still is today in parts of the Malaysian state of Pahang (Hill 1977: 160).

But natural marshes are limited in extent, and it is impossible to control the depth of the water, an important factor in improving yields. A rice-field should ideally be carefully levelled so that the depth of water is uniform, and in the absence of modern engineering this severely restricts field size. One Chinese agronomist, writing well after collectivisation and communisation had begun, gives the optimal size of an irrigated rice-field as under 0.1 hectare (Ding 1961: 294); a Japanese expert, pointing out that prewar the limit of a field's area in Japan was about 0.1 hectare, says that now with modern equipment this can be extended to 0.3–0.5 hectares (Kanazawa 1971: 15). This is minute compared with the wheat-fields of the American mid-West, where a single field may be several hundred hectares in size (Leonard and Martin 1963: 14).

To retain the water, low bunds (or little dykes – the French call them *diguettes*) usually less than 2 feet high are built round the carefully levelled field. Bunded fields are certainly of ancient origin. There is written evidence to show that poldered fields, technically more demanding than simple bunded fields (see p. 34) were already known in parts of the Yangzi Delta in the Spring and Autumn period (722–481 BC) (Bray 1984: 113), while clay models of bunded rice-fields are found in graves all over South China by the Han dynasty (206 BC–220 AD) (figure 2.1).

It is easier to construct level fields on land which is fairly flat to begin with, and most early wet-rice farmers settled in river valleys or deltaic plains, where natural rainfall could if necessary be supplemented as a water supply by streams or rivers. In peninsular Malaysia even today, the narrow coastal plains and river valleys are the only important wet-rice areas, though until recently much hill rice was also grown on swidden farms in the interior (Hill 1977: 173). In Thailand the historical spread of wet-rice cultivation can be traced from its earliest prehistoric roots in the river valleys and basins of the north, down to the central flood-plains where the kingdom of Ayutthaya (fourteenth to eighteenth centuries) was based, and eventually, in the nineteenth century, right to the marshy delta of the Chao Phraya around Bangkok (Ishii 1978b).

Moving from well-watered and well-drained valleys or plains to sloping hillsides or vulnerable flood-plains entailed the development of more sophisticated field types. First let us consider terraced fields. Terracing is essentially a means of levelling areas of soil so that hill-slopes may be cultivated. Agricultural terracing is a world-wide phenomenon,[1] and its purposes may be manifold. In some cases, as for example the presumably megalithic terraces (perhaps dating back to 2000 BC) of Gio-Linh in Quang-Tri province, North Vietnam, terraces were constructed as much for ritual or religious considerations as for agricultural purposes (Colani 1940; Wheatley 1965: 135). Sometimes people simply preferred to cultivate hillsides rather than valley floors for reasons of health. Agricultural terraces in the Cuzco region of Peru were also used for defence purposes (Donkin 1979), while the Shans of North Burma used their terraces as observation posts from which they could swoop down to levy tolls on passing travellers (Leach 1954). But most

Figure 2.1   Bunded field: clay model from a Han grave
Canton Museum

terraces had more prosaic functions: in China terraces are known as 'three-fold conservers', *san bao*, that is to say, they prevent erosion and conserve soil moisture and nutrients, and in many cases crops grown on terraced fields give yields several times higher than those grown in the same area under normal conditions. Raikes (1967) has characterised agricultural terracing as a form of proto-engineering for mitigating climatic stress. Liefrinck (1886: 40) describes how the productivity of irrigated terraces in Bali increases over the years as the irrigation water brings fertile sediments down from the mountainside which accumulate as a layer of rich topsoil. But the foremost advantage of wet-field terracing is that the terrace walls retain the run-off water, enabling irrigated crops to be grown on steep slopes which would otherwise have to be planted with dry crops, or even left bare:

Terracing means cutting steps in the mountain to make fields. In mountainous areas where there are few level places, apart from stretches of rock, precipices or similarly barren areas, all the rest, wherever there is soil, from the valley bottom right up to the dizzying peaks, can be split to make ledges where crops can be grown. If stones and soil are in equal proportion then you must pile up the stones in rows, encircling the soil to make a field. There are also mountains where the slope is excessively steep, without even a foothold, at the very limits of cultivation where men creep upwards bent close to the ground. There they pile up the soil like ants, prepare the ground for sowing with hoes [because the fields are too narrow to use ploughs], stepping carefully while they weed for fear of the chasm at their side. Such fields are not stepped but mount like the rungs of a ladder, hence their name of 'ladder fields'. If there is a source of water above the field, then all kinds of rice may be grown. (*Wang Zhen nongshu*: 11/2b)

Not all terraces, however, scale the dizzying peaks. The origins of agricultural terracing are far from clear,[2] but as Wheatley pertinently says:

the virtual inseparability of rudimentary terracing from wet-padi cultivation is a point to be borne in mind in any discussion of wet-field terracing in Asia. Although the act of bunding may produce initially only insignificant inequalities in the levels of fields, the potentiality is always present for increasing vertical differentiation as cultivation laps against a zone of foothills or is pushed towards the head of a valley. (1965: 132)

Such 'valley terraces', as Donkin calls them in contradistinction to 'cross-channel' and 'contour terraces', are common in rice-growing areas of East and Southeast Asia, for example in Negri Sembilan in Malaysia, and along the tributaries of the Upper Mekong in Yunnan, where the difference in level between the fields at the edge of the stream and those at the side of the valley can reach 30 feet or more (pers. obs.).

Woodard gives a description of the construction of low terraces in the Celebes, where he was cast ashore in 1793:

Many of the rice grounds are made on sloping lands, where the natives form little canals at about twenty yards distance from each other, in order to water the grounds. These divisions are levelled by carrying the higher part of the land to the lower, so as to form steps. This is performed by women and children, by means of small baskets. The land is overflowed six inches deep for about fourteen or sisteen [*sic*] days, when it becomes very moist. They then turn in about 20 bullocks, used to the employment, which are driven round the rice-fields to make the land poachy. The Malays term it *pruning*. This being done, they let the water in, which overflows it again, and renders the land fit for planting . . . (1805: 90)

Terraces on gentle slopes will usually be rather wide, with walls of earth, as in the Celebes, Yunnan and Negri Sembilan. Where slopes are steeper, the terrace wall must be faced with stone, and the fields are usually much narrower. Keesing distinguishes four types of terracing in Northern Luzon (1962: 312): the Lapanto-Bontoc type are faced with almost vertical stone walls to maximise the area of the field, while the South Kalinga terraces have stone walls capped with an inward lean of earth; the famous Ifugao terraces, which are commonly up to 20 feet in height and sometimes as much as 50, have stone walls more sloping than the two previous types, carefully sculpted to the terrain; the terraces of Tinguian, which are in the lowlands, do not have stone walls. All types are drained after the main crop to grow dry crops such as tubers or vegetables, and it is quite probable that rice cultivation in these terraces is a relatively late introduction.

Terraced fields can be built by single households or small groups of peasants, as was often the case in medieval China where impoverished farmers migrated from densely populated areas to carve a new living for themselves out of the mountainside. Terraced fields built in this way not only provided land for the landless, but also, since the newly opened land was often situated in inaccessible areas not inscribed on the land registers, they were generally not assessed for tax for some years at least (Li Jiannong 1957: 27). Often, however, the combined requirements of engineering the landscape and ensuring a reasonably equitable and efficient distribution of water have meant that large groups of farmers collaborated in constructing terrace systems. Wheatley, discussing the prehistoric stone terraces of Gio-Linh, describes complex systems of tanks and terraces, flumes and channels, bridges and causeways which were associated with objects such as menhirs and circular earth mounds presumably representing chthonic gods. This, he feels, suggests that the whole system was designed on the basis of a cult: 'the integral character of each of these systems is a sufficient indication that it did not develop piecemeal . . . [The units] were combined in such a way as to facilitate the management of an entire socio-economic unit, namely the territory and persons constituting a group of families or even a whole village' (1965: 136).

The *subak* irrigation systems of Bali offer a fascinating and well-documented study of how such organisations have worked in more recent times, though in this case on a secular basis. Liefrinck (1886) gives details of the *subak* under Dutch colonial rule, but points out that their organisation had remained essentially unchanged since pre-colonial days. Indeed *subak* groups still play an important role in Bali today (Geertz and Geertz 1975: 19 ff). Where a village becomes overpopulated, an enterprising group of villagers will form a society and select a suitable spot of uncleared land to build new terraces. Having obtained permission from the authorities to use the land, they hold a meeting to formulate the conditions of participation (usually the members of the *subak* share costs, labour and benefits equally), and when the season is suitable they construct the irrigation works and clear the land by collective effort. The land is then divided into individual holdings, which the original *subak* members can transmit to their heirs; cooperation between members remains the basis for maintenance and repairs (Liefrinck 1886: 7).

The terracing of rice-fields is a method of retaining water. But in many cases, when land is low-lying and the water-table high, it is more important to design fields so as to eliminate excess water. One of the most common forms is the poldered field, familiar to Europeans from Holland but also common in China, where it seems to have developed rather early. The first-century BC *Yue jue shu* refers to cultivated fields created amidst the flood near the ancient gate of Suzhou, a city in the Yangzi Delta (Bray 1984: 113), and Miao (1960: 140) quotes texts which indicate that poldered fields were being constructed in the area of Taihu Lake in Southern Jiangsu as early as the Spring and Autumn period (722–481 BC); Miao believes that poldered fields were quite common along the south bank of the Lower Yangzi until medieval times, probably linked to the flourishing of a local aristocracy, and various Tang dynasty (618–907) references describe powerful families in the Nanjing area reclaiming land along lake shores in this fashion. The Song writer Fan Chengda (1120–93) describes poldered fields with dykes several miles long, like great city walls, with rivers and canals inside and gates and sluices outside, which took extra water from the Yangzi in times of drought and were able to supply grain to neighbouring regions during famines (Bray 1984: 114).

Even when the dykes were much smaller, poldered fields were usually self-contained units, subdivided into separate fields with their own drainage channels; on the high dykes the farmers' houses were built and mulberries and other useful trees were planted (figure 2.2). Fei, an anthropologist native to Taihu Lake region, describes a village there in the 1930s which had about 1,500 inhabitants sharing 11 poldered fields, *yu tian*, about 180 hectares in all. Each unitary *yu tian* was subdivided into dozens of small plots (figure 2.3), and since the water came from the stream at the edge of the unit, the nearer a plot was to the centre the more difficult it was to supply and drain water. The levels of the plot therefore had to be graded like a dish, and to prevent the formation of a pool in the middle, the bunds between the plots were constructed parallel to the margin. In order to raise water from the stream outside into the outer plots, square-pallet chain-pumps (figure 2.4) were fixed at selected spots along the bank and the water was pumped into small channels which threaded between the plots, eventually depositing the water in a deep trench dug in the lowest part of the *yu tian*, from which it was then pumped back into the stream outside (Fei 1939: 156).

The construction of a variety of dyked fields is comprehensively described by the fourteenth-century Chinese agronomist Wang Zhen (*Wang Zhen nongshu*: ch. 11; see also Bray 1984: 113–23). Wang distinguished between two types, 'poldered fields', *yu tian*, which are built up above the level of the river or lake from layers of soil before being dyked, and 'encircled fields', *wei tian*, which are simply dyked; both of them may range in size, Wang says, between thousands of acres and a few acres (1313: 11/15b). Another way of reclaiming marshy land was to build 'strongbox fields', *gui tian*:

In 'strongbox fields' the soil is built up into a dyke to protect the fields, as for 'encircled fields' but a bit smaller. On all four sides are placed escape conduits, and the shape is similar to a strong-box and is convenient to cultivate. If the area is very marshy then the fields should be of smaller size, built with firm dykes on higher ground so that the water outside cannot easily get in but the water inside can easily be pumped out with a chain-pump. The parts which remain under shallow water should be sown with quick-ripening yellow rice (which only takes 60 days from sowing to harvesting and thus is not endangered by floods) . . . This is an excellent method of reclaiming marshy land. (*Wang Zhen nongshu*: 11/17b)

Silt banks and eyots might also be dyked to make 'silt fields', *sha tian*, which were more easily irrigated and drained than fields on the land, as well as having rich and fertile soil well suited to all kinds of rice: 'their advantage over other fields lies in their freedom from drought and flood' (ibid.: 11/24b).

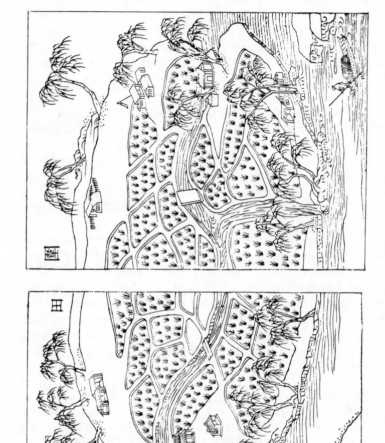

Figure 2.2   Poldered field illustrated in the Chinese agricultural treatise Shoushi tongkao *of 1742*
(ch. 14/5b)

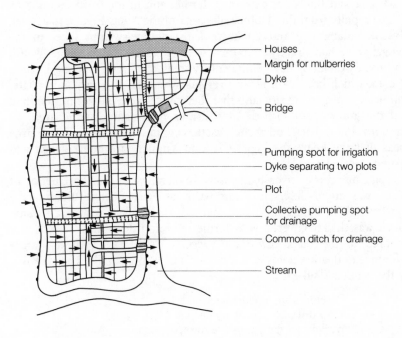

— Houses
— Margin for mulberries
— Dyke

— Bridge

— Pumping spot for irrigation
— Dyke separating two plots

— Plot

Collective pumping spot
for drainage

— Common ditch for drainage

— Stream

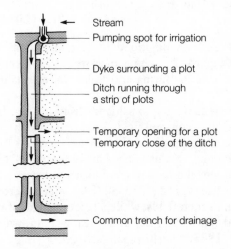

— Stream
— Pumping spot for irrigation

— Dyke surrounding a plot

Ditch running through
a strip of plots

— Temporary opening for a plot
— Temporary close of the ditch

— Common trench for drainage

Figure 2.3   Poldered field in the 1930s in the Yangzi Delta
(after Fei 1939)

Most dyked fields are extremely fertile, and in medieval China they spread rapidly from the Taihu Lake area of the Yangzi Delta to Hubei, Hunan, Guangdong and Guangxi. Most of the swampy lakes in the Yangzi Delta had already been turned into poldered fields by the twelfth century. By the mid-fourteenth century so much of the Dongting Lake in Hunan, which had acted as an overspill when the Yangzi was in spate, had been converted to dry land that there was severe danger of flooding, and the government forbade any further reclamation in the area (Li Jiannong 1957: 16). Today the practice continues to spread, and large areas of Lake Dian, the biggest lake in Yunnan, are being dyked and turned into fields.

If lake margins or river-banks were so marshy that the construction of dykes was impossible, in some parts of Asia floating fields were constructed. In China the usual method was to make a wooden frame which was thickly covered with fertile mud and dead water-weeds and tethered to the bank (*Chen Fu nongshu*: 1/2). The earliest literary reference to floating fields is in a sixth-century poem on the Yangzi River by the scholar Guo Pu:

> Covered with an emerald screen
> They drift, buoyed up by floating water-weeds.
> Without art the grains are sown,
> And fine rice-plants thrust up of their own accord.
> (See Amano 1979: 175)

Floating rice-fields were to be found in several regions of South China, including the Yangzi and Lake Dian, as well as in Kasumigaura in Northeast Japan, Lake Inlé in Burma and Lake Dal in Kashmir (Bray 1984: 121).[3] Finally there was the reclamation of saltlands from the sea. First a sea wall was built to cut off the projected fields from the tides, then a system of canals was constructed to leach out the salt with sweet water from a river. Initially salt-tolerant plants like barnyard millet (*Echinocloa crus-galli*) were sown to put the land in good heart, but after a few years the land was fit for any use. Wang (1313: 11/22a) refers to crops of rice and millet being grown in such fields, while a Japanese plan of reclaimed land, dating from 1300, shows that rice and wheat were grown as well as garden crops (Kuroda 1983: 61). In Japan 'salt dykes', *entei*, were first known from about the eighth century, when they were used in the construction of salt-pans, but it was not long before their scope for land reclamation was realised. Most of the early projects were only a qualified success, but by the eleventh to thirteenth century large-scale reclamation of this sort was common along the coasts of Honshū and Kyūshū. One

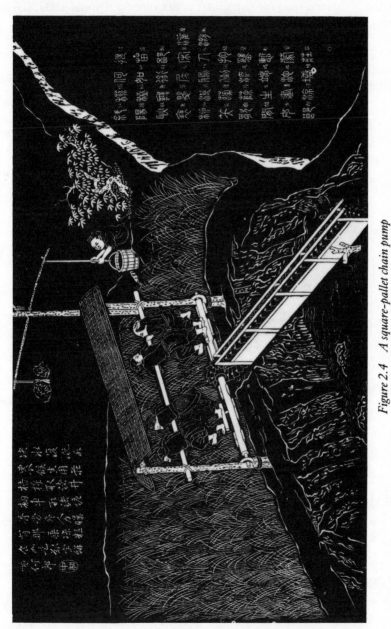

Figure 2.4 A square-pallet chain pump

(from a Qing edition of the *Gengzhi tu* (Agriculture and sericulture illustrated), perhaps copying the original Song illustrations of 1149)

project begun in 1238 in Aki (now Hiroshima) was subsequently referred to as the 'thousand *chō* [1,000 ha] of Tomita estate' (Kuroda 1983: 63) (figure 2.5). Such reclamation continued piecemeal right through medieval times and into the Meiji period. In Okayama (Southwest Honshū), for example, over 2,500 ha of rice-land were reclaimed in the river delta between 1590 and 1690 (Beardsley et al. 1959: 52).

Along the coast of Central China, sea-walls had been built in early

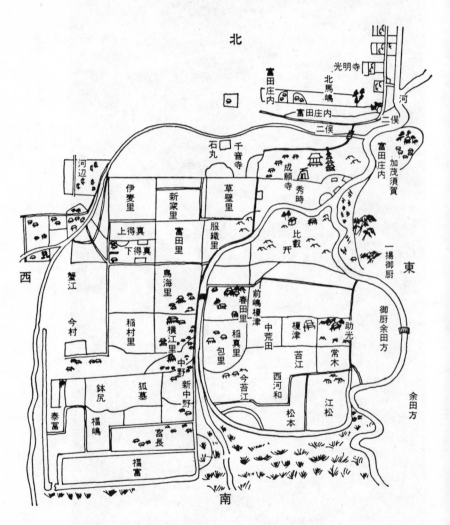

Figure 2.5   The Tomita estate
(from Kuroda 1983: 62)

medieval times which by the Song dynasty had fallen into disrepair. In 1026 the official Zhang Lun ordered the construction of several hundred miles of new sea-wall along the Jiangsu coast, and this project was brought to final fruition by the energetic statesman, poet and reformer Fan Zhongyan (1126–93). The local population were so grateful for the benefits brought by this scheme that many of them named their children Fan (Li Jiannong 1957: 15). Another great official benefactor was the Vietnamese mandarin Nguyên Công Trú, who administered two enormous projects for reclaiming salt-marshes, one in Annam (Thaibinh), and the other in Ninh-binh in the Red River Delta. These projects went under way in 1828, and the reclaimed land was distributed to groups of ten migrant households in lots of 100 *mâu* (1 *mâu* = 0.36 ha); the state also provided houses, buffaloes and ploughs. Over the next century the population of Thai-binh quadrupled, from 2,350 to over 10,000 tax payers, while the area of rice-fields increased from 19,000 to 24,000 *mâu* (Lê 1955: 39).

But not all such reclamation was officially sponsored. Watson (1975) describes how the founders of the Man clan, in flight from the Mongol invasion, arrived in the thirteenth century in what are now the New Territories of Hong Kong only to find that four other major lineage groups had already possessed themselves of all the best rice-land. Since they could fly no further, the Mans were obliged to occupy the only land left, a marshy, brackish area in the river delta draining into Deep Bay. The Mans built dykes with locks, enclosing the existing land and reclaiming extra land from the bay. The dykes retained the rain water and excluded salt water floods, and the locks were manipulated so as to minimise the salt content of the irrigation water. The process of reclamation was aided by the gradual geological uplift of Deep Bay and consequent silting up of the delta. In their 'new fields' the Mans grew one crop a year of special red rice highly resistant to salt. Although this rice gave only medium yields and was not considered of very high quality, the 'new fields' had the advantage of requiring no fertilisers and the red rice took very little labour. Nowadays the Mans have mostly given up farming for more lucrative pursuits, but the reclaimed salt marshes did provide them with an adequate if hardly bountiful living for over six centuries.

Although they were enterprises of considerable scale, requiring sophisticated design and organisation of manpower, these projects did not rely on heavy capital investment. This is an important feature of all the types of reclamation discussed. Most of the construction work involved shifting large quantities of earth, but this was done using such rudimentary equipment as baskets and shovels. Sometimes, as when building terraced fields or small 'strongbox fields', it was enough for a few households to cooperate. Even large-scale projects set up by officials or by great landowners depended principally on organising the necessary corvée labour. The expenses for repairing a broken sea-wall on the Takada estate of Yamato (modern Nara) came to 10 bushels of hulled rice, of which 8 bushels consisted of provisions for the corvée workers (2 pecks a man-day for 200 man-days), and the rest for such equipment as the corvée workers did not provide themselves, namely wooden posts and straw mats for cladding (Kuroda 1983: 66).

The expansion of world rice markets during the colonial period triggered the reclamation of vast areas of land in Southeast Asia. Migrants from the north flooded into the Burmese Delta between 1850 and 1900 and cleared large tracts of forest for rice-fields, which they farmed using extensive techniques (table 2.1). Between 1850 and 1880 the average holding size in the Upper Delta rose from 2.6 ha to 3.8 ha, while around Rangoon it rose from 4 ha to over 12 ha. The increase in the size of farms often led to over-hasty cultivation and underproductive methods (Adas 1974: 59, 62).

Considerable areas were also opened up for rice in Cochinchina and the Bangkok Delta at the same period, but in these regions land could only be rendered suitable for cultivation through the provision of large-scale drainage networks; this was undertaken at considerable expense by the French and Thai governments (see chapter 3).

As the supply of unoccupied land that can easily be converted to productive rice cultivation has shrunk, the costs of reclamation have risen, and there has been a corresponding shift from expanding the cultivated area to improving yields (table 2.2).

Raising yields

Here a highly simplified account of wet-rice cultivation is perhaps called for. As a rule, the farming cycle begins with the monsoon rains. Once enough rain has fallen to soak and soften the soil, the main field is tilled. The rice seed may have been sown meanwhile in a special seed-bed for transplanting, or it may simply be sown broadcast in the main field after tilling is completed. The young seedlings grow in standing water, and if irrigation is available the depth of water will be adjusted to follow the growth of the plant. The crop may or may not be fertilised and weeded. Just before harvesting any remaining water is drained off and the soil is allowed to dry out as much as possible before the reapers set to work. The grain is then dried and stored, threshed or unthreshed depending

Table 2.1 *Rice production in the Burmese Delta*

	1855	1905/6
Rice exports	162,000 tons	2,000,000 tons
Price per 100 baskets	Rupiahs 45	Rupiahs 120
Cultivated rice area	280–320,000 ha	about 2,400,000 ha

Source: Adas 1974: 58

Table 2.2 *Relative contributions of area and yield to total growth in rice production during the period 1955–73*

	A	B	C
Burma	1.98	1.13	0.84
Cambodia	−1.04	−2.76	1.54
Indonesia	2.84	1.31	1.50
Japan	0.64	−0.88	1.55
Korea	4.09	0.55	3.52
Laos	3.48	1.61	1.75
Malaysia	5.91	3.97	1.86
Philippines	2.78	1.11	1.62
Taiwan	2.00	−0.15	2.15
Thailand	2.84	1.78	1.06
Vietnam	5.27	1.08	4.18

A: Annual growth rate of output (in %)
B: Change in output due to change in area (in %)
C: Change in output due to changes in yield (in %)

Source: ADB 1978: appendices I–4.5c/d

upon the variety and the harvesting technique. These are the basic steps of wet-rice cultivation.

We shall now discuss the modifications and elaborations by which Asian farmers have increased and stabilised their yields, leaving aside for the moment the question of water control, which deserves a chapter to itself.

One crucial factor in determining the choice of cultivation methods is the amount of land available. As one might expect, the simplest and least time-consuming methods of wet-rice cultivation are practised in regions where suitable land is abundant. Often such cultivation systems carry a high degree of risk, for the rice crop is left to grow more or less at the mercy of drought, flood or pests. The methods used to intensify rice cultivation generally stabilise yields as well as raising them.

There is often a marked contrast between the methods used in areas of high population density and sparsely inhabited regions of the same country. The twelfth-century Chinese writer Zhou Qufei records such a contrast with disapproval:

The farmers of Qinzhou [southernmost Guangdong] are very careless. When tilling they merely break up the clods, and the limit of their sowing techniques is to dibble in the seed. Nor do they transplant the rice seedlings. There is nothing more wasteful of seed! Furthermore, after sowing they neither weed nor irrigate, but simply leave Nature to take care of the crop. (Shiba 1970: 53)

As his standard of comparison Zhou had the rich and crowded regions of the Lower Yangzi, where rice was sown in meticulously ploughed and harrowed seed-beds, transplanted, irrigated, fertilised with a variety of manures and commercial fertilisers, and weeded and fed several times before harvesting. No wonder he was shocked by what he considered the laziness and improvidence of the southern barbarians. Marked contrasts existed between the Lower and Upper Yangzi provinces until heavy migration from the Delta to Hunan and Hubei in the sixteenth and seventeenth centuries imposed the use of more productive techniques (Rawski 1972). Similar differences existed between Upper and Lower Burma up to the early twentieth century, when migrants from the densely settled plain of Mandalay introduced some technical improvements to the Burmese Delta (Adas 1974: 129), and between Tonkin and Cochinchina during the French occupation of Vietnam (Henry and de Visme 1928: 52). Sometimes migrants raise cultivation standards by introducing improved techniques; this has been a guiding principle in such policies as the Indonesian *transmigrasi*, whereby landless farmers from Java and Bali are given a new start in underpopulated and underproductive islands like Sulawesi (Charras 1982; Mantra 1981: 134 ff). On the other hand, when they find themselves in areas where land is plentiful, migrants not infrequently abandon the laborious techniques necessary in overcrowded regions in favour of less demanding methods. This was what happened when the French opened up the land market in Cochinchina to rich French and Vietnamese: although the landowners employed highly skilled farmers from Tonkin as their labourers, the cultivation methods used were far less intensive and productive than those of Tonkin (Robequain 1939: 96).

So many variations and combinations exist in wet rice cultivation techniques that an exhaustive examination would easily occupy a whole volume. An excellent study of historical and regional variation in Malaya (Hill 1977) gives an idea of the complexity of the subject. Here we shall simply mention a few of the more significant variations.

The least productive and reliable system of wet-rice cultivation systems is one where the fields are not accurately levelled or thoroughly tilled, the only supply of water is natural rainfall, the rice is sown broadcast, directly onto the fields, no fertilisers or manure are used, and the crop is not weeded or protected from pests. Such simple methods were to be found, for example, in large areas of Laos and Cambodia (Delvert 1961; Taillard 1972). A highly productive system would include careful water control, based on an adequate irrigation network; the fields would be accurately levelled, carefully tilled and manured; selected seed-grain would be sown in a separate seed-bed, to be transplanted into the main field in straight lines suitably spaced, the right amount of fertilisers would be applied and weeding would take place at frequent intervals, and herbicides and pesticides would be used to safeguard the crop. The success of the Green Revolution is premissed on such practices, but cultivation systems of comparable sophistication existed well before the 1960s, some of the earliest in parts of medieval China (Bray 1984: 597), and the most highly developed (which in many respects served as models for the agronomists of the Green Revolution) in early twentieth-century Japan and Taiwan (Dore 1969; Francks 1983; Ishikawa 1967: 59).

There are several discrete operations in wet-rice cultivation, each of which can be perfected separately or in combination – although in general all the operations will be at a similar level of sophistication. The question of seed selection and preparation has already been dealt with in chapter 1. Next comes the question of the seed-bed and sowing techniques. It is very wasteful to sow the seed directly in the main field, and the use of a separate seed-bed also permits more efficient and economical use of water and fertilisers. Here a medieval Chinese agronomist describes the preparation of the seed-bed:

In autumn or winter the seed-bed should be deeply ploughed two or three times so that it will be frozen by the snow and frost and the soil will be broken up fine. Cover it with rotted straw, dead leaves, cut weeds and dried-out roots and then burn them off so that the soil will be warm and quick. Early in the spring plough again two or three times, harrowing and turning the soil. Spread manure on the seed-bed.

The best manure is hemp waste, but hemp waste is difficult to use. It must be pounded fine and buried in a pit with burned manure. As when making yeast, wait for it to give off heat and sprout hairs, then spread it out and put the hot fertiliser from the centre to the sides and the cold from the sides to the centre, then heap it back in the pit. Repeat three or four times till it no longer gives off heat. It will then be ready for use. If it is not treated in this way it will burn and kill the young plants. Neither should you use night-soil, which rots the shoots and damages human hands and feet, producing sores that are difficult to heal. Best of all the fertilisers is a mixture of burned compost, singed pigs' bristles and coarse bran, rotted in a pit.

The seed-bed should be soaked and brought to a fine tilth, then sprinkled with chaff and compost. Trample them into the soil, rake the surface quite smooth, and then you can broadcast the seed. (*Chen Fu nongshu*: 5–6)

Nowadays the seed-bed is more likely to be prepared with a small rotary tiller, or even a tractor, and fertilised with chemical fertilisers, phosphates and nitrates. If the seedlings are to be tranplanted mechanically rather than by hand, then they may not even be sown in soil; instead specially treated paper is used, in sheets of a size which will fit directly into the mechanical transplanter. Transplanting takes place once the seedlings have grown to 20 or 25 cm, which may take one month or two depending on the variety. By thus reducing the period the rice-plants spend in the main field, the farmer may well be able to grow two or more crops where only one was possible before.

Transplanting also contributes to higher yields by strengthening the root system and encouraging tillering. If the plants are set in the ground in regular lines, then weeding and pest control are greatly facilitated. In China it appears that farmers tried to plant in straight lines, judging probably by eye, as early as the first century AD; this can be seen from numerous clay grave models depicting rice-fields.[4] Later methods became more sophisticated, involving the use of marker ropes, special 'seedling horses' (figure 2.6), or adjustable marking machines (Bray 1984: 279 ff). Straight lines also permitted the use of weeding hoes or, eventually, specially designed rotary weeders (apparently these were an eighteenth-century Japanese invention) which saved much painful bending (Bray 1984: 314 ff). Thus a switch from broadcasting to transplanting will easily increase yields by 40% (Grist 1975: 149).

The question of how the field is tilled is an interesting one, for it presents a striking contrast with the course of development in European agriculture, where increasingly powerful animal-drawn implements were developed to till as large an area as possible. The fundamental importance of animal traction in European agriculture was a crucial factor in the development of mechanisation. In the wet-rice regions of

Figure 2.6   A 'seedling-horse', yang ma, *illustrated in the* Nongzheng quanshu
(21/9a)

Asia, however, things developed rather differently. In underpopulated areas where land for rice and for grazing was plentiful and manpower was scarce, cattle were often used not to pull ploughs but simply to trample the fields to a good tilth; this was a common practice in parts of Malaya and Indonesia (Hill 1977; Woodard 1805). But the combined use of plough and harrow brings the soil to a much better consistency, and the simple but effective ploughs and harrows which are still in use in many parts of China were in use in the Canton and Tonkin area by the fourth century AD, as can be seen from surviving grave models (Bray 1984: 223). Very similar ploughs and harrows are to be found throughout East and Southeast Asia. Although they have frequently been dismissed as primitive by Westerners, in fact the shallow ploughing and thorough stirring of the soil into a thick smooth mud is exactly what is required for wet-rice cultivation. Deep ploughing may well break up the claypan below the mud which makes the rice-field impermeable, and the substitution of tractors for traditional ploughs requires much care (Berwick 1951). Where rice production is really intensive there is little land available for pasture; however manpower is abundant. Under these circumstances tilling methods frequently revert to what has been described as 'horticulture', that is to say farmers will till their fields with a variety of heavy iron hoes rather than with ploughs. Tokugawa Japan was a particularly conspicuous example; Ōgura Nagatsune depicts several hundreds of hoe types in his *Treatise of Useful Farm Tools* (*Nōgu Benri Ron*) of 1822. A few decades later, however, impressed by the superior efficiency of Western steel ploughs and deep tillage, Japanese agronomists were advocating a return to horse-ploughing, and in fact the horse-plough was widespread throughout Japan until the postwar period (Ishikawa 1981: 19). In other areas tractors or mechanical tillers have been substituted for more traditional ploughs, or for simple hoes. However it is well to remember that in wet-rice agriculture a simple tool such as the hand-hoe may well represent a more advanced technical stage than the more complex animal-drawn plough and harrow.

The choice of fertiliser also gives considerable scope for improving yields. Commercial nitrates and phosphates are an essential element of the Green Revolution package, and without them the HYVs often yield even less than traditional varieties, whereas with them they may yield more than twice as much (Yamada 1975: 184; Barker 1978: 66). But traditional varieties do not usually respond well to chemical fertilisers; they require the use of manure or other organic fertilisers. The simplest of fertilisers, used by almost all rice-farmers throughout history, are compost, manure and the ashes from the rice stubble, which is generally burned just before ploughing. Until ten years ago these were still the chief fertilisers in use in Kelantan, Malaysia; since compost and manure were in very short supply, these were usually reserved for the seed-bed, while the burnt stubble was the only fertiliser used on the main field (Bray 1985). Burning the stubble has often been condemned as wasteful and ineffective, but in fact it is a good source of potassium and phosphates, and the heat serves the useful purpose of killing the eggs of insect pests.

Farmers in the densely populated areas of China were experimenting with new sources of fertiliser in medieval times. As well as piling the mud from the irrigation ditches onto the fields and ploughing in weeds and other types of green manure, Chinese farmers purchased commercial fertilisers such as oil-cake, fish-meal and the waste from making bean-curd. The expense was not usually begrudged, for these commercial fertilisers were very effective: a single finely pounded oil-cake would fertilise a sixth of an acre of rice seedlings (enough to transplant an area as much as 25 times the size) (*Shen Shih nongshu*: 236). A thriving trade in fertilisers developed in medieval China, not only in the more industrial fertilisers like oil-cake but also in lime and in mollusc shells (used for the lime content), river mud, silkworm waste and human manure, all of which were sometimes transported over considerable distances.

The introduction of chemical fertilisers has led to very significant increases in rice yields. In 1937 a member of the Chinese National Agricultural Research Bureau calculated on the basis of experimental results that national rice output could be increased by 30% if the correct amounts of nitrates, superphosphates and potassium were to be applied throughout the country. In fact chemical fertilisers were already in fairly widespread use, especially in the coastal provinces, but domestic production was insufficient and between 1928 and 1933 China was importing 100–150,000 tons of chemical fertilisers annually, although for rice cultivation alone the application of some 6 million tons would have been necessary to achieve the 30% increase (Shen 1951: 38).

But chemical fertilisers by themselves do not always produce higher yields. Modern rice varieties must also be available, as many traditional varieties respond poorly or even negatively to their application (figure 2.7). It was the dissemination of improved varieties in the early decades of this century which led to the development of the chemical fertiliser industry in Japan (Francks 1983: 79). The provision of adequate water also has a significant effect on the efficiency of chemical fertilisers, as experiments in different regions of India and in Japan show (Ishikawa 1967: 119). The rapid expansion of irrigation networks in the Japanese colonies of Taiwan and Korea in the 1920s and early 1930s allowed the dissemination of improved varieties and of chemical fertilisers, bringing

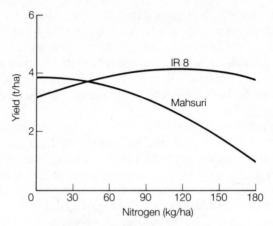

Figure 2.7   Response to nitrogen fertiliser
(from Barker 1978: 49)

average rice yields from about 1.5 t/ha to 2.5 t/ha by the mid-1930s (ibid.: 95).

Even under optimal conditions response to an increase in the amount of fertiliser applied is not linear, but reaches a level of maximum efficiency after which returns diminish; this level varies according to soil type, climatic conditions, rice variety and so on (Barker 1978: 49). In India from 1953 to 1963 the annual growth rate in the application of fertilisers was 19% and the annual increase in total agricultural output 2.5%; in Japan over the same period the annual increase in fertiliser application was only one-third as great at 5.8%, but the corresponding increase in agricultural production was one-third higher, at 3.3% (Ishikawa 1967: 106, table 2–7).

The point at which an increase in fertiliser application becomes uneconomic will be determined by the relative prices of fertilisers and of rice; for many Southeast Asian rice-farmers the oil crisis put chemical fertilisers almost completely out of reach for several years. By contrast, in Japan during the period 1965 to 1979, although the nominal value of fertiliser inputs more than doubled, in real terms it actually declined by 24% (Matsuda 1982: 441).

Weeding the rice may also contribute to significant increases in yields, for weeds not only deprive the rice plants of water and nutrients but also harbour pests and diseases. But weeding the rice-fields is very difficult unless the seedlings have been transplanted in regular lines, and often farmers preferred to invest their labour elsewhere rather than crawl through the mud. Labour-saving devices seem to have been developed as early as the Song period in China's Yangzi Delta, probably because the spread of double-cropping greatly increased the amount of weeding necessary. The fourteenth-century agronomist Wang Zhen, who described a number of innovations in the hope that they would be widely disseminated, writes of a weeding device

shaped like a wooden patten, a foot or so long and roughly three inches broad, spiked underneath with rows of a dozen or so nails . . . The farmer stirs together the mud and weeds between the rows of crops so that the weeds are buried in the mud . . . In certain areas I have seen farmers weeding their fields by hand, crawling between the crops on their hands and knees with the sun roasting their backs and the mud soaking their limbs – a truly pitiable fate, and so I have described the hand-harrow here in the hope that philanthropists may disseminate its use. (*Wang Zhen nongshu*: 13/28b)

These implements are still in use today, and are photographed in Hommel (1937: fig. 97). We have already referred to the rotary weeders invented in Japan. The great modern improvement in weeding has been brought about by the production of chemical herbicides, used in many areas before the Green Revolution and rendered all the more indispensable by the spread of double-cropping and chemical fertilisers (which of course fertilise the weeds as well as the crops).

Chemical pesticides are another important innovation, and one which is almost without historical precedent. True, in China at least, farmers used to mix their seed-grain with ashes, arsenic or aconite in order to prevent attacks by insects (Bray 1984: 250), but still the crop remained highly vulnerable to pests and blight. The helplessness felt by the farmers is well described in an eighteenth-century Chinese work on technology:

There are two disasters that strike rice fields in the mountains, which can be counted neither as flood nor drought although their effect is intensified by either. The peasants accept these disasters as inevitable; although they weep and curse them there is nothing they can do. Alas, how bitter is such a fate! The first disaster strikes in mid-autumn, when the grain has started well, has flowered, and is just heading. Suddenly a cold spell strikes several nights running – what the locals call 'freezing the cassia flowers' – the rice panicles are blasted by the cold, shrivel, and turn black and mottled. This is known as the 'dark wind'. The other strikes in midsummer, in stifling humid weather when the hot air presses down on the land so that clouds form in the mountains. Frequently this produces rain, and its arrival coincides with a strong southerly wind which carries the rain back and forth with it. Such constantly changing weather, veering from wet to dry, affects the grain in the fields, for leaf-hoppers appear and, munching noisily, devour all the leaves completely. The peasants say these two disasters fall from the heavens. (*Suo shan nongpu*: 1/4; tr. Bray 1984: 505)

Table 2.3   Rice yields in East and Southeast Asia

Country	Year	Yield (t/ha of unhusked rice)	
Japan	1950	4.25[a]	
	1956	5.06[a]	
	1962	5.79[a†]	
	1965	4.58[b†]	
	1977	5.14[b†]	
Taiwan	1926	2.12	(native rice)[a]
		2.31	(improved rice)[a]
	1967	5.1⎫	(C. Taiwan)[a]
	1972	5.7⎭	
China (PRC)	1921–5	2.56	(E. Central)[a]
	1949	1.89[c]/2.16[d]	
	1957	2.69[c/d]	
	1968	3.16[c]	
	1978	3.98[e]	
	1981	4.32[e]	
	1983	5.07[e]	
South Korea	1955	2.7[f]	
	1965	3.1[f]	
	1974	3.7[f]	
Burma	av. 1963/7	1.62[g]	
	av. 1971/5	1.71[g]	
Indonesia	av. 1963/7	2.13[g]	
wet-season	av. 1963/7	6.01	(Bimas programme, Java)[h]
wet-season	av. 1963/7	3.38	(non-Bimas control, Java)[h]
wet- and dry-season	av. 1968/79	3.70	(Bimas)[h]
wet- and dry-season	av. 1968/79	4.85	(Bimas Baru using HYVs)[h]
wet- and dry-season	av. 1968/79	3.17	(Inmas: free choice of inputs)[h]
	av. 1970/4	2.61[g]	
Malaysia	av. 1950/5	1.92	(main season)[i]
	av. 1963/67	2.42	(main season)[i]
		2.75	(off-season irrigated)[i]
	av. 1971/5	2.73	(main season)[i]
		3.20	(off-season)[i]
Philippines	av. 1963/7	1.30[g]	
	av. 1971/5	1.59[g]	
Thailand	av. 1963/7	1.86[g]	
	av. 1970/4	1.88[g]	

Some measures could be taken to control pests even then; Chinese works advise running a bamboo comb through the plants to kill lurking insects, or sprinkling lime or tung oil on the plants. But it is only with the twentieth-century development of the chemical industry that truly effective pesticides have become available.

The foregoing processes aim to increase the yields of rice. Once the rice is ripe, it is still possible to increase the amount of grain available for consumption or sale by improving harvesting, processing and storage methods. Storage is a serious problem. Grain stored unthreshed, in the panicle, as is usually the case when reaping-knives and not sickles are used, may last for several years without spoiling. But farmers who have adopted double-cropping, new high-yielding varieties and the sickle have to thresh their grain before storing it, and complain that this type of rice keeps much less well (Bray 1985). Both large- and small-scale storage present enormous problems, and it has been said that even today more grain is lost in store than is lost by natural disasters; in some countries losses in storage are said to reach 50%, and 12% seems to be a reasonable average for most parts of South and Southeast Asia (Grist 1975: 401; Tani 1975).

Rice yields throughout Asia have risen steadily in the last few decades, with improvements in water supplies, better cultivation practices, the dissemination of improved varieties and increased use of chemical fertilisers and pesticides (table 2.3). The question arises as to whether they can be increased indefinitely. Economic considerations will evidently impose certain limits on the further improvement of irrigation networks or on farmers' ability to increase their use of fertilisers. But it seems that the limits of the soil and of the rice-plant have not yet been reached. If we consider the case of Japan, which has the highest yields anywhere in Asia, we find that from 1965 to 1977 yields increased at an average annual rate of 0.97%. This surely gives grounds for optimism.

Sources:
[a] Ishikawa 1981: 3, table I–1
[b] Matsuda 1982
[c] *Agricultural Yearbook of China 1980**
[d] Wiens 1980*
[e] OECD 1985
[f] Ban et al. 1980: 45
[g] ADB 1978: 346, appendix I–4.4
[h] Palmer 1977: 103
[i] Taylor 1981: 53, appendix, table 2. 1
[†] Ishikawa and Matsuda both take their figures from the Ministry of Agriculture's *Economic Survey;* the break in progress after 1962 seems improbable, especially given the figures for Taiwan. Perhaps Matsuda's figures are in fact for polished, not unhusked rice.
[*] See Stone (1982) for an evaluation of these statistics.

Labour productivity and the mechanisation question

The productivity of labour can be increased through a variety of means. Fertilisers, herbicides and pesticides may all improve yields without raising labour requirements, indeed the use of herbicides and pesticides can release the farmer from hours of back-breaking labour. So too do improvements in the water supply, dealt with in chapter 3. Sometimes yields can be improved without any additional expenditure of capital or of labour, if work-patterns are reorganised so that labour is deployed more efficiently. According to studies carried out in Kelantan, Malaysia in 1973–4, an average of 203 eight-hour man-days per hectare were required in the off-season to produce 2.8 t/ha of rice (Fujimoto 1976a: 41; 1976b: 162). Although the greatest potential for increasing yields lay in the application of pesticides and fertilisers to the young seedlings, better *timing* of operations, it was found, would also improve yields by a far from insignificant amount, possibly totalling as much as 30% (Fujimoto 1977: 56).

The most obvious way of raising the productivity of human labour is to substitute some alternative form of energy. In Asian countries where pasture-land is scarce, draught animals may sometimes require almost as much labour for the provision of fodder as they save in the field. Water-power is another matter. The spread of water-raising equipment in medieval China must have brought about considerable savings in human labour (Needham 1965: 330–62; Li Jiannong 1957: 28–36).

The oldest piece of water-raising equipment was the swape or well-sweep (*shaduf* in Arabic), first known in Babylonia and Ancient Egypt and mentioned in a Chinese text of the fourth century BC; a hand-operated scoop-wheel which raised water into a flume was also in early use in China. The most typical Chinese and East Asian water-raising device was the square-pallet chain-pump, colloquially known as the 'dragon-backbone machine' (figure 2.4), which was in use by the second century AD. Though usually worked by human labour, it could also be geared up and turned by animal-or water-power, as an illustration from the seventeenth-century technical treatise *Tiangong kaiwu* shows (Needham 1965: 581–2). Water-wheels seem to have been a later introduction from the West, first illustrated in an agricultural treatise, the *Wang Zhen nongshu*, of 1313. But even though they contributed greatly to the spread of irrigation, compared to motorised pumps the efficiency of the traditional machinery was low. 'An ox would be able to irrigate, by turning a water-wheel, 0.3 *mu* [approx. 0.02 ha] in one hour; when operated by four labourers, only 0.1 *mu* per hour would be possible, but when equipped with a 3 HP electric motor it would irrigate over ten times as much' (Vermeer 1977: 190).

Perhaps more efficient in their replacement of human labour were the water-powered hammers and mills which hulled and ground the grain (Needham 1965: 390–405). Water-powered trip-hammers were said by one first century Chinese writer to be one hundred times as efficient as the traditional pestle and mortar, and by the fourteenth century Wang Zhen tells us of huge water-mills which could mill enough grain daily for a thousand families (*Wang Zhen nongshu:* 19/10a-b). As in medieval Europe, many of the Chinese mills were owned by abbeys or monasteries, or by rich merchants, though the government made repeated attempts to control them so as to reduce their profits and lower the prices paid by the poorer citizens.

To return to irrigation, there is no doubt that the introduction of small diesel and electric pumps has revolutionised the lives of millions of rice-farmers. In the Saga Plain in Japan, for example, the installation of specially designed electric pump-sets reduced the labour requirements for irrigation from 70 man-days/ha in 1909 to 22 in 1932 (Ishikawa 1981: 16), and output per man-day increased from 12.6 to 25.3 kg of rice in the same period (Francks 1983: 259); the considerations governing the choice of electricity as the energy source, as well as the size and design of the pumps, were very carefully considered beforehand (ibid.: 210–45).

Since pumps increase the output of the land as well as reducing labour requirements, it is not surprising that unavailability or lack of capital seem to be almost the only obstacles to their adoption. Before 1949 few Chinese farmers had been wealthy enough to purchase pumps, but collectivisation permitted the rapid mechanisation of irrigation in most parts of China (though 'dragon backbones' are still in use in some poorer areas [Wertheim and Stiefel 1982: 30]). Although the figures are far from accurate, it seems that between 1949 and 1956 the number of HP of installed pumps quadrupled from 100,000 to 396,000, while the area irrigated by these pumps rose from 370,000 ha in 1954 to 883,000 ha in 1956; by 1965 it was claimed that over 7 million HP of pumps were installed, irrigating some 6.6 million ha of land (Vermeer 1977: 193, table 34).

The mechanisation of other processes in rice farming has, however, often met with both technical and social obstacles. Here we shall deal briefly with some of the technical problems encountered and their solution. The suggestion has often been put to me that the only real obstacles to the large-scale mechanisation of rice-farming must be social, since rice cultivation in the USA and Australia (and to some degree in

Southern Europe and Africa) is very highly mechanised indeed, to the point that in the USA the crop is often sown by plane and may require only five man-days per hectare in all. It is certainly true that in most Asian rice-growing regions high population densities, scattered holdings and acute shortage of capital do hinder easy rationalisation, though they can be counteracted to some extent by such institutional measures as land reform or the provision of rural credit. Dumont (1957: 150) points out that when a programme of land consolidation was implemented in Japan after the Second World War that of itself led to a 15% increase in production. And in Kelantan, Malaysia, where in the 1970s the Agricultural Development Authority made tractors available for hire at heavily subsidised rates, their use was quickly adopted by all but the poorest farmers, even though they often damaged the bunds separating the fields and impacted the soil (Bray and Robertson 1980).

There is an important natural obstacle to the adoption of heavy machinery in Asia, namely the paddy soils. The agronomist Grist explains (1975: 198):

Where land can be cultivated during the dry season and flooded in the wet season, or where a firm bottom or pan provided by heavy clay soil exists and water control is good, the machines and system of cultivation for paddy differ but little from those employed in cultivating a dryland cereal such as wheat, although the technique must be adjusted to conditions arising from imperfect water control. Soils of this description are found in the rice areas of the United States, the Guianas, Australia, and parts of Europe and Africa. It is in these countries, therefore, that paddy cultivation is highly mechanised. A great deal of paddy land in Asia is in deltas, coastal strips and along the banks of rivers; much of it is swamp and consists of clay silts, silts and silty sands – providing a deep 'mud' in which machine wheels cannot find adhesion, so that the flotation method appears to be the only one for heavy implements.

The demands of terrain and water control form a further obstacle to the use of large machines, for they often severely restrict field size. This is not simply a by-product of population pressure or partible inheritance: there is little that can be done, for instance, to broaden terraced fields on a steep slope. The intensive demands on skilled labour typical of rice cultivation are a further obstacle to the use of machinery. First, the high degree of skill required has made it difficult even to substitute hired labour for family labour, so that farms have tended to become smaller as methods become more intensive, and secondly, the more skilled and complex a human task is, the more difficult it is to design a machine that can perform it as well. For instance, where a farmer using a sickle finds no difficulty in cutting every panicle of rice in the field, a combine-harvester will miss a swathe round the edge and in the corners which, especially in a small field, may make a substantial difference to the total yield. Corners are always a problem with machinery: farmers in Kelantan who hired tractors to plough their fields then had to till the corners themselves, using heavy iron hoes.

A subsistence farmer relying on family and exchange labour may not count the cost in man-hours of his rice crop, particularly if he has few opportunities to invest his labour elsewhere. But the introduction of double-cropping, the need to use hired labour, the possibility of increasing his income through cash-cropping or off-farm employment, all bring increasingly acute pressures to bear on his time and capacities. When double-cropping was introduced in Kelantan, rice-farming became a year-round occupation instead of occupying only six or seven months, and since large blocks of land were irrigated according to the same schedule, it became difficult for farmers to overcome the bottlenecks of transplanting and harvesting by exchanging labour. With barely one month between the harvesting of one crop and the planting of the next, pressure on labour became intense, and so most farmers who could afford to do so switched from buffalo-ploughs to tractors, despite the disadvantages mentioned earlier (Bray and Robertson 1980).

Experiments with the mechanisation of rice cultivation in Malaysia, as in most Asian countries which were once Western colonies, go back to the 1920s and 1930s, and were until recently based almost exclusively upon the modification of Western-style heavy machinery. Not surprisingly, such experiments were usually only a qualified success (e.g. Berwick 1951). The real breakthrough was to come from Japan.

Farm size in Japan had long been small: in 1910, 70% of farmers operated less than 1 hectare and only 3% operated more than 3 ha (Agric. Bureau 1910: 8), but land ownership was far less equally distributed. After the Second World War an extremely effective programme of land reform was implemented (Dore 1959). In 1945, 46% of Japan's total farm-land had been cultivated by tenants, but by 1950 the figure had dropped to 10% and it continued to fall thereafter (Ogura 1967: 70); it is important to note, however, that the total number of farms remained almost unchanged, at 5.4 million in 1908 and 5.2 million in 1970 (Tsuchiya 1976: 85). The Agricultural Land Law of 1961 prohibited farmers from acquiring holdings of over 3 ha. Since smallholding had been institutionalised, there would clearly be a market for appropriately small-scale machinery. As the economy recovered after the war and decentralised light industries started to expand, many of which used a putting-out system similar to that of Europe in its early phase of industrialisation, opportunities for commercial cropping and for part-time employment off or on the farm increased; moreover, these occupations were more profitable than rice-farming. The traditional Japanese attachment to the family rice-farm, coupled with a costly government policy of rice-price subsidies, prevented farmers from abandoning rice cultivation, but they were anxious to have as much free time as possible to engage in more lucrative activities. They also had more capital to invest in their farms. Clearly the time was ripe for the mechanisation of rice-farming.

The principle obstacle to the rapid introduction of farm machinery was the lack of suitable equipment. Results from experimental farms in Japan generally showed that large-scale machinery as used in the West was not suitable for use in the typical tiny paddy-fields: even on cooperative farms where land consolidation had been carried out, although its use greatly improved the productivity of labour this often entailed a considerable reduction in rice yields (Tsuchiya 1976: 180). It took some time for suitable small-scale machinery to be perfected. The first item to be developed was the power-tiller, now a familiar sight all over the world. This first came into use in Japan in the 1950s, and by the 1960s had become a standard item of farm equipment. The Japanese Institute of Agricultural Machinery, one of whose duties is to test all new farm machinery on performance, durability and handling, tested over 400 models of power-tillers between 1955 and 1975 (Grist 1975: 233), and certainly played a key role in the more recent development of successful small-scale harvesters and (most difficult of all) transplanting machines.

Japanese agriculture mechanised rapidly. From 1955 to 1966 power-tillers were the main machines in use, and transplanters and small-scale reaper-binders were first introduced in about 1967 (Tsuchiya 1976: 186); their dissemination was rapid, following immediately on the perfection of efficient models. The transplanter was undoubtedly the greatest challenge. Although over one hundred models of various types had been developed in Taiwan alone by the early 1960s, none had given satisfactory results; by that time engineers in China as well as Taiwan were competing with the Japanese, and progress was speedy. More than ten efficient models were launched on the Japanese market in 1969, varying in price from $300 for a hand-operated machine to $1,000 for a powered type (Grist 1975: 221). In 1970 only 1% of Japanese farmers owned a transplanter, but the figure had risen to 61% by 1979. Reaper-binders, which became common in the late 1960s, were gradually superseded after the mid-1970s by the more efficient combine-harvesters; in 1982, 55% of farmers owned reaper-binders, and 31% owned combine-harvesters (Matsuda 1982: 444). But the figures for ownership of farm machinery do not represent the full extent of their use, for farmers in Japan tend to share their machines although very few rent them out for profit (ibid.: 450); the development of group and contract farming has also extended the use of machinery in recent years (Morio 1982).

The integrated mechanisation of rice cultivation, from ploughing to winnowing, has now been achieved in Japan, and since the process began in about 1955 there has been a transition from small- to medium-sized machinery. This was facilitated by a programme of land improvement whereby fields were regularised and enlarged and drainage improved; such improvements have been carried out on 43% of Japan's rice-land so far, but the very largest plots are no more than 0.3 ha in size, and the remaining 57% still consists of plots of less than 0.1 ha (Matsuda 1982: 447). A similar programme of land consolidation was initiated in Taiwan in 1962, but technical problems and corruption brought it to a halt in 1971 with only about 200,000 of Taiwan's 750,000 ha of arable land having been consolidated. As in Japan, the resulting fields were still tiny by Western standards. For example in San-lin in Central Taiwan field-size was doubled, yet this still only brought the average from 0.085 ha to 0.17 ha (Huang 1981: 121, 127).

The care and effort which have gone into designing appropriate machinery have ensured that yields in Japan have not suffered through its introduction: in fact, thanks to modern fertilisers and pesticides and improved water control, land productivity has continued its steady increase in Japan, rising by 12.2% between 1965 and 1977; labour productivity increased by 6.5% per annum over the same period, but although initially the price of machinery was low relative to rice prices, enabling many farmers to make this capital investment, from 1965 to 1977 the productivity of mechanical investment dropped rapidly, by 9.8% per annum (ibid.: 441).

Similar patterns of small-and medium-scale mechanisation have also occurred in South Korea, especially since the third Five-Year Plan of 1972–6 which set the modernisation of agricultural techniques as a priority (Ban et al. 1980: 71, 189), and in Taiwan, following an ambitious programme of land consolidation (Huang 1981: 121, 134). In both these countries, as in Japan, a rapid expansion of the economy and the growth of rural employment opportunities outside rice farming made farm mechanisation both possible and desirable. Much of the farm machinery has been imported from Japan, presenting problems of maintenance and repair (ibid.: 141).

Most Asian countries have experimented with Japanese power-tillers and threshers, but each region has specific technical requirements, which means that imported machinery may prove unsuitable, and in none of the other rice-growing regions of Asia are economic conditions as favourable as in Japan, Taiwan and South Korea. In quite a few regions, for example the Muda Scheme in Malaysia (see chapter 3), large-scale machinery still predominates; it is usually owned by private entrepreneurs who keep hire-prices at their uppermost limit, beyond the means of poor farmers who are also deprived of the opportunity of hiring out their labour (MADA 1980). Although some progress has been made towards modifying large-scale machinery to suit the local conditions of the Muda region, for instance reducing the size of the tractors from 60–70 HP to 35–40 HP, the use of heavy combine-harvesters is still damaging fields and making deep ruts, causing difficulties for the new tractors. At the same time:

Virtually no progress has been made in the mechanisation of transplanting despite years of development effort undertaken by various government agencies in cooperation with Japanese scientists. Initial attempts centred around the development of transplanting attachments for four-wheel tractors . . . A number of 8-row prototypes were tested . . . but were eventually abandoned owing partly to the high rate of missing hills created by tractor tyres as well as manoeuvrability problems. (MADA 1980: 6)

Here is a clear case of inappropriate technology applied to one process impeding the development of appropriate technology for another.

Quite apart from technical difficulties, financial obstacles must be presumed to play an important role in discouraging mechanisation, at least in the 'free' economies. Although tractors, mechanical threshers and other machinery are usually explicitly incorporated in the Green Revolution package, figures indicate that while poorer farmers have eagerly adopted improved varieties and fertilisers, which raise yields and income, they have lagged significantly behind larger farmers in investment in all forms of mechanisation or labour-saving products like pesticides (Barker and Herdt 1978: 91). In countries like Java, Thailand and India few tractors are to be found at all.

In the socialist economies financial difficulties are more easily circumvented, as brigades or communes can make more economical use of capital equipment than individuals. Ideological considerations have led the Chinese government to pursue a variety of policies on agricultural mechanisation, emphasising the virtues now of the Russian *kolkhoz*, now of intermediate technology, now of Wheat Belt-style farms. But ecological factors have confined large-scale Western-style machinery largely to North China and Manchuria, and in the rest of China, especially in the rice regions, efforts have been concentrated on producing small-scale equipment similar to that used in Japan, if somewhat heavier and sturdier (American RSID 1977: 151). Stavis (1978: 264) concludes that ideological pressures have in the main been overridden by a general pragmatic concern to improve rural living standards and increase production. Although supporting evidence is not yet available, it seems highly probable that the expansion and diversification of China's rural economy under the 'responsibility system' will lead to a rapid increase in small- and medium-scale mechanisation, as it did in Japan under similar circumstances. In a speech given in London in July 1985 He Kang, the Chinese Minister of Agriculture, said that from 1978 to 1984 the average annual increase of HP for farm machinery was 8.8%; this represents an emphasis on small machines, for in the year 1983–4, while the number of full-size tractors was expected to increase by 1.9% to 857,000, the number of power-tillers was expected to increase at ten times the rate, by 19.6%, to 3.3 million.

Japan has shown how the technical obstacles to mechanising rice-farming can be overcome. The most important achievement of small- and medium-scale mechanisation in Japan, Korea and Taiwan has been to reduce the labour requirements of rice cultivation and allow farmers more free time for more profitable alternative employment *without* exacerbating income differentials between rich and poor farmers and *without* depriving poorer farmers of opportunities for farm work. It has also been a significant factor in reducing the gap between rural and urban incomes, which is one reason why many economists consider the implications of the Japanese experience to be crucial for developing countries where land is scarce and labour plentiful.

3

Water Control

The chief objects of water control, as far as the rice farmer is concerned, are to reduce the risk of flood and drought, to ensure an adequate and regular supply of water which can be let in and out of the fields as required, and thus to increase the rice crops and even, if the water supply is sufficient, to allow the cultivation of more than a single crop a year. In dry areas where previously only low-yielding dry crops could be grown, or in flooded areas where farming was impossible, the introduction of water control means that new rice-fields can be constructed, increasing the arable area as well as intensifying production.

A comparison of the countries of monsoon Asia made by Ishikawa in the 1960s, based on statistics provided by the FAO and national government agencies, shows a clearly positive correlation between the irrigation ratio (the proportion of irrigated to total cropped area) and land productivity (the total cereal output per unit of cropped land) (1967: 74, chart 2–3). A study by UN(ECAFE)'s Bureau of Flood Control published in 1950 also shows that rice yields in those regions of Asia where water control systems do not exist are significantly lower than where water control is practised (figure 3.1). Japanese economists distinguish two landmarks in land productivity in Asia. The first is an average rice yield of about 2.3 t/ha, the second of about 3.8 t/ha (ibid.: 77). Amano (1954) estimates that the first level had been reached in China as early as the tenth century; Japan had reached it some time before the Meiji Restoration of 1868.[1] Ishikawa suggests that this first landmark in productivity can only be achieved where water control is practised (1967: 78; 1981: 30). The second level of 3.8 t/ha, reached by the 1950s in the deltas of the Yangzi, the Pearl and Red Rivers, and in Japan, seems to depend on more complex improvements over a large range of inputs which include not only water control but also improved crop varieties and fertilisers (ibid.: 122).[2] The crucial role of water control in raising rice yields is in any case clearly demonstrated.

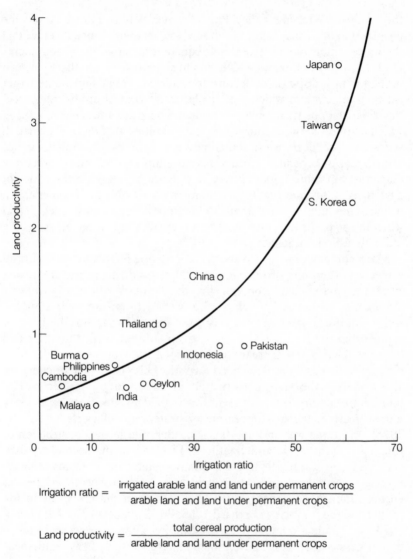

Irrigation ratio = $\dfrac{\text{irrigated arable land and land under permanent crops}}{\text{arable land and land under permanent crops}}$

Land productivity = $\dfrac{\text{total cereal production}}{\text{arable land and land under permanent crops}}$

Figure 3.1   Land productivity and irrigation ratio
(from Ishikawa 1967: 74)

Water control and institutions: the debate

Water control systems came in all sizes, from a single tank or well used by an individual farmer, to the vast irrigation networks of the Punjab and the proposed Mekong Valley Project which was to have involved the cooperation of China, Laos, Cambodia and Vietnam. Since it is rare that the water supply in any system is adequate to meet all the requirements of all the users, strategies which minimise or resolve conflicts between users are an indispensable feature of water control systems. The larger the total system into which a particular water control unit is integrated, the wider the potential range of conflict. There are a number of ways in which conflicts between individuals, communities, regions or even nation states may be dealt with: sometimes a system has in-built technical safeguards, or technical efficacy may be improved to meet increasing demands, but more important (at first glance anyway) are the codes of customary rights and regulations, enforced through careful supervision, which sometimes prove difficult to incorporate into national legislation when the state (or Irrigation Authority) replaces the village elders as the ultimate arbiters of justice.

Many contemporary Asian states are investing heavily in water control projects in the hope of raising agricultural productivity and improving rural incomes. Their concern for their voters' prosperity reflects attitudes of earlier Asian rulers who wished to ensure their subjects' well-being for a variety of reasons: pure humanitarianism, the hope of suppressing the rebellious instincts which so often welled up after bad harvests, the desire to increase the volume of taxes, or the ritual duty of a monarch who symbolised the good fortune of his people. Other concerns also underlay the state construction of water control projects. The fourteenth-century rulers of Ayutthya wished to link their capital city more directly to the sea, for reasons of strategy as well as trade (Tanabe 1978), and trade was an important consideration in the construction of canals in Transbassac and Southern Thailand in the second to sixth centuries (Stargardt 1983: 199). Many waterways in China, though serving a secondary purpose for irrigation, were primarily designed to ensure efficient movement of the grain tax from the provinces to the capital and the frontiers (Eberhard 1965: 80; Twitchett 1970: 84; Huang 1974: 51), while a number of large-scale irrigation projects undertaken by successive Chinese governments were designed as settlement schemes for landless peasants (Bray 1980). In feudal Japan local lords built canals in part to ensure their political control over the area (Kelly 1982b: 14), while in nineteenth-century Siam the royal house established water control facilities in vast areas of the swampy Bangkok Delta to provide estates for impoverished nobles (Tanabe 1978).

In the nineteenth century Marx and Weber suggested that there were strong links between the technical and social demands of water control and the emergence of centralised, monolithic states in Asia, associating such centralisation with the inhibiting of local initiative, with economic stagnation and with the development of a complex bureaucracy and social hierarchy which also impeded economic growth. Such hypotheses were subsequently elaborated by historians like Chi (1936) and Wittfogel (1931; 1957), who saw the necessity for centralised management of water resources as the key factor in determining the political and institutional forms of Asian societies. Chi in fact used the geographic expansion of state water control to explain a political and historical dynamism in Chinese society, but Wittfogel took Marx's notions of stagnation and repression further, postulating an equation between 'hydraulic society' and 'Oriental despotism'. Numerous subsequent studies have shown that centralisation and bureaucratic control are not necessarily concomitants of Asian water control systems, even when these are integrated into very large networks,[3] yet the concept of 'hydraulic societies' retains its fascination; it is interesting that, while repudiating Wittfogel's negative evaluation of the Chinese state, Needham too adheres to the idea that Chinese society was essentially organised around a monolithic 'feudal bureaucracy', derived in large part from the managerial requirements of predominantly large-scale water control (Needham 1974).

One of the main arguments that underlies such theories as 'Oriental despotism' and 'hydraulic societies' is that only a highly centralised state can mobilise sufficient capital and technical and administrative expertise to construct and run huge irrigation systems such as the Angkorian network described later in the chapter. It is certainly true that both Hindu and, later, Buddhist monarchs all over Southeast Asia saw it as part of their kingly role, an act of the highest religious merit, to donate generously from the royal treasuries to provide the necessary materials and funding (usually this meant stone, timber and the rice to feed corvée labourers). But kings were not the only instigators of such works. Temples, dignitaries, or even rich villagers often gave endowments to construct or maintain irrigation works on different scales. Such donations were usually recorded in inscriptions set, for example, in the wall of the tank thus financed; the stages of construction would be accompanied by religious rituals and the whole work consecrated upon completion (Stargardt 1983: 187).

Although the acquisition of religious merit was an important motive, we must not forget that it was usual for the builder of such a work to retain rights over the water which passed through it. In medieval Ceylon, for example, farmers paid something akin to a tithe to the owners of the tank which watered their fields. Since the provision of irrigation water improved yields, both farmer and donor stood to benefit materially, and if it was a monarch who was responsible for the improvement, he could count on an increase in his tax revenues, paid as a proportion of the farmer's produce which, even during times of peace and prosperity, might amount to over one-fifth of the harvest.[4] Often kings would donate tanks to religious foundations; again this was an act of merit which increased the revenues of the monastery or temple. As Stargardt (1983: 197) rightly points out, Southeast Asian societies were equally aware of both the religious and the economic benefits to be derived from hydraulic works, and to regard either motive as predominant would be a distortion.

Turning to the Far East, the link between 'feudalism' and water control has also been insisted upon by Japanese historians, departing from the early twentieth-century Marxist analyses of Japanese history which take water and its control as an essential fourth factor of production (together with land, labour and capital) (see Kelly 1982a: 9). The organisational requirements and political potential of irrigation agriculture are seen by most Japanese historians, whatever their period of study or political persuasion, as crucial in determining the persistence of small-scale peasant agriculture (shōnōsei), the 'feudal' subordination of the individual to a hierarchical community (hōkensei) and the eventual emergence in early modern Japan, from previously more autonomous agricultural groupings, of the village as a corporate body (kyōdōtai) corresponding to the basic unit of irrigation (e.g. Kanazawa 1971: 13–16; Kelly 1982a: passim).

One reason why Japanese social scientists of every political hue take such a lively interest in water control is that it is seen even today as a key element in the agricultural modernisation debate, intimately related to the fate of Japanese rice farmers. The post-Second World War land reforms were closely linked with legislation reorganising irrigation management (the Land Improvement Law of 1949), and with heavy government investment in irrigation projects (Ogura 1967; Shimpo 1976; Kelly 1982a: 15). The mixed results did little to resolve the debate as to whether it was social and political factors which determined the technical organisation of irrigation and levels of agricultural production, or vice versa. Scholars such as Kanazawa (1971: 16) and his colleagues of the 'feudalist' persuasion believe, for example, that prewar irrigation management was largely determined by forms of land tenure and political control, and hold that radical legislative reforms were (and remain today) an indispensable precondition for technological improvement and the breaking-down of a crippling system of smallholder agriculture. On the other hand, Shinzawa Kagatō and his followers, who have been highly influential in shaping state policy, maintain that state investment in technological improvement can resolve the social contradictions which hitherto impeded the rationalisation and modernisation of Japanese agriculture (Kelly 1982a: 22).

Much Japanese scholarship on water control focuses on the contradiction between common management of water and individual ownership of land. This preoccupation with the dialectic between communality and individualism, and the necessity for breaking traditional moulds, is to some extent historically determined in the case of Japan. In other parts of Asia different factors may be more important. The famous *subaks* or irrigation societies of Bali may be said to exhibit a degree of communal pressure towards individual participation similar to that of the Japanese irrigation groups, yet in the next-door island of Lombok, where regional rulers intervened much more directly in village life, popular participation in the running of the *subak* is small even in areas of Balinese population (Gerdin 1982: 71). Groslier (1979) points to the preponderantly ritual factors which determined the form of the elaborate irrigation networks of classical Angkor. Taking contemporary examples in Sri Lanka, Chambers (1980: 48), while allowing the importance of prevailing technological levels in shaping the organisation of water control, maintains that such features of a society's culture as the degree of hierarchy or egalitarianism are also major determinants.

The debate as to whether technological change determines social evolution or vice versa is implicit, if not explicit, in almost all works on modern development, and as it applies to the question of water control it is of special relevance to the rice economies of Asia today. Many national governments and international aid agencies are currently investing heavily in the construction of large-scale irrigation schemes in areas where water control was previously small-scale or even non-existent. Official planners have become ruefully aware of the social complexities and difficulties attendant upon such technical change, and the literature on water control has grown rapidly in consequence. Since the conflict of interests between individual and community, so meticulously documented in the Japanese studies, is common to all water control systems, most social science studies have focused mainly on the institutional features of water control, treating the technical features as secondary. But the classification of water control management according to criteria such as 'centralisation' or 'decentralisation' lends itself to ideological bias. Furthermore, at least in so far as wet-rice cultivation is concerned, it is undeniable that certain social and economic characteristics (such as the small scale of fields and farms, and the necessity for cooperation at various levels between the farmers in a single water control unit) are common to all the societies in question, whatever higher political or economic forms may prevail. It is also clear that these characteristics are imposed by the technical requirements of irrigated rice cultivation.

A technical classification of water control systems

The technical concept of 'water control' (*shuili* in Chinese, *suiri* in Japanese, literally 'turning water to advantage') is perhaps peculiarly Asian.[5] It covers three interlinked categories: irrigation, drainage and flood control. Although Westerners usually connect rice principally with irrigation, in fact any or all of the three may be necessary for its successful cultivation, depending on topography and climate. Irrigation proper, the supplementing of an insufficient water supply, may be carried out on almost any scale from the individual household to a whole province or nation. Drainage, the removal of excess water, tends to require greater investments of labour and other resources, and cannot usually be carried out without the cooperation of a relatively large community or the intervention of a wealthy family or institution. Flood control along the great rivers of monsoon Asia requires enormous investments in construction and maintenance, but since it is literally a matter of life and death for thousands if not millions of their subjects, and often a matter of national survival as well, Asian monarchs have made it a primary concern since very early times.[6] While irrigation and drainage functions tend to be complementary, those of irrigation or drainage may well conflict with those of flood control, often with disastrous results. One thinks, for instance, of the peasants of North China breaching the Yellow River dykes to irrigate their wheat-fields (Needham 1971: 228), or of the rich landowners of Central China draining so much of the shore of the Dongting Lake to make dyked fields that the lake could no longer serve as a proper overspill for the Yangzi when it was in spate. Generally speaking, in the rice-growing regions of monsoon Asia irrigation and drainage systems were constructed independently of flood-control dykes and canals. Today, given the vastly increased financial and technical resources available, it is possible to construct water control systems integrating all three functions.

In this chapter we shall follow a broad classification of water control systems based primarily on their functional and technical characteristics.[7] We shall demonstrate some of the important factors in their historical expansion and change, briefly linking institutional to technical forms, and considering the implications for contemporary development.

Gravity-fed irrigation networks

Many of the world's most impressive irrigation systems have been found in arid zones, hardly surprisingly, for in such areas, although subsistence agriculture may often be sustained without supplementing the meagre supply of rain water, it is only by providing extra water, and especially an assured and regular supply of water at the main growth period of the principal crops, that surpluses can be produced. The effect of irrigation is equally impressive for dry crops like wheat or cotton and for wet crops like rice or sugar-cane. The Sudan's Gezira Scheme allowed good cotton to be grown under almost desert conditions (Gaitskell 1959); the irrigation schemes of the Punjab have allowed abundant crops of wheat, cotton and rice to be grown (Dasgupta 1977; Farmer 1981); more anciently, irrigation water from the Yellow River and its tributaries gave rise to the intensive production of millet, wheat, sorghum and other cereals and in particular maintained a steadily high level of production in the Wei River valley, a naturally arid region in the northwest where Chang'an, the traditional capital of China, was located (Bray 1984).

Wet rice, like dry crops, flourishes under irrigation in arid zones, but a more regular and abundant supply of water is required if crop growth is to be maintained, especially where rainfall is not only low but irregular. Very often rainfall patterns differ significantly within a relatively small area, and irregularity, poor seasonal distribution and high evaporation are just as important obstacles to successful agriculture as low rainfall, which is why it is not unreasonable to speak of the 'dry zones' of Sri Lanka and South India, for example (Mendis 1977: 13; Farmer et al. 1977: 10). In these areas, as in other 'arid zones' of monsoon Asia, annual rainfall may vary by as much as one-third from good year to bad (Nakamura 1982: 8).

The rice-plant's maximum water requirements occur between flowering and ripening. Since the rice has to be sown during the rains, its period of maximum growth often extends into the dry season, rendering harvests precarious in the absence of irrigation. In Upper Burma, for example, the annual rainfall of 700–1,050 mm is barely sufficient to produce a rice crop (Stargardt 1983: 196). But if water can be regularly supplied to the fields during the dry period production can easily be doubled, and indeed sometimes double-cropping becomes possible as in the case of Angkor in the ninth to twelfth centuries, when the Khmer empire was at its height (Groslier 1974: 103; 1979: 174–8). Stargardt (1983: 119) computes the increase in rice production in the Satingpra peninsula in Southern Thailand as irrigation techniques developed from the fourth to fourteenth century (table 3.1) and, if her computations are correct, the differences between fourth- and sixth-century production figures clearly show how irrigation could contribute to the growth of cities and elaborated economies. It is not simply the rise in average production, but the comparative reliability of irrigated rice crops, that permits such a leap from village to city, as Groslier says of the parallel stage in Khmer Cambodia (1974: 113): 'ce qui est certain, c'est que par rapport à l'ancienne économie de subsistance, on était passé à un système de production intensive et . . . dans toute la mesure du possible à l'abri des écarts du climat'. Ishikawa shows clearly that in Asia the productivity of rice, as well as of other crops, is directly correlated to the proportion of arable land which is irrigated (1967: 75) (figure 3.1).

It is important to remember, however, that, as Stargardt has shown (1983: 185–205), the vast and impressive irrigation systems characteristic of the Southeast Asian arid zones, those which supported the Pyū and Pagan dynasties of Upper Burma, the Pallava and Chola kings of South India and Ceylon, the kingdoms of Kediri and Majapahit in Java, and the Khmer empire in Cambodia, developed gradually from pre-existing small, local irrigation systems and, generally speaking, represented an increase in scale and sophistication of management rather than any great leap forward in technical expertise. Indeed they usually relied heavily for

Table 3.1   *Rice production at Satingpra, fourth to fourteenth centuries*

Century	area under rice (ha)	rice production (kg)
4th (pre-urban)	19,200	16,400,000
6th–9th (urban)	50,000	48,000,000
9th–13th (urban II[a])	130,000	130,000,000
9th–13th (urban II[b])	130,000	202,000,000
13th–14th (urban III[a])	37,000	35,200,000
13th–14th (urban III[b])	37,000	44,400,000

[a] Assuming single-cropping of long-season varieties.
[b] Assuming double-cropping of one long-season and one short-season traditional variety.
Source: based on Stargardt 1983: 119

their construction, maintenance and management on the contribution of villagers whose skills had been developed over centuries.

Ponds, tanks and reservoirs

The main evidence for both the early networks of tanks or ponds, and for the great irrigation systems of Southeast Asia, is archaeological, though some early inscriptions survive in Bali and Java (van Setten 1979: 33, 61) which refer to irrigation works or officers, while for South India there is considerable epigraphic evidence for the medieval period as to how revenues for irrigation works were raised, workers paid, rights allotted, and so on (Stargardt 1983: 186).

The typical dry-zone irrigation systems of Southeast Asia are situated in the valleys of small rivers or on the edges of the alluvial plains of great rivers like the Mekong or Chao Praya (Stargardt 1983: 200–5). Sometimes rainwater was collected in small tanks sited on natural depressions or excavated in alluvial soils, as in early South India and Sri Lanka. Such tanks were widespread in Andhra Pradesh and Tamil Nadu; sluices in the earthen walls controlled the flow of water into distributary channels which led down the natural slope of the land to water the fields below (Stargardt 1983: 186). Similar tanks go back at least to the third century BC in Sri Lanka (Brohier 1934–5; cited Stargardt 1983: 190–1), where they may originally have been connected with Naga worship. Small tanks filled by rainfall or natural percolation from the high water-table were used for domestic as well as irrigation purposes. These small tanks, and field canals, originated in the fourth to sixth centuries in the Satingpra sites (see Stargardt 1983: 80–2); navigable canals were first dug in the sixth century (ibid.: 82).

It is not easy to enlarge rain-fed tanks much beyond the scale of a single household in zones where rainfall is in any case sparse, and very often such tanks dried out soon after the rains unless the water-table was high and rainfall was supplemented by percolation. But if a stream or small river is trapped or diverted much larger volumes of water can be stored. Spencer (1974: 86) says that the technique of damming a small valley with an earth barrier is Indian in origin, and is found in Southeast Asia only in zones of Indian influence (including the Cham region of Vietnam). In early Cambodia, the plains of Upper Burma, South India and Ceylon, larger streams and rivers could be trapped since the stronger earthen or stone dams were carefully designed to withstand water-pressure and were provided with sluice controls leading off into distributary channels.

Shifting the dam further downstream allowed the tank to be enlarged, sometimes to enormous capacity. Leach (1961: 18) describes the village tanks of contemporary Sri Lanka as being about 7 feet in depth. 'Very roughly, the full tank covers much the same area of ground as the land below which it is capable of irrigating.' But where larger works were undertaken the dams or bunds were usually short relative to their capacity. The site would be carefully chosen to correspond to a natural depression, and as Stargardt points out 'the basic principle in the technology employed was to achieve an inverse ratio between the scale of bunding work and its effect' (1983: 192). The Mahendratatāka tank, built in the early seventh century by a Pallava king of South India, contained sufficient water to irrigate land almost 13 km away (Venkayya 1906: 203; cited Stargardt 1983: 188), and some South Indian tanks held enough supplies for 15 months, a necessity since their sources of supply could be extremely erratic (ibid.).

In mountain valleys the danger of rivers destroying their dams at the height of the rains meant that it was preferable to build a feeder canal rather than dam the river directly, diverting a more easily regulated portion of the river waters to fill the tank. Such works were common in Pyū (*c.*sixth- to eighth-century) and Pagan (mid-ninth- to late thirteenth-century) Burma, and could also attain enormous capacities. One Pagan royal tank irrigated about 15,000 ha, and several served areas of 7–10,000 ha (Stargardt 1983: 195).

Without doubt, however, the most impressive irrigation network in Southeast Asian history was that constructed around the capital of Angkor when the Khmers were at the height of their power in the ninth to twelfth centuries. At one point the Angkorian irrigation works supplied some 167,000 ha along the northern plain of the Tonlé Sap basin (Groslier 1979: 190). The city of Angkor was founded in the ninth century, on a sweep of fertile alluvial soil watered by numerous rivers and close to the rich fisheries of the Tonlé Sap. It also happened to be the geographical centre of the Khmer empire.[8] The 'hydraulic city' was developed under Indravarman (r. 877–89), who like Hindu rulers elsewhere in Southeast Asia strove to achieve the kingly virtues of Rāmā and to ensure the happiness and prosperity of his subjects, not only through his own spiritual perfection, but also by active intervention. The monarch was the 'Lord of the lords of the soil' (Groslier 1974: 114); as the Old Javanese version of the Rāmāyana has it:

> Care of the farmlands is always the king's responsibility
> For from these comes all the produce for the kingdom's welfare.
>
> (tr. van Setten 1979: 78)

The layout of Angkor was highly symbolic, for it was not a city in the European sense, but a political and ritual centre which interpreted the cosmos as a whole in terms of stone, soil and water. Thus as Groslier points out, to draw any distinction between *urbs* and *rus* in the case of Angkor would be wrong, for here *urbs* actually represents *rus* and nature, incorporating in itself the gods of fertility and the soil (1974: 111). The Khmer rivers and waterways, in the Angkorian philosophy, represented the triple course of the Ganges (Mekong means 'mother Ganges'), the temple which they surrounded represented the sacred mountain of Meru.

The early Khmer monarchs had inherited from the Funanese a huge network of canals which, as well as facilitating transport, drained and desalinated the northern plains between the Gulf of Siam and the Lower Mekong, and provided irrigation through a number of dams and tanks. Following the Hindu cosmological ideal, however, the tanks, canals, moats, temples and cities of Angkor were strictly geometrical in shape. The huge tanks, or *baray*, were not natural depressions but were built *above* or *below* the natural plain, to trap the waters of a small river. A double channel was dug around the site of the proposed *baray*, and some of the excavated soil was used to build the square retaining dyke between the channels, while the rest was used to fill in the stone monument or temple-mountain built in the centre of the *baray* (figure 3.2). The *baray* of Indravarman's capital, Lolei, was 300 ha in area and held at least 10 million cubic metres (Groslier 1974: 100). The clay and sand soils used to build the dyke formed an impermeable layer, preventing losses from seepage. The river water was fed into the *baray* through a series of dams and feeder canals. Since the natural slope of the land was northeast-southwest, the water moved naturally southwest through the distributary canals, and was let into the fields and led from one to another (the fields were square, and about 80 m across) by the simple expedient of making a small breach in the banks. The water supply from these huge reservoirs seems to have been sufficient to allow the Khmer to grow two crops of rice a year.

Being fed by gravity alone, the irrigation network was limited to an arc of between 30° and 45° below the *baray*, and the only way to expand the system was to build a new *baray* upstream. Each new king, therefore, founded a new temple with its associated *baray* and irrigation network, proceeding gradually northwards. It is not certain, though, that all the old systems remained operative and that the system expanded arithmetically with time, for the silt carried by the feeder canals tended to settle in the reservoirs. No cleaning was carried out, for this would have meant the enormous task of draining the whole *baray* (and depriving a whole district

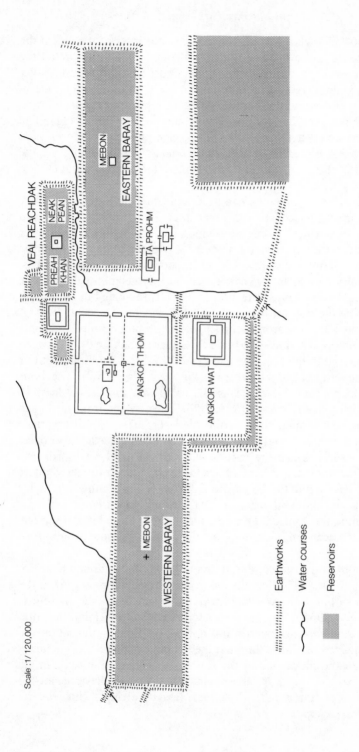

Scale :1/120,000

VEAL REACHDAK

PREAH KHAN
NEAK PEAN

EASTERN BARAY

MEBON

TA PROHM

ANGKOR THOM

ANGKOR WAT

WESTERN BARAY

+ MEBON

Earthworks

Water courses

Reservoirs

Figure 3.2 *General plan of Angkor*
(based on Coèdès 1948)

of crops for at least one season). As the *barays* silted up and the irrigation water carried less fertile silt into the fields rice yields would fall, and eventually – and suddenly – the water flow would cease altogether. Then the whole agricultural area dependent upon that *baray* had to be abandoned, for as the fields dried out a ferrous hard-pan formed which made the land irreversibly sterile.

The inbuilt obsolescence of the *barays* was probably a significant factor in the decline of Angkor from the fourteenth century. The Siamese conquered the Khmer capital in 1364, and thereafter continuous civil wars which lasted on and off for five centuries prevented any attempt at reconstruction of the Angkorian canals. Cambodia shifted back to the old zones of habitation in the north, and to the old agricultural techniques, which remain in use today. Rice yields are low, much land is left fallow and irrigation techniques are rudimentary or non-existent (Delvert 1961: 353). After the fourteenth-century Siamese invasion the Cambodians reverted to a subsistence economy, using extensive techniques where sometimes the rice-harvest gave only three times the amount of seed-grain. The population fell steadily, thanks to poverty and war, to an estimated 1 million in 1879 when the French moved in (ibid.: 425). The old agricultural heartlands around Angkor were soon overgrown by scrub (*veal*), except in the immediate vicinity of reservoirs and rivers, where the modern villages stand on ancient Angkorian sites (Groslier 1974: 105).

Much the same happened on the Satingpra peninsula in Southern Siam (closely linked by trade, culture and technology with the Mōn and Khmer empires across the South China Sea). Satingpra too was destroyed by the Siamese in the fouteenth century, at a time when it was probably already weakened economically by the deterioration of its irrigation network and consequent decline in agricultural production (Stargardt 1983: 36). Today aerial photographs show the faint outlines of the ancient square rice-fields, which had produced two crops of irrigated rice each year. They lie beneath the bunds of the modern strip-shaped fields in which a single crop of unirrigated rice is produced (ibid.: figs 37–9).

It was not always the case, however, that the fall of a kingdom meant a reversion to less intensive cultivation methods. Leach tells us that in Ceylon the large central reservoirs and feeder canals built and controlled by the state during the Sinhalese kingdom of Anurādhapura (*c.*second century BC to thirteenth century AD) fell into decay with the fall of the kingdom to be repaired very much in their ancient form under British rule. But village tanks in the same region, which had not always been linked to the larger systems, were constantly being built and repaired, and although very few can claim to have survived intact for more than a few centuries, many have been constructed on sites where ancient tanks had previously stood (1961: 15 ff). In Burma too, parts of the Kyaukse irrigation works have functioned continuously for over two thousand years (Stargardt 1983: 197). So while a few ancient centralised systems created almost irreversible damage to the environment as they decayed, others were able to survive indefinitely in segmented form.[9]

It is also important to bear in mind the crucial contribution of local farmers and dignitaries to such hydraulic works, of whatever size. Without the funds, materials, labour, management skills and technical expertise provided locally, hydraulic works on whatever scale would have been impossible. As we have seen, the huge works of Angkor or medieval Ceylon and Burma simply applied tried and tested technical principles on a much larger scale than hitherto. They did not represent any intrinsic technical advance, which is why such systems were often able to survive for centuries in segmented and uncoordinated form long after the centralised state which had built them had disintegrated. Although the initiative for large irrigation schemes, as for other public works, may have come from high up, they depended for their success on close collaboration between state and village. In many of these societies, the titles given to villagers who acted as engineers or organisers of labour were of much earlier origin that the inscriptions which record their contribution.[10] The interpretation of such titles is often difficult, but village officers certainly appear to have included elders in charge of the construction of local irrigation works, surveyors of dams and officers in charge of maintenance (van Setten 1979: 60 ff). Royal officers, on the other hand, had the role of mobilising and, where necessary, arbitrating between different villages.[11] Usually it was the royal treasury which provided the rice rations during construction work for the locally levied corvée labourers, but once the work was complete, individual villages became responsible for the normal running and maintenance. Village committees, often elected for fixed periods (e.g. Stargardt 1983: 189 on South India, 196 on Burma), had the power to levy taxes on the irrigated land, part of which contributed to the royal revenues; the rest was used to pay labourers to clear out channels, to remove silt or repair bunds; carpenters and other craftsmen were paid to mend boats and sluices, and so on (Venkayya 1906; Stargardt 1983: section V passim). In some cases village labour was not paid, but each farmer contributed a certain amount of labour and materials during the dry season (e.g. in medieval Sri Lanka; Stargardt 1983: 192).

The level of local skills and knowledge which the medieval kingdoms of Southeast Asia could command was not inconsiderable:

The degree of expertise shown in levelling and aligning the bunds was very high and further exhibited in the excellent alignments followed by the canals – sometimes covering long distances and managing by means of tunnels to cross from one watershed to another. Excessive water pressures on the tank bunds were mitigated by the construction of high- and low-level paved sluices to regulate outflow and even by the introduction of further sophisticated devices such as valves and stone facings on the bunds. (Stargardt 1983: 192)

But these techniques, though sophisticated, had originally been developed by small communities and were therefore limited in potential. The great states of Southeast Asia were able to increase the scale of such works, but did not develop new technologies which would have enabled them to adapt to more challenging environments. The irrigation systems we have described were typical of upland valleys and plains, watered by small streams and rivers, in areas where natural rainfall was sparse and erratic; they were fed by natural gravitational flow. Thus the Khmers of Angkor were able to expand their irrigation network north of the Tonlé Sap and east of Angkor to the edge of the plains (Groslier 1974: 103), but their skills were not sufficient to master the meandering lower course of the Mekong. It was not until the colonial era that attempts to master the great rivers of Southeast Asia and to drain their deltas became feasible. The technologies and other skills and resources involved will be discussed further on in this section.

In the hilly regions of Southern and Central China, and in Japan, one of the most ancient forms of storing and redistributing water was a system based on small ponds which, like the small ponds or tanks of South Asia described earlier, supplied anything from a single farm to a small hamlet. But given the greater abundance and regularity of the natural rainfall in East Asia, the proportion of stored water to irrigated area could be much smaller, as low as 1: 5 instead of 1: 1:

On high land, identify the places where water accumulates and dig out ponds. Out of 10 *mu* [approx. 0.6 ha] of land you must be prepared to waste 2 or 3 *mu* for water storage. At the end of the spring when the rainy season comes heighten the banks and deepen and widen the interior. Strengthen the banks by planting mulberry or silkworm-thorns[12] to which buffalo may be tethered in the shade as their nature requires. Meanwhile the buffalo by trampling the banks will strengthen them, the mulberries will be well watered and grow into fine trees, and even in the dry season there will be sufficient water for irrigation, yet in heavy rains the tank will not overflow and harm the crops. (*Chen Fu nongshu*: 2)

Small ponds were constructed by rice-farmers throughout Central and Southern China at an early period, as can be seen from the large number of clay models (figure 3.3) found in graves of the Later Han dynasty (AD 25–220). In Sichuan, the Yangzi region, Guangdong and Guizhou, as well as in the Tai kingdoms of Yunnan, individual farmers dug small ponds which served to grow lotuses and water-chestnuts and to raise fish and turtles, as well as to irrigate the rice-fields (Bray 1984: 110; Yangzi 1979: 59). A text of slightly earlier date than the grave models, relating to the provinces just north of the Yangzi, refers to much larger ponds, in fact reservoirs, covering an area of one or more *qing* (i.e. well over 50 ha);

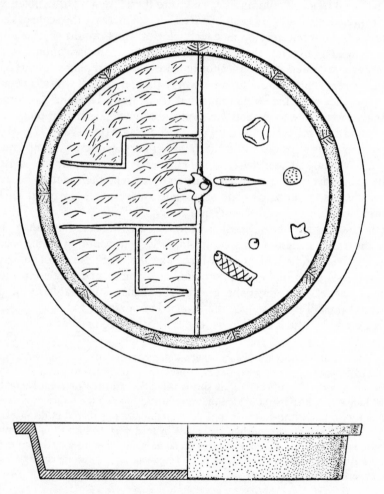

Figure 3.3   Han grave-model of irrigation pond and rice-field, from Guizhou (the right-hand section, the pond, contains fish, water-chestnuts and other aquatic plants)
(from *Wenwu* 1979: 5, fig. 17)

these, it says, would irrigate four times the area of rice-fields.[13] Such reservoirs had become common by the early Song dynasty (960–1127), and Ma Duanlin, a twelfth-century scholar, writes:

Along the Central and Southern Chinese coast there are reservoirs everywhere. Generally the lake lies higher than the rice fields, which in turn are higher than the river or sea. When there is a drought they release the lake water to irrigate the fields, and when it is too wet they drain off the water from the fields into the sea, so that there is never any natural disaster. (tr. Bray 1984: 110)

Large and small ponds are still important sources of irrigation water in many parts of Central and Southern China today (Gustafsson 1984: 144). In the Meiquan district of Hubei province, irrigation water is now supplied by one medium and 30 small reservoirs, and by 6,010 ponds; in all the irrigated area is about 8,000 ha, which shows how small the majority of the ponds must be (Nickum 1981).

Ponds are the most ancient type of irrigation supply in Japan. They were probably introduced from Korea in about the fifth century AD, together with new rice varieties and iron-tipped tools (Tsukuba 1980: 61; Kelly 1982a: 2). Tanaka (1983: 31–3) characterises these small ponds or reservoirs in which, according to archaeological evidence, the water was often retained by a simple dam of poles and logs, as typical of the economy of the Kofun period (third to sixth centuries AD). Recent archaeological excavations in the Nara Basin, however, indicate that 'saucer ponds' dug into the upper slopes, which could water a greater area by natural gravity flow and which were very common in early China, were extremely rare in Japan before the Kamakura era (1185–1392); only during the Tokugawa period did they come to predominate as a water supply for rice cultivation (Farris 1985: 96). A great deal has been written on the social organisation associated with pond irrigation in Japan (e.g. Tamaki 1979: 24–32), and we shall return to this in chapter 6. But as the feudal warrior class started building up their local bases and expanding the area of cultivated land under their control, larger irrigation networks based on small rivers and derivation canals became increasingly common. The proportion of land in Japan irrigated by ponds fell steadily, until by the turn of this century only one-fifth of the irrigated land in Japan was watered from ponds (Agric. Bureau 1910: 21). Today the proportion has fallen to one-sixth (Kelly 1982a: 3).

Nevertheless the Japanese still construct ponds for irrigation purposes where the terrain is suitable. Beardsley et al. point out in their study of Niiike in Southern Honshu, where as well as new canals a large pond was built to supplement the irrigation supply during the national programme of land improvement in the 1920s, that pond-water has the great advantage that it does not need to be pumped up into the fields (1980 edn: 145). And the Japanese encouraged the construction of large numbers of storage ponds in Northwest Taiwan after they gained control of the island in 1895 (Wang and Apthorpe 1974: 33).[14]

More recently still, tank irrigation was introduced to the Khorat plateau of Northeast Thailand, using American capital and technical aid, during the 1950s. These tanks vary in size, irrigating on average a few hundred hectares. Because local ecological conditions and distribution requirements had been insufficiently studied, the tanks have not proved very successful (Kaida 1978: 223).

Contour canals

Another method of gravity-fed irrigation is typical of the low mountain ranges of East and Southeast Asia, where rainfall is often higher and more regular than in the neighbouring plains. Under such conditions it is not necessary to store the water seasonally in reservoirs so as to distribute it more evenly throughout the year. Instead the supply is perpetual. Water is diverted from mountain streams, springs or small rivers, and led (again by natural gravity flow) along a series of small contour canals, distributary channels and water pipes to the rice-fields. (It is desirable to water the fields from diversion canals rather than directly from the stream, as this facilitates control over the quantity, depth and speed of water available.) One of the earliest irrigation systems of this type is to be found in the Gio-linh highlands of Vietnam, which as we have already mentioned (p. 30) seems to have been designed according not only to technical criteria but also to ritual precepts. In the Hinduised cultures of medieval Java and Bali cosmological principles also played an important role in spatial organisation. Round a mother village four more villages would be grouped, on the corners of a square based on the cardinal points. The group of five villages formed a unit called *mancapat*, which sometimes was extended to include the eight compass directions (van Setten 1979: 58–9). But despite their cosmological sensitivities, topographical and tenurial complexities did not permit the Balinese and Javanese to construct their irrigation works according to the strict symmetries of Angkor; indeed the intricacies of Balinese waterworks are more reminiscent of interwoven spiders' webs.[15]

Irrigation systems based on exactly the same principles as the Balinese *subak*, if slightly less complex, are common in North and Northeast Thailand, Southern and Southwest China and the Philippines. The Funanese had built terraced rice-fields in the northern hills of their Cambodian domain well before they were conquered by the Khmers in the late sixth century (Groslier 1974: 97). While the Lao have traditionally preferred to grow rice along river-banks in the flat plains, the White Tai of the Laos hills, descended from Chinese soldiers who intermarried with Tai women in about 1600 after a campaign along the northern border between Laos and Tonkin, brought with them agricultural and engineering skills which generally impressed French diplomat de Reinach: 'Ils savent admirablement tirer parti des ressources du sol. Par d'ingénieux canaux établis à flanc de coteau, ils amènent les eaux nécessaires à l'irrigation de leurs rizières de montagne; ils savent également capter les sources *souvent fort éloignées* pour les employer au même usage' (1952: 205).

Such systems rely on very simple tools but sophisticated design. Most rivers in the steep mountain valleys of the area are fast-flowing, prone to flooding and difficult to control. The Minangkabau rice-farmers of North Sumatra and Malaya built mud and brushwood dams across smaller streams in their territory during the wet season (Hill 1977: 132), but since the dams had no sluices, control over the supply to the fields was limited and there was always the danger that in heavy spate the stream would burst the barrier. A more effective solution is to build contour canals which water the terraced rice-fields from above. Since the stream is captured higher up, the dam does not have to be particularly high or strong, provided the gradient of the conduits is carefully regulated; for this the Balinese use a simple type of water-level (*geganjing*) 'employed with remarkable skill' (Liefrinck 1886: 50). Small dams might simply consist of a few tree-trunks laid at such an angle as to force water into the conduit, while larger ones are made of stones held together in bamboo baskets or gabions.[16]

The complex layout of conduits, check-ponds to trap silt, sluices and overflows, tunnels and aqueducts found in Balinese *subaks* is described in detail by Liefrinck (1886). Though the tools and materials used are simple, the design is by no means so. Considerable natural obstacles have to be overcome: for example it is not uncommon for water to be taken by tunnels up to a mile long under a ridge, or led by a stone or wooden aqueduct across a valley or into another watershed.

Such technology must be of ancient origin in Asia. Many of its elements are first described and illustrated in the *Wang Zhen nongshu* (ch.18), and Wang's notes often contain excerpts from much earlier writers. For instance Du Shi, a high official of the Han dynasty (fl. *c.*25–57 AD) and the inventor of the first Chinese water-wheel, had already alluded to the bamboo pipes which Wang describes and illustrates (figure 3.4): hollowed bamboos, joined end to end, were used to bring water from mountain springs or streams, across valleys, slopes or

Figure 3.4   Bamboo aqueduct
(*Wang Zhen nongshu*: 18/20a)

level ground, to fields which were often a considerable distance away. Wang also shows a wooden aqueduct or flume (figure 3.5), again used to transport water over long distances. If a village was at a distance from any water source, Wang says (ibid.: 18/21b), all the families would join forces to construct such a flume. As long as the source was a spring high above the village, the water would run down all by itself as was its nature, but if it came from a low-lying pond or ditch then it would have to be pumped up into the flume. These flumes, Wang says, crossed valleys on stilts and went in tunnels through spurs of high land. Sometimes, especially if the gradient was steep, the water would be full of mud and silt by the time it ran into the fields, in which case if would be filtered through a fine-meshed bamboo basket (ibid.: 18/35b).

Where water distribution is as complex as in these systems of valley irrigation, numerous social problems also have to be taken into account. The Balinese *subak*, as explained earlier, does not correspond to the social unit of the village but comprises a group of individual farmers whose fields are watered from the same source. Sometimes potential conflict between *subaks* can be eliminated by technical means: where a conduit borders on another *subak*'s ground, for instance, an underground tunnel can be built to prevent water theft; or two conduits coming from different sources may cross, in which case an aqueduct or tunnel can be constructed. While the *subak* members regulate their internal affairs according to their own very strict rules, in the case of disputes between *subak* organisations over rights to land and water, government officials will be called in to mediate; in pre-colonial times these were court posts (Liefrinck 1886: 11 ff; van Setten 1979: 45).

The irrigation system of Mandalay was also constructed with simple tools but sophisticated skills.[17] First built by the Burmese kings, it was subsequently repaired by the British and is still in use today, though over the centuries some of the smaller canals have fallen into disuse, only to be replaced much later by other canals following almost the same bed. Like the Balinese, the Burmese are well aware of the importance of building their canals and conduits at the right gradient, which varies according to soil type, the upper and lower limits being imposed by the necessity of preventing both silting-up and erosion. It is necessary to obtain a flow from the canals which will provide the fields with a total of about 2 m depth of water over the four months' growth period of the rice. A device called the *khaichein*, a graduated board to which a plumb-line is attached, is used to calculate the gradient during the construction of the canals, and the speed of flow and weight of water is measured by floating cups along the stream. The canals, main, feeder and derivation, are worked and maintained by the state, but the small channels, ditches and

架槽

Figure 3.5   Wooden flume
(*Nongzheng quanshu*: 17/20b)

drains are the responsibility of the local farmers under the direction of a canal chief, elected by the villagers, who organises corvée labour for maintenance: for every acre of field a farmer must repair 50 feet of bank along both sides of the channel.

Systems of similar antiquity and durability operate in parts of Thailand. In the Chiangmai valley and other valleys of North Thailand, the dams are called *fai* and the contour canals *muang*. There are 'many small-scale traditional systems which are operated and maintained by villagers . . . Accounts of the ancient Chiengmai irrigation systems given in the book *The Laws of King Mengraaj, King of Lannothai*, written in 1292, are sketchy and incomplete but are still apt descriptions of the irrigation works as they exist today' (Potter 1976: 81). Irrigation was essential to the economic viability of the early states of North Thailand, hence the provision of a legal code for water management, but the traditional networks were, and still are, organised and maintained without direct government intervention (Moerman 1968: 51). Although irrigation administrators were appointed only with state approval, like their subordinates they had to be chosen by the villagers, and this remains largely true today even of the irrigation canals of recent construction financed by the government. The traditional *fai* and *muang* networks cannot be expanded beyond limits imposed by rainfall and topography. If it is wished to bring more land under irrigation then integrated headworks systems must be constructed. The new irrigation networks are also gravity-fed systems with weirs and contour canals, but because they are constructed of more modern and expensive materials (concrete rather than brushwood and gabions), the main weirs and water-gates are built and maintained by government workmen instead of villagers (Potter 1976: 83). 'But even in [these] large-scale state-backed irrigation systems the terminal network beyond the lateral channels employs the old *muang*, and the organisation for operation and maintenance has changed little . . . In their form, and in the engineering principles involved, the smale-scale, traditional *fai* and *muang* systems and the larger gravity irrigation systems can be considered similar' (Kaida 1978: 211) (figure 3.6).

Bacdayan documents a case in Northern Luzon where the new dam and contour canals necessary to expand the existing irrigation system in the 1950s were planned, designed and constructed by the local people without any outside help: 'this remarkable engineering feat . . . was made possible only through the people's detailed familiarity with the territory through years of hunting and foraging' (1980: 179).

In Japan it seems that contour-canal irrigation began to develop in the medieval period, gradually surpassing village-based pond irrigation in

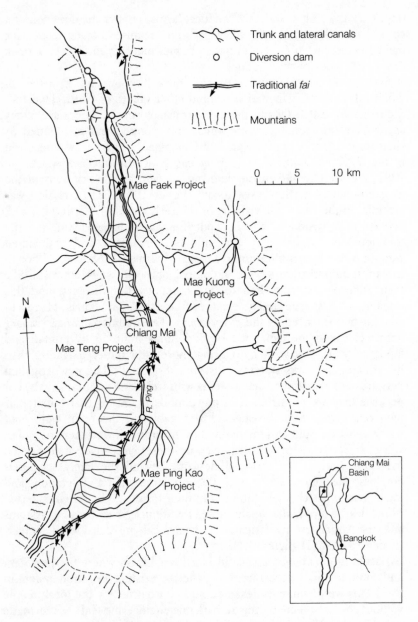

Legend:

〰️ Trunk and lateral canals

○ Diversion dam

═══ Traditional *fai*

⎜⎜⎜⎜⎜⎜ Mountains

0　　5　　10 km

Mae Faek Project

Mae Kuong Project

N

Chiang Mai

Mae Teng Project

R. Ping

Mae Ping Kao Project

Chiang Mai Basin

Bangkok

Figure 3.6　Irrigation systems in the Chieng Mai Basin

(from Kaida 1978: 212)

importance as the power of the court nobility waned and local warrior chiefs gained increasing economic and social control over the countryside. Irrigation networks spread from small mountain basins to the larger river plains as the warrior chiefs' ambitions grew: new technology made flood control and canal construction possible even along larger rivers by the fourteenth and fifteenth centuries (Kelly 1982a: 2), and these irrigation networks were improved and added to continuously over the centuries (table 3.2; also Shimpo 1976: ch. 1). A

Table 3.2   Main canals along the Aka River (Northeast Honshū) in the Tokugawa period

Century	Period of construction	Estimated area served
Daihōji	unknown	40 ha
Gokamura	unknown	200 ha
Sankason	unknown	40 ha
Shōryūjigawa	c.1609	4,100 ha
Shida	c.1610?	510 ha
Nakagawa	c.1615	3,000 ha
Inaba	1607–22; 1689–92	1,150 ha
Kumaide	1661?	40 ha
Etchū	1703–4	40 ha
Ōgawa	1706	260 ha
Tenpō	1831–8	50 ha

Source: Kelly 1982b: 18

major drawback of this type of irrigation, however, is that the water supply is limited, being confined to a single river system (and Japanese rivers are not the mighty giants of the mainland). As the area irrigated by any one network grew, water shortages became endemic, and increasingly strict and complex regulations became necessary to prevent open conflict between different groups of users (see chapter 6). The Japanese traditional networks, like those of Southeast Asia, have survived and expanded over the centuries, and in many cases it has been possible to incorporate them into modernised irrigation systems, solving the problem of water shortage by the construction of a large concrete dam at the head of the central system. But in such cases, although the consequent technical changes required in irrigation methods have not been enormous, the regulations governing water allocation, which had often remained unchanged for centuries, required considerable modification. In the case of the irrigation network in Shiwa (Northeast Honshū), which was first developed in the early seventeenth century following the establishment of the Tokugawa shogunate, a codification of the irrigation rules was recorded in 1672 and, apart from one minor adjustment in 1895, these remained in effect until the opening of the new Sannōkai dam in 1952 (Kelly 1982a: 55; Shimpo 1976: 21 ff).

Institutional difficulties frequently arise because the modernisation and extension of water control facilities threatens the delicate balance of rights and obligations between water-users. It may even be that farmers oppose certain forms of technical improvement rather than sacrifice their place in the traditional hierarchy established in Japan over centuries of wrangling and rivalry:

As one follows the route of the [Twelve-Gō] canal [in Niiike, Okayama] and its branches today, one comes across a few control and diversion structures of recent date and modern aspect standing side with very humble, primitive arrangements. Prefectural loans have helped to build [two] concrete water gates ... [between which] sections of concrete or rock retaining walls alternate with heavy piles or stakes interwoven with bamboo strips to support the banks. Some diversion ditches that water the fields in the vicinity are no more than holes in the bank. At other places there are crude diversion devices made of piles of submerged rocks and pine trunks laid across the canal, of calculated thickness and depth beneath the surface to control the amount of water diverted. These simple arrangements are readily displaced by accident or high water, and their reinstallation becomes a matter of sometimes acrimonious arbitration; it is difficult to replace them with more precisely measured modern devices, not only because of the expense involved, but because of jealous fears that one side or other will come out on the short end. (Beardsley et al., 1980 edn: 148)

Perhaps the most venerable and impressive of all irrigation networks based on contour-canals is to be found in China, in the Chengdu Basin of Sichuan, where the Min River, a tributary of the Yangzi, flows swiftly down into the plain from the sheer foothills of the Tibetan plateau. The Guanxian irrigation works were started under the direction of Li Bing, who was appointed Governor of Sichuan in 250 BC; he died in about 240 BC and the scheme was completed under his son, Li Ergang, some ten years later. Needham calls Guanxian 'one of the greatest of Chinese engineering operations which, now 2,200 years old, is still in use and makes the deepest impression on all who visit it today. The Guanxian irrigation system made it possible for an area of some 40 by 50 miles to support a population of about five million people, most of them engaged in farming, and free from the dangers of drought and flood. It can be compared only with the ancient works of the Nile' (1971: 288).

Li Bing tamed the tumultuous floodwaters of the Min with a device of great elegance and simplicity: at the point where the Min reaches the plain, he divided the river into two huge feeder canals by means of a division-head of piled stones called the Fish Snout (figure 3.7). One feeder canal serves only for irrigation, the other also acts as a flood channel. The flow of water into the irrigation canal is regulated by means of dykes and connected spillways so that when the floodwaters rise above the level of safety they automatically spill off into the flood channel.

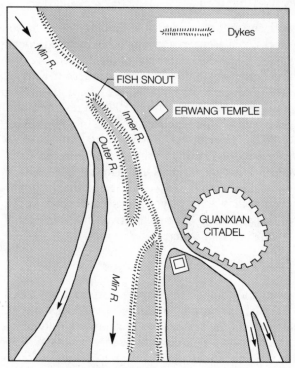

Figure 3.7   The Fish Snout at Dujiangyan
(after Wuhan 1979: 68)

Each year there is a cycle of operations corresponding to the flow of water . . . Throughout the centuries, the advice of Li Ping to clear out the beds and keep the dykes and spillways low has been faithfully followed, and if it has been possible to preserve the system so closely as he left it, this is partly because the river is not extremely silt-laden, and partly because its annual fluctuations have permitted incessant and effective maintenance. Every year, about mid-October, the annual repairs begin. A long row of wooden tripods is placed across the outer feeder canal at its inlet and covered with bamboo matting plastered with mud to form a cofferdam, thus diverting all the flow into the inner canal. The bed of the outer canal is then excavated very actively to a predetermined depth, and any necessary repairs to the division-heads are carried out with the aid of gabions. About mid-February, the stockade-dam is removed and re-erected at the intake of the inner canal, so that all water flows to the right, and similar maintenance of the inner system is effected. On the 5th of April, the ceremonial removal of the cofferdam marks the opening of the irrigation system and gives opportunity for a general celebration, even in these days of slide-rules and plans for power-stations. (Needham 1971: 293)

It is significant that the original technology used to construct the Guanxian works, while cheap and simple, has proved effective enough not only to allow for gradual expansion of the network over two millennia but also to render largely redundant more modern irrigation technology and materials. Between 1949 and 1959 the area under irrigation almost doubled, from half a million to 930,000 acres, and the Irrigation Authority envisaged an eventual irrigated area of no less than 4.4 million acres (ibid.: 289). Nevertheless, when I visited Guanxian in 1980, the works still remained essentially unchanged both in form and construc- tion. Wooden posts, bamboo mats and gabions filled with stones were still the essential materials used to maintain the Fish Snout and to control the water flow; the only obvious concession to the twentieth century was that the inner bank of the river just above its division had now been reinforced with concrete.

'Creek' irrigation[18]

The tank, pond and contour-canal systems we have described so far are basically designed to provide irrigation alone; this means they can generally supplement the seasonal water shortages without necessitating recourse to pumps or lifting devices: gravity-flow is sufficient. But in areas such as the great river deltas, where the land is flat and swampy and the flow of water sluggish, drainage becomes as important as irrigation. In deltaic areas where the water-flow is very slow, 'creeks' serve not only as irrigation channels and drainage ditches but also as storage for the water. Since the land has no natural slope which will allow the water to run from field to field inside an irrigation unit, all fields must take their supply of water directly from the creeks. This means that an intricate network of waterways must be developed to serve all the fields – usually each network will take its water directly from a river and discharge it into the same river further downstream – and a rather high proportion of the surface area is occupied by waterways rather than fields. To ensure adequate supplies of water it is necessary to dredge the bed of the main river as well as the creeks, and dykes have to be built around the fields to prevent flooding. Of course since the creeks are below the level of the land, it is necessary to raise the water into the fields by pumps or other devices.

It is not usually possible for individual peasants or even groups of farmers to construct the large, complex and coordinated networks of ditches and channels that will convert deltaic flood-plains to fertile rice-fields. Not surprisingly, this 'creek' irrigation as the Japanese call it was a relatively late development which depended on considerable investment by very wealthy landowners or even the state.

This can clearly be seen in the Chinese case of the Yangzi, or Jiangnan, Delta. Although the inland areas of the Delta had become an important agricultural region in Tang times (seventh to ninth centuries), the marshy coastal zones could not easily be occupied unless extensive hydraulic works were carried out to prevent flooding and salinisation, and for this new hydraulic techniques had to be developed as well as administrative skills.

As mentioned in appendix B, by the eleventh century the Song state was under considerable pressure to increase agricultural production in the Yangzi area, and the high fertility of the land already reclaimed by wealthy landowners from lakesides and river-banks probably gave impetus to the official policy of deltaic reclamation which began in the early Song. The techniques of constructing dyked and poldered fields had already been mastered (chapter 2), but the design and maintenance of intricate water networks still presented problems. The Song *Dynastic History* for 1158 tells us that in previous times creeks had been opened up in great numbers joining the Taihu Lake to nearby rivers or to the sea, but that now they had all silted up because the troops in charge of their maintenance had been withdrawn, and the peasants' fields had in consequence become submerged. The estimated cost to restore them to their former state was more than 3.3 million man-days, an equal number of strings of cash and over 100,000 bushels of grain. Thereafter, 24 creeks were opened up between the Taihu Lake and the Yangzi, and 12 more were opened up directly to the sea; according to the statesman Fan Zhongyan some 6,000 or 7,000 farmer-soldiers[19] were settled in the Suzhou area specially to maintain the system and prevent flooding (Nishioka 1981: 127). Large areas, then, were already being reclaimed during the Song (e.g. Elvin 1978: 81 on the Ningbo region).

This is reflected in the agricultural treatises of the time, which devote long sections to dyking fields, to water management and to water-raising devices. The square-pallet chain-pump had been known in China for over a thousand years, as had many other water-lifting devices like the *noria* or 'Persian wheel', and the swape or well-sweep, but their use spread rapidly during the Song (Needham 1965: 530 ff; Li Jiannong 1957: 28 ff). The Song also saw the publication of five works specially devoted to water control, *shuili*; during the 90 years of the ensuing Yuan dynasty (1279–1368) nine works on water control were published; during the three centuries of the Ming dynasty (1368–1644) no less than 81 works on water control are known to have been produced (Shen Baixian 1979: table 5.1, pp. 517 ff). While the spread of water-pumps demonstrates that there must have been a steady expansion of creek-irrigated fields, the explosion of books on water control proves the keen interest taken by government officials and the landowning class alike in this subject.

As we have already said, cooperation across the board was necessary to reclaim and maintain large tracts of swampy land at the mouths of large rivers. Only the state had sufficient resources and authority to organise and finance the dredging of the main rivers, using corvée labour to carry out the work.[20] During the early Ming (up to about 1500) the dredging of creeks and repairing of dykes was organised by local landowners, most of whom resided on their land at that period. The labour was provided by their tenants and was levied according to the length of their land bordering on the creeks and dykes. Landlords also organised collective drainage, a practice which remained necessary until the adoption of pumping-machines in the twentieth century. So in the Song and early Ming state authorities, landowners and peasant farmers all cooperated to keep the fertile dyked fields in working order. As the saying went: 'If Suzhou and Taihu Lake have a good harvest, then all China will be well-fed' (cited Nishioka 1981: 150).

But the Song and early Ming were periods of unprecedented economic expansion, and as the monetary economy advanced two phenomena developed which necessitated radical changes in the management of creek irrigation in the Yangzi Delta. The first was the growth of a class of absentee 'gentry' landowners, who by the later Ming greatly outnumbered resident landlords. These gentry landlords, thanks to their position as bureaucrats, had sufficient income to acquire much larger amounts of land than the resident landlords, whose incomes were restricted to their rents. A would-be reforming official writing in the mid-sixteenth century took as a standard case a landlord owning 1000 *mu* (approximately 60 ha), and thus having at least 100 tenants on his land (Hamashima 1980: 87). However these tenants were not available as corvée labourers for the maintenance of local irrigation works, because as bureaucrats the gentry landlords were exempted from all corvée responsibilities. Furthermore, as the economy of the Yangzi Delta became increasingly commercialised and the relative price of rice fell, peasant farmers relied more and more on commercial crops (such as cotton) and on small-scale commodity production to earn cash with which to pay their rent, formerly often payable in kind.[21] The slack season for rice cultivation had been the time when irrigation work was carried out, but it was no longer a slack season as far as peasant farmers were concerned, and they stood to lose heavily if they were obliged to give up their time to irrigation repairs. The burden on the independent peasants, and on the tenants of the remaining resident landlords, was increased by the non-participation of gentry landlords in corvée labour schemes.

In order to prevent the total deterioration of the creek irrigation networks and to diminish popular resentment and antagonism towards the gentry, Ming officials worked out a series of reform measures. First, the privilege of corvée exemption was denied in as many cases as possible. Secondly, a landowner's corvée responsibilities were calculated not according to the length of land beside the waterways, as hitherto, but according to the total area, a much more equitable arrangement now that the concentration of land-ownership was increasing. And finally, not only were gentry landlords obliged to provide corvée labour by sending their tenants to join in maintenance work, but the government guaranteed the tenants some compensation for their work, issuing them with ration cards for rice which they then claimed from their landlord; in case of default, the tenant was allowed to deduct double the amount from his rent. Needless to say, reforms of this kind were fiercely opposed by the gentry landlords, but Geng Ju, the official who proposed them in this particular form, managed to put them into effect in the region under his jurisdiction in the early seventeenth century. They were then gradually adopted throughout the Delta region, and continued to provide a model up to the twentieth century.

It is interesting that in the village near Shanghai described by Fei in the 1930s drainage of the dyked *yu* fields was still carried out with communal labour. With the entrenchment over the centuries of absentee landlordism, tenants had in fact gained rights of permanent tenancy approximating to ownership, and so the labour contributions were calculated on the basis of farm size (Fei 1939: 172). No technical changes had taken place in the system of creek irrigation until the very recent introduction of small modern pumping machines, which at the time that Fei carried out his study was presenting the villagers with considerable organisational problems. The advantages offered by collectivisation in such circumstances are obvious.

In Japan creek irrigation is confined to the few flat deltas, most notably the Saga Plain in Kyūshū, which has been the focus of intensive study by Japanese scholars, since it is considered to be the region which had the most advanced rice-growing technology in the 1920s and 1930s. Traditional creek irrigation was firmly established in the Saga Plain in the mid-Tokugawa period, when the local *daimyō* family, the Nabeshima, carried out extensive improvements to the local canal network (Francks 1983: 102). Irrigation and drainage were extremely arduous tasks, relying on constant use of man-powered water-wheels similar to the Chinese square-pallet chain-pumps; Saga farmers hired labourers to man the pumps in the high season (Kelly 1982a: 34). 'Rationalisation' began in the 1920s, as the development of mining and industries in Kyūshū attracted the labourers away from agriculture. In response to the resulting severe labour shortage, which coincided with a boom in rice prices, local government officials and prefectural Farmers' Associations, *nōkai*, working in consultation with the farmers, began to investigate suitable methods of mechanising pumping. After several experiments which failed, a suitable small electric pump was developed which could cover units of between 5 and 20 ha (Francks 1983: 119), usually consisting of plots belonging to a number of farmers. The pumps were operated jointly by the cultivators of the fields they served, so that each individual farmer might participate in several pump groups. The households in each pumping unit were responsible for providing the labour required to set up the new pumping facilities, but the local Irrigation Society or *kumiaia* bore all the capital costs of installation and management, and was responsible for the initial designing of the infrastructure. The installation of the electric pumps reduced labour inputs for irrigation from 70 man-days/ha in 1909 to 22 man-days/ha in 1938 (Ishikawa 1981: 16, table 1–3).

In Tonkin, where the danger of flooding was acute, the few modern irrigation works constructed under French colonial rule were akin to creeks: 'des canaux 'bas', qui peuvent à l'occasion servir au drainage et qui ne risquent point d'inonder les rizières environnantes' (Gourou 1936: 105). These new irrigation facilities regularised the supply of water, but in the absence of mechanical pumps the labour requirements were no less than those of the traditional irrigation networks: in a good field about 11 man-days were necessary, using a swape, to provide 10 cm of water (the optimal depth for growing rice-plants) for 1 ha of land, and much more time was required on most land (ibid.: 103). But most of the

Tonkin Delta had been under intensive rice cultivation for centuries; the dykes which prevented the Red River from flooding were very ancient, and had been reinforced and properly organised as early as the Trân dynasty in the thirteenth century; a programme of canal-building was initiated in the fifteenth century, while sea-walls were used to reclaim the salt-flats from the fourteenth century, and especially large areas were reclaimed under the direction of Nguyên Công Trú in the early nineteenth century (ibid.: 130, 135, 207). By the time the French took over Tonkin there was little scope left for reclaiming land or extending water control (Robequain 1939: 249). In Cochinchina, in the Mekong Delta, however, the situation was quite different.

Cochinchina was practically uninhabited when the French arrived, but it clearly had great potential for development as a rice-exporting region.[22] The French invested heavily in water control from 1870 on, setting up a system of primary, secondary and tertiary canals, and the area under rice cultivation increased fourfold between 1880 and 1937 (table 3.3). To

Table 3.3   Rice in French Cochinchina

	1880	1900	1937	Increase 1880–1937 (%)
Cultivated area (ha)	522,000	1,175,000	2,200,000	421
Exports from Saigon (tonnes)	284,000	747,000	1,548,000	545
Pop. of Cochinchina	1,679,000	2,937,000	4,484,000	267

Source: Robequain 1939: 243

recoup the costs, large concessions of land were made to 'Europeans' (many of whom were in fact naturalised Annamites, as well as to companies. To get the land off their hands quickly the government sold at low prices and in large units, many rice estates being between 500 and 1,000 ha in size (Robequain 1939: 96); in 1930 some 120 French *colons* held around 100,000 ha of land between them (ibid.: 214). The labour force consisted mainly of migrants from the Northern provinces of Tonkin and Annam, who were taken on as tenants under a bailiff, and given lots of about 10 ha (Brocheux 1971: 149).

Although the investment in water control considerably increased rice production in Cochinchina, cultivation methods were extensive and yields lower than the fertility of the soil and the abundance of water might have led one to expect.[23] Most of the migrants came from regions where intensive cultivation techniques were practised, but when they took up their tenancies most of them were destitute and had to rely on the landlord to provide tools, draft animals and seed-grain, as well as loans of rice and money; their lots of 10 ha were immense compared with the farms of Tonkin, where the population density was such that a majority of peasants owned less than 0.2 ha (Gourou 1936: 360), and the shortage of labour in Cochinchina meant that even if tenants had been in a position to hire or exchange labour there simply was not enough available to practise intensive methods. In fact, given the prevalence of absentee landlordism and the poverty of the migrant peasants, landowners found it easier to make their money by usury than by high farming: 'Ces fermiers sans ressources, souvent instables et inquiets, reçoivent des propriétaires des avances en argent et en grains. C'est sur l'intérêt de ces prêts *autant et plus que* sur l'amélioration progressive des rizières que compte le propriétaire' (Feyssal 1934: 18; my emphasis). Even with low rice yields, the landowners did extremely well: the investment in canal-building in Cochinchina cost about 48 piastres/ha and gave a return of over 40% (Henry and de Visme 1928: 58). The peasants, on the other hand, did badly: not only were they debt-ridden and harassed by frequent bad harvests,[24] but furthermore poor seed-selection and cultivation methods meant the rice produced was of low quality. Indochinese rice found difficulty competing with Thai and Burmese rices on international markets, and this led to a severe crisis during the Depression (Henry and de Visme 1928; Henry 1932).

The Lower Delta of Siam too had remained almost uninhabited until it was developed to produce rice for export in the late nineteenth century, when creek-style waterways and poldered fields were constructed in large numbers. Under natural conditions the Delta is not only uninhabited but uninhabitable: in the rainy season the whole area of a million hectares is submerged, and in the dry season the mud parches and cracks and 'desert conditions prevail on a large scale. People cannot even find enough water to drink' (Takaya 1978: 187). The hardships suffered by early migrants to the region are vividly described by Hanks (1972). But although the Delta presents few attractions as a human habitation, it is an ideal natural habitat for rice, being almost uniformly flat and subject each year to very gradual flooding, the waters eventually reaching a depth of about 1 m – in fact the Delta is by far the most favourable natural environment for rice in the whole of Thailand (Takaya 1978: 181).

The Siamese state had been exporting rice grown in the northern regions to Malacca and elsewhere since the sixteenth century. Until the mid-nineteenth century all international trade from Siam, including that of rice, was in the hands of the king, who obtained the rice as a tax in kind on agricultural produce – the *akon* tax or tithe (Ishii 1978b: 32). But with the signing of the Bowring Treaty between Britain and Siam in 1855 the royal trade monopoly came to an end, with especially important implications for the rice trade: 'Through this treaty, rice exports were liberalised and grew rapidly in response to the increasing demand on the international rice market; accompanying this, rice production expanded sharply, particularly in the young Delta' (ibid.: 39).

Canals to provide rapid and efficient transport between the inland regions and the Gulf of Siam had first been constructed through the Delta region in the Ayutthya period, but in order to open the Delta up and to provide irrigation and drainage for rice cultivation it was necessary to expand the network considerably. While the corvée system had provided the labour force for such work in earlier periods, from the mid-nineteenth century a more reliable and productive work-force of Chinese immigrants was employed (Tanabe 1978: 49). This cost vast sums of money: for instance the construction of the 27 km Mahasawat canal required a total investment of 88,120 baht, most of which was provided by Rama IV, who then (for the first time in Siamese history) claimed ownership of the land bordering the canal (some 2,500 ha), which he granted to his sons and daughters to use as rice-land. It was supposed to be cultivated by corvée peasants, *bao phrai*, or debt-slaves, *that*. Other canals were financed by nobles or wealthy Chinese, who also claimed possession of land along the banks (ibid.: 154). But much of the land remained uncultivated, and that which was brought under cultivation was underproductive: it was not until the sytem of corvée and debt slavery began to disintegrate in the late nineteenth century that the Delta began to realise its agricultural potential. In 1877 the government published a document entitled 'The Regulation of Canal Excavation' in which the wastefulness and underproductivity of the old ownership system was criticised; a new policy had been introduced in the 1870s whereby migrant free peasants were encouraged to contribute their labour or capital to the construction of new canals, in return for which they were granted ownership of a tract of land constituting a household farm, together with tax concessions; they also had to pay a canal fee for the irrigation water (ibid.: 58 ff). As a result of these institutional changes, large tracts of the Delta were swiftly brought under cultivation in the 1870s and 1880s, but as the productivity and thus the value of the land rose, the peasants began to lose their relatively privileged status. Not only did a lively market in land grow up and the pawning and mortgaging of their land by peasants become frequent, but the government changed its policy of undertaking canal construction as public works. Instead it gave concessions to wealthy nobles, Chinese, or companies, who made their profit by selling the land:

In 1888 the Siam Canals, Land and Irrigation Company, whose shareholders were royalty and Chinese, began construction of a canal system and land reclamation in a vast tract of wasteland in the delta flat region to the northeast of Bangkok. In this famous Rangsit canal system, the government contract recognised that all unowned land within forty *sen* (sixteen hundred metres) on either side of the new canals would become the possession of the company from the time of construction. In this way the company was able to sell huge areas of land to royalty, noble officials, and peasants.

The Rangsit canal system comprised a trunk canal, the Rangsit canal, and a lattice of several tens of canals. The Rangsit canal differed from the conventional canals in having lock gates at either end at the junction with the rivers, through which the water level could be controlled and the drainage and irrigation function raised. And the project was not only epoch-making in its technological aspects; historically it was greatly significant in the process of disorganisation of the old system, marking the affirmation of landownership of the adjoining lands that led to the development of an extensive new landlord-tenant system aimed at the collection of landrent. (Tanabe 1978: 65)

Here is a clear instance of the way in which technological advance can disrupt social organisation.

It is interesting that although otherwise the rice economy of Malaya was generally much later in its development than that of Siam, the northern kingdom of Kedah became a rice-exporter at an early date, and it was not long before the *raja* initiated land reclamation schemes to expand production.[25]

The Portuguese traveller Pires had mentioned as early as 1512 that Kedah had rice in quantities, but rice only became an important export crop after the founding of the East India Company settlement at Penang seriously threatened Kedah's control over trade in the region. The ruler decided to ensure his wealth through a new form of trade: the export of Kedah rice to Penang and other ports. The capital, which had hitherto been situated on the estuary of the Muda River, was moved inland to Alor Setar, on the flat, flooded plains which are the heart of the Muda scheme today. By 1785 Kedah's total rice exports amounted to 80,000 *piculs* (over 10,000 tons), and by 1821 she was exporting that amount to Penang alone. Migrants from Patani in Southern Siam and from the Indonesian islands had started reclaiming swampland in the Muda plain for paddy-fields in the sixteenth and seventeenth centuries, and a proportion of their crop went to the ruling class as tax. To increase their rice revenues the Kedah rulers were prepared to construct canals, which served the dual purpose of draining the swampy land and of facilitating transport of the tax rice. The first canal was built in 1664–5, an extension was constructed in 1738 and two further canals had been built by 1816, thus providing a large area of the Muda plain with the basic infrastructure for the colonisation of padi-land. These early canals were built with corvée labour, *krah*, and although the settlers had rights of usufruct over the land they opened up, its ownership remained vested in the state. The state thus incurred very few costs for this early reclamation programme, but derived considerable benefits. After a period of disruption following the Siamese invasion of 1821, the Kedah rulers were anxious to encourage the peasants who had fled to return and new migrants to settle in the region. In 1885 the Prime Minister built a main north-south drainage canal 20 miles long, at a cost of $250,000 Straits Settlement dollars; several more followed before indirect British rule was imposed in 1909, and by 1915 Kedah had a network of 250 km of drainage canals.

This network, together with a certain amount of gravity-fed irrigation provided by temporary brushwood dams across the rivers, permitted the cultivation of a single crop of padi in the main season. In the 1960s a major plan was drawn up to double the area of rice cultivation and to provide sufficient water for double-cropping throughout the scheme. The increase in the water supply was to be achieved principally through the construction of two large dams providing gravity-fed irrigation, thus transforming the Muda plain from an area of predominantly creek irrigation (or 'controlled drainage irrigation') to one of predominantly gravity-flow irrigation (Taylor 1981: 41, table 2.6):

The construction of infrastructural facilities took place between 1966 and 1970, at a cost of $245 million [Malaysian] ($2,550 per ha). The principal infrastructural components were the Muda and Pudu dams and their associated reservoirs, connected by a 6.8 km tunnel; a conveyance system comprising an existing river channel, a diversion barrage, 115 km of main conveyance channels, and several regulators; an internal network comprising 965 km of primary and secondary distribution canals spaced from 1.2 to 2.0 km apart, 865 km of drainage channels, 770 km of laterite surface road, and many minor structures; and a 100 km coastal embankment to control tidal intrusion and enable drainage outflow from the scheme. The Muda scheme is designed to receive about one-third of its water supply from streamflow, rainfall, and the Muda and Pudu reservoirs respectively. (Taylor 1981: 44)

The scheme now covers an area of 96,000 ha. Management is provided by a special body, the Muda Agricultural Development

Authority (MADA), set up in 1970. Compared with other water control schemes in Malaysia, the Muda scheme has performed well: double-cropping and the adoption of new varieties and modern inputs are almost universal, and by 1975–6 mean annual yields of padi had risen to 7.66 t/ha, compared to 3.63 t/ha in the Kemubu irrigation scheme (see below), and 1.12 t/ha in Pahang, where water control facilities are more or less non-existent (ibid.: 43). The land consolidation which accompanied the extension of the canal infrastructure in the Muda area has facilitated mechanisation, and even large-scale mechanisation, on the scheme (Jegatheesan 1980), and the rapid commercialisation of padi production, with the increasing capital requirements which this entails, is believed by a number of observers to have set in train the differentiation of the Muda peasantry and the emergence of capitalist farming (de Koninck 1978; Gibbons et al. 1980; Lim et al. 1981: p 2). This will be discussed at greater length in chapter 6.

Pump irrigation schemes

In areas where the land is flat and the water-table low, drainage presents few problems. However the provision of irrigation water has, in the past, been next to impossible. The only exception was well irrigation.

Before the dissemination of artesian and diesel pumps which made them an attractive alternative to the capturing of surface water, wells were more typical of dry regions than of high rainfall areas.[26] In regions where there was a long dry season, as in medieval Ceylon, these limited sources of irrigation water, serving individual farmers or small groups, might stand in direct contrast to vast and complex gravity-fed irrigation networks whose growth and decay often seemed symbolic of the states which constructed them.

Typically an individual farmer digs a well on his own land and uses it only for his own purposes. If the water-table is low, then animal power or diesel pumps may be necessary to raise the water to ground level, and the necessary capital investment may limit the use of wells to richer farmers and landlords, unless the state provides loans or subsidies (Vaidyanathan 1983: 18). Networks centred on wells seldom attain the size of irrigation networks served by rivers or other types of surface water.[27]

Pasternak (1972a: 27–34; 1972b: 205) describes the social changes which occurred when the government installed pumps in a Taiwanese village in the mid-1950s. Previously the villagers had relied on an integrated irrigation system, run by an elected irrigation association. As pressures on the supplies and the demand for water grew, sharp conflicts became endemic and the irrigation association played a crucial role in arbitrating over disputes. Once the new pumps were installed and came to constitute the chief source of irrigation water, the role of the irrigation association dwindled and real authority developed upon 'natural groups consisting of the twenty-five farmers who drew water from a single pump' (ibid.).

The invention of powerful mechanical pumps has permitted the development of irrigation facilities where none were possible before. This is the case of the Kelantan plain on the east coast of peninsular Malaysia. Rice cultivation techniques which were advanced compared to the rest of Malaya, by which transplanted wet rice was grown in fields bunded to retain the rainwater, were probably introduced from Siam in about the sixteenth century, but the shortage of water meant that only one crop could be grown a year. Furthermore in many places the water was not sufficient to grow even one crop of wet rice: instead dry rice was grown by various methods (Hill 1951; Dobby 1957). It is notable that wet-rice land was valued according to its elevation, which determined the amount of available water and so, to a great extent, land productivity: low-lying land, *tanah dalam*, was the most productive, intermediate land, *tanah serderhana*, gave lower yields of wet rice, while high land, *tanah darat*, could only be used for dry rice (Bray and Robertson 1980: 226). Despite their industry and skill, Kelantanese farmers could only obtain low yields of wet rice, averaging about 230 *gantang*/acre (1.5 t/ha); dry-rice yields were often as low as 150 *gantang*/acre (less than 1 t/ha), and their harvests were extremely vulnerable to drought (Haynes 1932: 14; Baker 1936: 20; Fedn of Malaya 1953: 84).

The first small irrigation schemes in Kelantan were set up in the 1930s under the newly formed Department of Irrigation and Drainage, but they could only be established in a few specially favourable areas (Haynes 1933: 13; Moubray 1937: 23). No significant progress had been made by the early 1950s, when the Rice Production Committee received numerous complaints about the uncertainty of the water supply and the unsatisfactory arrangements for its control (Fedn of Malaya 1953: 87). However in 1967–73 the federal government invested about $75 million Malaysian ($3,770 per ha) in infrastructural work to create the Kemubu irrigation scheme, of about 19,000 ha, which together with four smaller schemes totalling some 12,500 ha is now managed by the Kemubu Agricultural Development Authority (KADA), created in 1973. The water is all pumped from the Kelantan River:

The Kemubu Scheme infrastructure involves the Kemubu pumphouse with five diesel pumps, each having an hydraulic capacity of 250 cusecs; two private-sector pumps with a capacity of 275 cusecs; 374 km of irrigation canals, almost one-half of which are tertiaries; 344 km of drainage channels and a variety of structures to control and facilitate the movement of water within the irrigation distribution system, including tertiary offtakes that are gated and equipped with measuring devices (although not all function properly). The scheme has an irrigation canal density of about 18m per ha and is designed so that each tertiary offtake serves an irrigation unit of about 20 ha. Prior to the current phase of upgrading irrigation facilities in Malaysia's large-scale schemes, the irrigation infrastructure in Kemubu was probably the most extensive in Malaysia. The many micro-undulations in the scheme's topography, however, make timely and equitable distribution of irrigation water throughout the scheme area difficult. (Taylor 1981: 45)

Double-cropping is now possible in most of the Kelantan plain, and although yields are still much lower than in the Muda area, averaging only 3.63 t/ha in 1975–6 (ibid.: 43), most farming families now have an assured subsistence – indeed 50–65% of families market padi in varying amounts (Shand and Mohd. Ariff 1983: 241). But average yields still do not exceed 2.5 t/ha even in the main season, and often drop sharply in the off-season if, as is not infrequently the case, there are difficulties with the irrigation. Despite a substantial increase of 36% in the Guaranteed Minimum Price of padi in 1980, in the following year there was a 35% drop in average padi output per farm, from 4.3 to 2.8 t (ibid.: 177). This can be attributed partly to a preference for more remunerative off-farm employment, and partly to the difficulties farmers often experience if they do try to produce two crops of padi a year. The improved varieties grown in Kelantan do not mature particularly fast, and in consequence the official irrigation schedule is so intensive that farmers often fall behind in their operations and have to miss a season. Or they may be obliged to miss a season if there is a pump failure (Bray and Robertson 1980: 234). The uniformity imposed by the schedule no longer allows the labour bottlenecks of transplanting and harvesting to be avoided through staggered timing and labour exchange, and family labour must therefore be supplemented with hired labour. Three-quarters of Kemubu padi farmers felt they had suffered from labour shortage in 1981, and two-thirds hired extra labour to cope, thus reducing their already meagre profit-margins; for a number of reasons, mechanisation does not seem to offer the solution at present (Shand and Mohd. Ariff 1983: 105; 119 ff).

Another problem Kemubu farmers have had to face is the change in value of their land. While formerly low-lying land was the most valuable, now it is often so waterlogged that it can only be cultivated in the off-season, if at all. Large areas of dry land formerly used for growing rubber, fruit, tobacco or vegetables, which are relatively profitable sources of income, now lie below the water-table and must be used instead as poor-quality rice-land (Bray and Robertson 1980: 232). The reduced opportunities for generating farm income from crops other than rice was a contributing factor in the drop of overall incomes of 12% between 1979 and 1980, from $3236 to $2862 Malaysian (Shand and Mohd. Ariff 1983: 221). It is hardly surprising that young people in Kelantan prefer almost any employment to padi farming, and as they leave the region in search of work more and more rice-land lies fallow.

Each tertiary offtake in the Kemubu scheme serves an irrigation unit of about 20 ha, and in the absence of a proper network of quaternary channels, the majority of fields receive their water from neighbouring fields rather than directly from an irrigation channel (Taylor 1981: 163). Generally, the nearer a field is to a secondary irrigation channel, the higher its yields, and the value of land is changing accordingly (Bray and Robertson 1980: 232). Farmers often express frustration at the impossibility of controlling water effectively at terminal level – not to mention the much wider problem of pump failure: the total area of over 19,000 ha is served by only seven pumps, each of which thus supplies over 2,500 ha (ibid.: 164). A programme of terminal-level improvement is envisaged by KADA; in the meantime, groups of farmers often cooperate to dig small irrigation channels to provide a better supply to their fields (pers. obs.).

A rather different problem presented itself at first in the Muda scheme and in other Malaysian schemes. At the outset MADA staff experienced serious difficulties in enlisting the support of the Muda farmers in irrigation work. Conflicts over water between individuals or groups of farmers were frequent and sometimes fatal (Afifuddin 1978: 277), and it was feared that the lack of traditional village cooperative organisations would constitute a serious stumbling-block to development. Discussing similar problems in the nearby Krian irrigation scheme, Horii suggests that this is in large part attributable to the lack of any native experience of irrigation organisation; 'the weakness and immaturity of self-governing organisation and village solidarity in traditional Malay society were probably largely responsible for the problems associated with rice irrigation in the country' (1981: 36).

While Horii's explanation does carry certain condescending overtones of the Japanocentric concept of 'tightly structured and loosely-structured societies', it is certainly true that where farmers have no previous experience of water control they tend to remain indifferent to the struggles of technicians and administrators trying to increase the efficiency of a new scheme. Studies of state irrigation schemes in Thailand refer to the 'minimal' level of peasant participation and to local farmers' lack of both knowledge and enthusiasm (Kaida 1978: 223, 231). This does not seem particularly surprising, however loosely or tightly the society may be structured, if the scheme is a completely new implantation. One might expect that the problems would be greatest where new, modern pump-irrigation schemes were installed rather than where pre-existing gravity-flow or other types of network were expanded and modernised. But of course it is not unknown for officialdom to encounter local obstructiveness when attempts are made to introduce innovations into a 'tightly-structured' society with long experience of water control, as we saw earlier in the case of Niiike in Japan. And speaking of Northern Thailand which has, as we have seen, a long tradition of local-level water control, Wijeyewardene maintains that 'both government and farmers consider the provision of irrigation water a duty of the state' (1973: 99).

On balance, however, it seems that local experience is to be valued rather than distrusted. Discussing China, Vermeer points out that certain regions 'had a long-standing experience in managing and distributing the scarce and often unreliable river water supply for irrigation. This experience, both in management and in irrigation techniques, is not easily taught. Examples that are quite illustrative have been given in China of the differences between old irrigation districts and newly-established ones in the successful use of irrigation facilities' (1977: 133). In their efforts to overcome local ignorance and inertia, governments have sometimes resorted to bringing in skilled outsiders to inject a little knowledge and enthusiasm. In the sixteenth and seventeenth centuries, Ming and Qing officials brought farmers skilled in irrigation methods from the Yangzi Delta up to Zhili (the area around Peking) to teach intensive rice-farming methods to the northerners who had been settled on newly constructed irrigation schemes in the province (Brook 1982: 684). Ecological conditions were against them, however, notably the danger of salinisation; similar attempts to establish wet-rice cultivation in North China since the establishment of the People's Republic have also met with very limited success (Vermeer 1977: 165, 233). Similarly successive Indonesian governments have encouraged Balinese and Javanese rice-farmers to migrate to the Outer Islands where their skills in water control and intensive cultivation methods would set a good example to less industrious local farmers (p. 44 above). The success of this particular policy is difficult to gauge. An alternative is to set up an institutional framework which encourages, or even compels, local farmers to participate actively in irrigation groups which meet the precise technical demands of the system, as happened in Taiwan in the 1950s (Ishikawa 1981: 62).

But the flexibility and good sense of the farmers themselves should not be underestimated. The Muda scheme is a case in point: despite their initial gloom, MADA officials were delighted to find that 'after a faltering start, the peasantry manifested high resiliency and ability to adapt, improve and innovate. This was very much a result of increased economic incentives and the formation of a new, workable organisational framework [the Farmers' Associations, which provide a forum for discussion between officials and farmers in Malaysia]. As a result, the infrastructure even though absent at the critical tertiary levels was made to work productively although at levels below its potential' (Afifuddin 1978: 289).

Patterns of growth and change

Let us now propose a few generalisations on historical trends in the evolution of water control systems. For a start, these Asian systems display a surprising degree of technical and institutional continuity.

Asian rice cultivation seems to have begun in naturally marshy areas and spread rapidly into regions where rainfall was sufficient to grow a crop in small bunded fields. From there it was but a step to the construction of small-scale gravity-flow irrigation networks like the pond-fed or canal-fed systems typical of the hills of East and Southeast Asia. The skills and techniques involved could be developed to a high degree of sophistication which could easily be applied to larger-scale works based on the same technical principles, the huge tank-fed irrigation networks of medieval Ceylon and Angkor, for instance, or the *fai* and *muang* (dam and contour canal) networks which ensured the economic survival of the early states of Northern Thailand. Small communal units could be integrated into larger networks, or basic techniques applied to constructing works on a larger scale, the chief difference being that as networks grew in size and complexity, management usually diverged so that two distinct levels appeared. First, there was a local level of irrigation officers, usually chosen by their villages, though sometimes the posts were hereditary; they were responsible for regular maintenance and management, the labour and materials being provided by the farmers who benefited from the water. Secondly, there were state officers appointed at national level, who were responsible for coordination, for the organisation of large-scale construction projects (which were often financed by the central state), for the maintenance of the primary waterways and for arbitration in disputes between localities.

As water control systems become larger and more complex, the higher administrative levels acquire an increasingly dominant role. In cases such as the development of networks of tank-and-canal irrigation in medieval Ceylon and Burma, this process was in fact reversible: the technical and financial requirements remained divisible so that, when centralised control of the hydraulic network disintegrated, elements of the system (in this case village tanks) could still survive independently. But some types of water control system cannot be subdivided. The combined irrigation-and-drainage networks which we have considered under the heading of 'creek irrigation' depend for their efficacy on intricate and extensive canal networks which spread excess water over a sufficiently wide area to prevent deep flooding and to allow control by pumping. 'Creek irrigation' networks are not subdivisible below a certain size requiring considerable capital investment and coordinated organisation. In China, where the state had a long-standing tradition of investment in agricultural projects, the first systems of creek irrigation were established in the Yangzi Delta in medieval times; in Tokugawa Japan it was feudal lords anxious to secure their personal economic base who financed creek irrigation projects in the few deltaic plains. But the huge, marshy flood-plains of the Mekong and Chao Praya had to await the mid-nineteenth century growth of international rice markets before they were drained and opened up to rice-farmers, often at considerable expense.

Since the late nineteenth century the governments of almost all Asian states have taken an increasingly active role in expanding and developing national water control facilities. It is often supposed that 'modern' hydraulic works represent a qualitative break with 'traditional' systems, but this is an exaggerated point of view. It is true that certain types of hydraulic network, for example the *fai* and *muang* networks of Northern Thailand, cannot be expanded by traditional means beyond certain limits imposed by rainfall and topography, but the old network of dams and contour canals requires little modification to be incorporated into a new, expanded network served by modern headworks (Kaida 1978: 211). In the Malaysian state of Kedah, the famous new Muda irrigation scheme represents the extension and improvement of an infrastructure of drainage canals initiated by the Sultan in 1664 and subsequently developed by private interests. Similarly in China and Japan a great number of modern hydraulic networks represent the coordination and integration of smaller traditional networks, often supplemented by the construction of one or more large reservoirs or headworks (Gustafsson 1984: 144); it has been calculated that 70.9% of ponds and reservoirs and 73.7% of the river irrigation systems which existed in Japan in the 1960s had been constructed before the Meiji Restoration of 1868 (Francks 1983: 32).

Apart from changes in size, hydraulic networks have also changed in construction materials and design. Most simple networks were constructed largely of earthworks, wood and gabions, and brick was also used in India (Tada, forthcoming), but in the larger systems it was not unusual for stone to replace the earthworks, for instance in the Hinduised states of Southeast Asia. In China in the Ming dynasty (1368–1644) a large number of earthen dykes and other hydraulic works, which had required yearly maintenance by a large labour force, were rebuilt in stone (Yangzi Region 1979: 165). Nowadays concrete is largely replacing earth and stone in structures such as dams and water-gates, as well as being used for the lining of canals (e.g. VanderMeer 1980: 227). Although the installation and maintenance costs of concrete channels are not necessarily less than those of earthen channels, the concrete lining prevents loss of water through seepage and can contribute to significantly higher yields of rice (Taylor 1981: 157). In the near future polyester flumes reinforced with fibreglass may prove even more effective (ibid.: 188).

The design of water control systems has been continuously improving over the centuries, although naturally always subject to constraints imposed by environment and materials. Again it is difficult to draw a hard and fast line between 'traditional' and 'modern'. The application of Western science has not necessarily transformed the field overnight. Although theories of hydraulics were sufficiently advanced to constitute one of the subjects studied by engineers in Europe by the late eighteenth and early ninteenth centuries, their application even today has to be tempered by experience and adapted to local environment and resources (Tada, forthcoming). The importance of the 'human element' in water control cannot be underestimated but is impossible to quantify (Levine 1980). Discussing water control in the People's Republic of China, for example, Gustafsson points out that most Western-designed water control is very wasteful, since water is usually considered by Westerners to be an abundant and free commodity; this leads to a preoccupation with the installation of sophisticated 'hardware' and a neglect of local social organisation and the consequent management requirements (1984: 128). On the other hand, while Chinese administrators from the Song dynasty (tenth century) onwards failed to develop a mathematically derived science of hydraulics, they devoted considerable thought to the political and social as well as technical and fiscal factors involved in the effective management of water control systems (Shen et al. 1979).

Many practical design features – effective locks, sluices and valves, for example, retaining dams which are short relative to their capacity, and complex networks of overspill and feeder canals – have been in existence

for centuries (Stargardt 1983: 192; Needham 1971: passim), and
frequently modern schemes have largely incorporated the pre-existing
infrastructure, although sometimes the potential scope of modern
technical improvements has been limited by traditional social rivalries, as
in the case of Niiike in Japan, mentioned earlier. On the other hand, in
the very same district of Niiike, improvements in engineering technology
made possible a complete remodelling of the canal network and field
layout, enormously improving the irrigation facilities and cutting down
on wastage of arable land (Beardsley et al. 1980 edn: 135).

One area in which undeniable technical advances have been made in
the twentieth century is in the raising of water. Many gravity-flow
systems were so designed that no water-raising was necessary to irrigate
the fields, but 'creek irrigation' cannot work unless the water is raised by
pumps or some other device, and many new irrigation networks are
entirely dependent on powerful electric pumps which pump water up
into the feeder canals from low-lying rivers (often the earlier lack of
irrigation in these places was largely due to the difficulty of raising
sufficient water in the absence of mechanised water-raising technology,
as for instance in many parts of Malaya). The earliest water-raising
devices of East and Southeast Asia were probably swapes, still in
common use in Tonkin in the 1930s (Gourou 1936: 103), and even
found in some parts of Japan in the 1950s (Beardsley et al. 1980 edn:
145). More effective than swapes are the wooden foot-pumps, square-
pallet chain-pumps, which can raise water to a height of up to 5 m
(Needham 1965: 339). These first appeared in China almost two
millennia ago, and continue in use in certain areas today. But the first
motor-pumps were introduced into the Yangzi Delta in the late 1920s,
an innovation which greatly eased labour demands, though it presented
considerable organisational problems as the *raison d'être* of the communal
pumping groups was destroyed (Fei 1939: 172). The adoption of small
electric irrigation pumps by the farmers of the Saga plain in Japan also
entailed considerable institutional reorganisation (Francks 1983: ch. 7),
but cut labour requirements by as much as two-thirds (Ishikawa 1981:
16). In many recently constructed irrigation schemes central pump-
houses serve very large areas: in the Kemubu scheme in Malaysia seven
centrally located pumps are designed to irrigate a total of 19,000 ha
(although tests have shown that in practice they operate at only about
72% of their original design capacity) (Taylor 1981: 164). The adoption
of improved pumping machinery can revolutionise farming efficiency by
allowing more effective use of water, in some cases providing extra water
and so permitting more intensive cropping patterns, for example the
introduction of double-cropping on most Malaysian irrigation schemes,

in others enabling a more effective timing of water use, as in the development of 'rotation irrigation' in Taiwan (VanderMeer 1980). It is also important to note that the effectiveness of fertilisers is greatly increased when a controlled water supply is assured.

We have seen how historically water control systems have spread from easily mastered environments to meet more and more difficult technical challenges, requiring greater investments of labour and capital, and higher levels of management expertise. In the last century developments in water control have been a major factor in increasing rice production in most countries in monsoon Asia.

In China and Japan water control facilities were already highly developed at an early stage,[28] and the scope for increasing the area, at least in the heartlands, has therefore been relatively limited. Buck (1937: 187) shows how extensive water control facilities were in the rice-growing provinces of China by the 1930s (figure 3.8). Although the irrigated area in China was expanded by some 13 million ha between 1965 and 1975, most of this was in North and Northwest China, and in Central Asia. Even so, there was still some scope for expansion in the south: the area under water control along the Yangzi was expanded from 4 million ha in 1949 to 10 million in 1974 (Vermeer 1977: 187–8).

In Japan by the end of the nineteenth century there were few possibilities for expanding the area of rice under water control, and the government turned its attention instead to the colonies of Taiwan and Korea. When the Japanese took over Taiwan in 1895 the percentage of irrigated arable was 36.6%; by 1946 it was 69.6%; a maximum of 77.6% was attained in 1966, but since then the proportion has fallen somewhat, reaching 52% in 1973 (Shen et al. 1979: 209–10). After the Japanese annexed Korea in 1910, their efforts at first were concentrated on rehabilitating existing water control systems, but from 1920 new systems were constructed too. Between 1920 and 1933 the irrigated area was expanded by 165,000 ha, and over a similar period rice yields increased from 1.7 to 2.5 t/ha (Wade 1982: 24–5). This effort was continued after the war. The irrigated area in South Korea was expanded from 350,000 ha (28% of the total padi area) in 1952, to 585,000 ha (46%) in 1974 (Ban et al. 1980: 95).

In Thailand, as we have seen, gravity-fed irrigation was an early development in the north, but the reclamation of the flood plains did not begin until the late nineteenth century. Since then the central government has continued its efforts to improve water control facilities, and the total irrigated area has increased from 608,000 ha in 1917 to 1,824,000 ha in 1967 (Motooka 1978: 311), of which 1,445,000 ha are state projects (Wijeyewardene 1973: 95). In 1917, 592,000 ha were

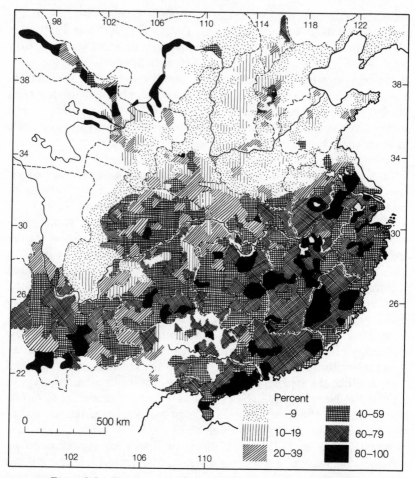

Figure 3.8   Percentage of cultivated land in China under irrigation
(from Buck 1937:187)

under irrigation in the Bangkok Delta and 16,000 ha in Northern
Thailand; by 1967 these figures had increased to 1,408,000 ha and
172,000 ha respectively (Motooka 1978: 311).

In Indonesia, water control was already highly developed in the Inner
Islands of Java, Madura and Bali before the Dutch took power, but
almost non-existent in the Outer Islands. The Dutch invested heavily in
improving the networks of Java. It has been estimated that between 1880
and 1939 they spent 250 million guilders on water control (Geertz 1963:

145), both on improving existing networks and on expanding the irrigated area. In Pasuruan Residency alone, 58 waterworks were constructed between 1856 and 1868 (Elson 1978: 11). Since independence further heavy investments have been made to rehabilitate and improve water control facilities in Java, but success has been hampered by the lack of appropriate local-level organisations (Birowo and Hansen 1981: 19).

The Dutch also planned reclamation schemes in the swamplands of the Outer Islands, in particular in Kalimantan, in the 1920s, with a view to providing rice-land for migrants (the transmigration scheme referred to earlier), but the projects were overambitious and the areas reclaimed remained limited. Further plans, even more ambitious in the areas involved though perhaps more realistic in the technology required, have been drawn up at various stages under the post-independence Five-Year Plans: for example in 1967 a plan was made to reclaim 5 million ha of saline swamp in Kalimantan over a period of 15 years; since then pilot projects have been carried out and the plan reduced to 250,000 ha (Hanson 1981: 222).

In fact today much of the land in monsoon Asia which is naturally suited to water control has already been brought into use, so that the continued expansion of water control facilities has now reached a point of diminishing returns, where the costs of construction are high and the corresponding improvements in production relatively low. The stage has been reached in several countries where expanding the area under water control has become a less rewarding exercise than improving facilities already in existence (e.g. Taylor 1981: 137, 187; Kaida 1978: 236). And although there is certainly scope in many existing systems for improvements in the 'hardware', especially at the terminal level (i.e. the supply to individual fields), where wastage of water tends to be particularly high (Taylor 1981: 188), it is widely agreed that the greatest scope for increasing the effectiveness of water control now lies in the improvement of management: working out better scheduling, adjusting terminal-level supplies, reducing the size of management units, encouraging positive participation by local farmers, reducing tension and conflicts between users, and so on (Taylor 1981: 188; Kaida 1978: 230 ff; Vermeer 1977: 131 ff).

The importance of involving local farmers directly in decision- making and planning is clearly shown by examples from Japan, Taiwan and Korea. Building on their own traditions and experience, the Japanese introduced the equivalent of their own irrigation associations, *suiri kumiai*, to both their colonies, where they have flourished and developed along very similar lines:

The Irrigation Associations bring together farmers under the same irrigation system to organise and operate it themselves, employing staff who (at least in principle) are responsible to farmers' representatives, and dividing up the operating and maintenance expenses between themselves. Such a form provides for effective liaison between staff and farmers, and disciplines the staff to operate the system effectively through the mechanisms of accountability of staff to farmers. (Wade 1982: 9)

Decentralisation of water management is an important means of increasing the efficiency and equity of water distribution, as the contrasting cases of Meiquan in the People's Republic of China and Dhabi Kalan in Haryana, India demonstrate (Nickum 1980; Vander-Velde 1980: 259). Indeed it is widely acknowledged that the lack of decentralisation on the sub-continent adversely affects the efficiency of water control projects (Vaidyanathan 1983: 76–85). But successful decentralisation often presupposes skills and knowledge, as well as a willingness to cooperate, on the part of local farmers. These are more likely to be found where irrigation or water control associations were already in operation, that is to say, where water control facilities were already in existence. Thus improvements to the traditional irrigation systems of Northern Thailand involve certain modifications to the traditional irrigation organisations, but can rely upon their support and are generally successful, whereas the introduction of completely new water control facilities to Northeastern Thailand has aroused the local farmers, innocent of any experience of water control, to nothing more than apathy and indifference; even on the technical level, the schemes must be judged only partially successful. The mandarin approach to water control can be highly counterproductive. Instructing and involving local farmers so that new or enlarged schemes can function more efficiently may be no easy task, but it is perhaps the most urgent problem now facing agricultural planners (Afifuddin 1977; Tamaki 1977; Chambers 1980; Vaidyanathan 1983).

4

Rice and the wider economy

The specific technical and organisational requirements of rice cultivation
have a pervading influence on the rural economy as a whole, which is
manifested at a number of levels. The relatively inflexible ratio of
irrigated to non-irrigated land will influence crop choices, for example,
while the demands of operating an irrigation system will determine the
timing of all agricultural operations, as well as the organisation of labour
within the community as a whole. The intensive but intermittent labour
requirements of rice cultivation have the effect of tying large numbers of
skilled workers to the land, at the same time leaving considerable scope
for investing surplus household labour in commercial cropping or petty
commodity production. This chapter will examine how the specificities
of rice cultivation affect the development of other types of economic
activity.

'Skill-oriented' and 'mechanical' technologies

There is a significant divergence between the evolution of agricultural
systems like those of Northern Europe and North America, which
emphasise the importance of increasing the productivity of labour (see
appendix A), and of those like the rice economies of Asia, which stress
raising the productivity of land. These distinct processes involve distinct
types of technical change: in the first, labour is the scarce or costly
resource and there is a historical trend towards the subsition of
machinery for labour; in the second, there is an increase in the use of
skilled manual labour accompanied by the development of managerial
skills, and in effect labour is substituted for land.

For purposes of easy reference it would be useful if one could make a
simple terminological distinction between these two types of technical

change, and indeed between the two types of technology which they engender. A contrast between 'technical' and 'technological' change (i.e. change based on the one hand on the development of low-capital labour and management skills, and on the other of the development of capital-intensive equipment and machinery) might have seemed appropriate, given the common vernacular usage of 'technique' as skilled performance and 'technology' as sophisticated equipment, were it not for a generally accepted convention among economists and other specialists that 'techniques' are in fact constituent elements of a technology, though how far a 'technology' extends beyond being simply a combination of related techniques is subject to much debate. Unfortunately 'nothing better indicates the underdeveloped state of technological studies than the basic disagreements over fundamental terms' (Layton 1977: 198). Some of the difficulties inherent in attempting to define or subdivide such a vague and complex notion as 'technology' are outlined by Rapp (1985: 128–9). Mitcham (1978) proposes a functional typology, distinguishing technology-as-object (apparatus, tools, machines), technology-as-knowledge (skills, rules, theories), technology-as-process (invention, design, making, using) and technology-as-volition (will, motive, need, intention); the first two categories might at first appear to provide the distinction sought here, but closer inspection shows that they are not in fact appropriate. Economists have described technical change which involves no new capital investment in equipment (for example organisational improvement) as *disembodied* technical change, and that which does require new investment in plant and equipment as *embodied* (Freeman 1977: 227), but it does not follow that one can contrast 'embodied' and 'disembodied' technologies, and as the contrast focuses on the presence or absence of capital in a single instance rather than on long-term characteristics, it too seems inadequate for present purposes.

In the absence of any more appropriate terminology and in order to avoid clumsy circumlocution, it is proposed here to use the terms 'skill-oriented' and 'mechanical' to denote respectively technologies which tend towards the development and intensive use of human skills, both practical and managerial, and technologies which favour the development of equipment and machinery as a substitute for human labour. Technological trends in Asian rice economies would then be characterised as 'skill-oriented', and those in modern Western agriculture as 'mechanical'. Of course the distinction does not imply that managerial and practical skills are absent from 'mechanical' technologies, nor that the development of 'skill-oriented' technologies precludes the use of complex equipment, including labour-substituting machinery. But as chapter 2 showed, there are often considerable technical difficulties in developing suitable machinery to substitute for highly skilled labour; furthermore if the principal requirement is to raise the productivity of land, the benefits of mechanisation may be restricted to equipment which eliminates bottlenecks and permits the intensification of land and labour use.

Any technical innovation in agriculture is likely to provoke shifts in the allocation of resources which will benefit certain social groups to the disadvantage of others. The capital-intensive nature of most agricultural innovations in early modern Europe encouraged a polarisation of rural society into entrepreneurial farmers and landless labourers. One of the advantages of a 'skill-oriented' agricultural system such as wet-rice cultivation, which provides little scope for economies of scale and depends far less upon capital investment, should be that technological advance does not promote economic inequalities to the same extent.

The new inputs typical of many phases of development in rice agriculture are *divisible*, that is to say, new seed or improved fertilisers can be bought in any quantity according to the farmer's inclination or financial situation. Innovation is thus within the scope of farmers of all income groups. Often organisational improvements or a more careful carrying out of operations can make important contributions to increasing output without requiring any increase in capital outlay at all.

Since in a 'skill-oriented' technology like rice cultivation efficiency depends less upon the range of equipment than on the quality of labour, and since economies of scale do not operate as they do, for example, in the European case described in appendix A, a skilled and experienced smallholder or tenant farmer is in just as good a position to raise the productivity of his land as a wealthy landlord[1] (see chapter 5). Indeed as productivity rises, the costs of adequately supervising the many tasks involved in wet-rice farming become prohibitive: inspecting an irrigated field for weeds is almost as onerous as weeding it oneself.

So although prices of land rise as production is intensified and yields increase, and although there are often very high rates of tenancy in areas where wet rice is intensively farmed, the difficulties of effective supervision mean that landlords find little or no economic advantage in evicting their tenants to run large, centrally managed estates. Instead they generally prefer to leave their tenants to manage their small farms independently, shouldering all or part of the risks of production. Thus, contrary to the pattern set by the development of the 'mechanical' technology of Northwest Europe, in wet-rice societies there has been little trend towards the consolidation of landholding and the polarisation of rural society into managerial farms and landless labourers. Units of management remain small, usually at the scale of the family farm (table

Table 4.1 Farm sizes in Asia

		Farm size (ha)	Wet-rice area (ha)
Japan	1960[a]	1.00	0.56
	1978[a]	1.15	0.64
Korea	1965[b]	0.91	
	1979[b]	1.02	
Taiwan	1965[c]	1.05	
	1979[c]	1.02	
Java	1969/70[d]		0.8
Central Java	1971/2[e]	0.5	0.5
Thailand (Rai Rot)	1972[d]		6.0
Philippines (Laguna)	1966[d]		2.2
	1975[d]		2.2
Malaysia (Kelantan)	1971/2[e]	0.9	
Sri Lanka	1972/3[d]	0.8	

Sources:
[a] Hou and Yu 1982: 131
[b] ibid.: 206
[c] ibid.: 611
[d] Taylor 1981: 89
[e] IRRI 1978: 8–9

4.1), and the producers are not separated from control of the means of production (see chapter 6, and appendices B and C for the historical cases of China and Japan). The small-scale independent management units controlling land and skills are, however, inextricably linked into much larger-scale cooperative units for the management of water and the redistribution of labour. The paradox between the individual and the communal nature of rice cultivation has frequently been remarked upon by Japanese social scientists (e.g. Kanazawa 1971; Tamaki 1979).

The specificity of wet-rice agriculture

Wet-rice cultivation shapes and divides a landscape decisively, imposing a technical, economic and linguistic distinction between wet and dry.

Flying over Kelantan [Malaysia], one is immediately struck by the contrast between the wide tracts of flat green riceland with the irrigation channels glinting in the sun, and the distinct patches of dark wooded land which hide the homesteads from view. Near the coast the sea of ricefields is most extensive, the islands of woodland becoming larger and more contiguous as one flies westward, until they finally merge into dense jungle. The distinction between riceland (*bendang*) and village land (*kampong*) is determined primarily by the elevation of the land. The low-lying areas, usually with moist heavy soils, are suitable for rice farming and not much else; land which is even a few feet higher is comparatively dry and safe from floods, providing a natural place to build houses, plant trees for shade and protection from the wind, and grow vegetables, spices and fruit. This distinction between padi fields and village land (respectively 57% and 35% of the land area) looms large in the life of Kelantanese communities. *Bendang*, or padi fields, provide the staple rice necessary for subsistence; no individual *kampong* crop is necessary to physical survival, but together these two types of land provide a varied diet and a source of cash income. (Bray and Robertson 1980: 217)

The same distinction and complementarity are found in all rice-growing regions. Rice-fields which are undrained and permanently waterlogged are suitable for very few other crops apart from semi-aquatics like taro, ginger, indigo and sugar cane (Bray 1984: 112). On the whole dry and wet land are not interchangeable, and rice-farmers must make a long-term choice as to the proportion of land to be allotted primarily to rice and that given over to other crops. The concentrated periods of heavy labour requirements are also a determining factor.

Some crops compete with rice for land, labour and water, and cases where rice-farmers have given up producing their subsistence requirements to turn their wet-fields over entirely to commercial crops, though comparatively rare, are not unknown. In fifteenth-century Fujian province, China, many farmers chose to devote their wet-fields principally to sugar, which fetched a high price on the export market, and to buy their rice from other provinces (Rawski 1972). And in nineteenth-century Java the 'Culture System' produced intense competition between sugar-cane and rice, for land, irrigation-water and labour. As a result localities where the sugar quota was high tended to produce only a single crop of rice a year; at the same time rice production intensified in localities where little sugar was grown, and such areas supplemented the food needs of the sugar districts.[2]

Of course the farmer's choice as to how to allocate his resources will be determined by the demands of the market as well as by technological constraints, and in fact a fair degree of technical flexibility is possible. In the Japanese village of Niiike, studied by Beardsley and Hall, rice was grown only for subsistence until the 1930s, and cotton was the most important economic crop, grown in hillside fields throughout the area:

The farmers of Niiike have shifted in recent years to an increasing emphasis upon paddy farming for a number of reasons, among them the increased importance of cash-crop farming, the collapse of the market for locally grown cotton, and the improvement of hitherto marshy paddy land ... Cotton was [formerly] a major product of the Okayama Plain, where some of Japan's largest spinning mills had been built after the Meiji Restoration. The mills later turned to the cheaper and more plentiful cotton imported from the United States and southern Asia. The market for domestic cotton thus declined sharply after 1910. The Niiike farmers turned to raising mat rush, the basic material for the covering of floor mats. A swamp plant, this rush could be grown as a second crop even in hard-to-drain paddy fields. Intensive use of chemical fertilisers began about the same time. [With the programme of rice-land improvements of 1925 to 1930] household labour was needed now in the paddy fields or could be profitably employed in weaving the mat rush into *tatami* covers. Gradually cultivation of the hillside dry fields was abandoned, and pine trees were planted ... Niiike became a paddy farming village. All parts of the valley floor low enough to lead water are utilised for paddy. (Beardsley and Hall et al. 1980 edn: 134–6)

Greater flexibility in the redeployment of limited land and labour resources can sometimes be achieved through mechanisation, and the possibility of mechanising certain agricultural operations has recently permitted many Asian farmers to make the transition from subsistence to commercial cropping. To take two examples from Thailand, the introduction of tractors permitted the Lüe farmers of Ban Ping in the north to open up a large area of new fields in a nearby flood-plain for the commercial production of non-glutinous rice, although they continued to use the plough in the home fields where they grew glutinous rice for their own consumption. The case of the Ban Ping farmers is interesting, as they were very quick to adopt tractor ploughing but continued it only for a few years, to clear the new land and also to till it quickly at a period before local water control networks had been constructed which eliminated seasonal flooding. The Lüe farmers preferred using ploughs to tractors, partly because ploughs are said to give higher yields, and they only used the tractors for a brief period; nevertheless tractors were an essential element in the transition to commercial rice-cropping (Moerman 1968).

Nearby, in the Chiengmai Basin, rice-farmers wishing to supplement their incomes turned not to commercial rice production but to the cultivation of dryland crops, opening up new fields on higher land where they grew groundnuts, garlic, chilli and maize. But in order to free enough household labour for such enterprises they too started using machinery for certain rice-growing operations (Bruneau 1980: 426).

Fields that can be drained can be used for other crops. An early

Chinese description of drainage techniques is given in the *Wang Zhen nongshu*:

High fields are tilled early. In the eighth month they are ploughed dry [that is, without waiting for rain or irrigation as is usual before ploughing] to parch the soil and then sown with wheat or barley. The method of ploughing is as follows: they throw up a ridge to make lynchets, and the area between two lynchets forms a drain. Once the section has been tilled they split the lynchets crosswise and let the water drain from the ditches; this is known as a 'waist drain'. Once the wheat or barley has been harvested they level the lynchets and drains to accumulate the water in the field which they then plough deeply. This is vulgarly called a twice-ripe field. (*Wang Zhen nongshu*: 2/5b, tr. Bray 1984: 111)

The climate in China's Yangzi valley was sufficiently warm to allow the alternation of summer rice with winter barley or wheat, and this double-cropping system spread rapidly after the fall of the Northern Song dynasty to the Mongols in 1127. A twelfth-century work says:

After the fall of the Northern Song many refugees from the Northwest came to the Yangzi area, the Delta, the region of the Dongting Lake and the Southeast coast, and at the beginning of the Shaoxing reign (1131–63) the price of a bushel of wheat reached 12,000 cash. The farmers benefited greatly, for the profits were double those of growing rice. Furthermore, tenants paid rent only on the autumn crop, so that all the profits from growing wheat went to the tenant household. Everyone competed to grow the spring-ripening crop, which could be seen everywhere in no less profusion than to the north of the Huai River. (*Ji le bian*, tr. Bray 1984: 465)

Further south in China barley was preferred to wheat as it matured earlier and was better adapted to humid conditions and poorly drained land (Shen 1951: 208). In South Japan wheat, barley and naked barley (collectively known as *sanbaku*) were the most common second crops in drained rice-fields. The incentive to convert undrained fields, *shitsuden*, into drained fields, *kanden*, was provided by access to the commercial markets which developed during the Tokugawa and Meiji periods (Francks 1983: 59, 108), and later *kanden* expanded further as the development of pumping equipment made it possible to drain low-lying fields (Ishikawa 1981: 43).

Uniformity and systemic change

The constraints of efficient labour use and water control impose a degree of technical uniformity and cohesion on rice-farmers, as well as requiring cooperation between them. All the farmers within a single irrigation unit will have to fill and empty their fields at the same time, which means they will have to plant varieties with a similar ripening period. They will usually cooperate on the maintenance of their joint irrigation channels, and will also be obliged to cooperate in order to fulfil their labour requirements during the periods of peak demand.

It has been pointed out that if rice-farmers had restricted their farm size to the area which they could manage with family labour alone, they would often not have been able to produce enough for their own subsistence (Wong 1971). To some extent such problems could be mitigated by spreading one's efforts over several different plots and by planting a number of rice varieties. Lewis (1971: 49) describes the tactics of Filipino farmers in the lowland *barrio* of Buyon, all of whom grew early and late, glutinous and non-glutinous rices in the same season, in order to split up fields and the timing of operations and so spread out their labour requirements; thus one household could cope alone with several plots amounting to over an acre where it would have been unable to manage a single field of the same area. In most rice-growing societies, however, farmers supplemented their family labour through labour exchange or, much less frequently, labour hire.

Labour exchange systems have been found in almost every society where rice is grown. Some regions have formal, permanent labour-exchange societies, in others arrangements may be *ad hoc*, or several kinds of arrangement may co-exist. In Kelantan, Malaysia, for instance, two systems of communal labour co-existed until very recently. For *berderau*, exchange labour proper, a group of friends, relatives or neighbours would get together to plant rice on a rota basis, 10 or 12 families in a group. These groups were of long duration, as the advantages of having one's field planted first had to be rotated among the members of the group over several years. *Pinjaman*, literally 'borrowing', was a system more akin to hiring labour: a farmer would provide a good meal for a day's work, and was under no obligation to work in the other farmers' fields (Bray and Robertson 1980). In Japanese villages exchange labour for transplanting was called *kattari* or *yui*; there too the *kattari* group was formed of about a dozen families on a permanent basis. There were also a number of other types of cooperative group, covering activities from repairing irrigation channels to organising funerals (Embree 1946: 99); a similar range of cooperative groups was to be found in Korean villages (Reed 1977: 19).

Many exchange organisations are based on simple proximity, but in Southwest China, 'far from being confined to the village, the exchange of labour is commonly practised among different localities. Since such transactions, based as they are on reciprocity, really constitute a credit system, some form of security is needed, and this is provided by ties of kinship. Thus we find that exchange of services among relatives is considered most desirable' (Fei and Chang 1948: 64). It is perhaps not surprising that in a strongly patrilineal society like that of China cooperation between kin is preferred, whereas in Malaya, where descent groups are bilateral and the word for 'kinsman' and 'friend' is the same, the choice is not so obvious. In other cultures still other criteria may apply. In the Madras area of India exchange labour is confined to members of the same caste (Nakamura 1972: 161).

It is important to bear in mind that exchanging labour does not increase the amount of labour available, but redistributes it so that it can be deployed to best effect. It seems that labour exchange is usually confined to rice farming alone, and does not extend to cash crops, for which extra labour is hired if necessary (e.g. Potter 1976: 42). In Tokugawa Japan the institution of labour hire developed as the rural economy expanded and diversified, but was in large part confined to commercial crops and rural manufactures (Smith 1959: ch. 8). But in Tonkin labour hire had a completely different nature and origins. French colonial rule put paid to what few rural industries there were and laid a heavy stress on rice monoculture. The introduction of monetary taxes (which as usual laid a far heavier burden on the poor than on the rich), together with rapid population growth, had led by the 1930s to the development of a landless labouring class, who found their only employment in rice-farming, and consequently to the disappearance of cooperative organisations (Popkin 1979: 155; Fforde 1983: 56).

Another almost ubiquitous form of cooperation in rice-growing areas, at least where water control of any sophistication is practised, is represented by the various irrigation groups and associations referred to in chapter 3. Irrigation associations are not necessarily egalitarian, although it has been alleged that the communal nature of water control in rice-growing societies counteracts the tendency towards economic polarisation inherent in the private ownership of land (see Kelly 1982b: 12). But although hierarchies do exist in irrigation societies and the least powerful members are often unashamedly exploited (see chapter 6), all the farmers however humble do belong to the group.

Communal organisations such as labour-exchange groups and irrigation societies greatly reinforce the technical uniformity and cohesion imposed on rice-growing societies by the physical demands of rice cultivation. They often prove a highly effective, rapid and acceptable channel for popularising innovations and standardising techniques. The sharing and reinforcement of skills and resources is especially important where a single technical change entails a transformation of the whole system, as is frequently the case in rice cultivation. Changes in rice cultivation come not singly but in 'packages'; in fact one might characterise such change as systemic: new varieties allow double-cropping but require more water and fertilisers, as well as an intensification of labour use which transforms previous patterns of organisation. Let us take as an instance what happened in Kelantan, Malaysia when an irrigation scheme was constructed by the Kemubu Agricultural Development Authority (KADA) to permit double-cropping of rice.[3]

Each irrigation unit serves over 20 ha. The water is supplied by KADA for a charge of M$25 per hectare per annum, according to a very strict timetable calculated for each district every season. Sufficient water has to be supplied to soften the soil for ploughing, and after transplanting there must be 15 cm of water standing in the fields during the period of maximum growth. It is also advisable to change the water in the padi-fields every week or so.

Every season KADA issues a timetable to each district prescribing the exact day on which each operation is to begin and finish (figure 4.1). It is necessary to follow this timetable almost without deviation if two crops are to be grown successfully. In particular, if transplanting is not completed on time, then the crop is likely to fail through lack of water. If the timetable is to be adhered to, then the farmers must set to ploughing and sowing almost as soon as they have finished harvesting. In the old days the month or two after the harvest was a time of rest and celebration, with feasts, plays, dancing, kite-flying and other amusements, and even now the farmers feel they deserve a rest after the harvest. But there is no time allowed for resting under the new system, and so it happens that the farmers begin to lag behind the new timetable, one season by only a few days, the next by a few days more, until eventually they have to forfeit a whole season. In Bunut Susu, the village I was studying, half the farmers lost the monsoon season of 1976–7.

It is essentially the presence or absence of water which determines which land can or must be used for rice, and over which period of the year. It is instructive to see what happens when the water-level changes as it did in Kelantan. Before the construction of the KADA irrigation scheme permitting the double-cropping of rice (see chapter 3), poorly drained land, although it produced the highest yields of rice, was usually left idle in the dry season; slightly higher land, especially where soils were sandy, would produce good crops of vegetables or tobacco.

The old varieties of rice cannot be grown in double-cropped fields because their growth period is too long. Over the past five years a number of new, high-yielding varieties have been introduced, mostly by KADA, though some of the most popular varieties were in fact found by

Figure 4.1   KADA timetable for rice cultivation
(photo courtesy A. F. Robertson)

the farmers themselves. Under favourable conditions the new varieties give much higher yields than the old. In some parts of the KADA area the average yield is as much as 5 t/ha, but the highest yields reported for Bunut Susu, which had problems with its water supply, were 3.75 t/ha, and on poorly drained or dry soils yields of less than 2 t/ha were usual.

KADA recommends the use of 7.5 bags of chemical fertiliser per hectare each season, and almost invariably the farmers comply. In 1977 it cost M$135 to fertilise one hectare. A disadvantage of chemical fertilisers is that they encourage the growth of weeds, and regular weeding of the standing crop is now often necessary.

The new varieties ripen at five months. As soon as double-cropping and the new, looser-grained varieties were introduced, the farmers of Bunut Susu gave up the use of the reaping-knife and started harvesting with sickles. Instead of cutting the stems halfway down and storing the rice in bundles to be threshed as required, the farmers now cut the stems at ground-level and thresh the grain immediately into wooden tubs. The new method of harvesting means that all the rice, ripe, over-ripe and under-ripe, is cut at once, but the sickle is much quicker than the reaping-knife. Previously it might have taken a month to harvest all the rice grown on one farm, and reaping was all done with family labour. Now most farmers hire three or four men to help, and five men can easily harvest a hectare in five or six days. Most farmers also hire tractors now to prepare their fields in the short time available between the two crops.

This has led to a transformation in the organisation of labour. In the old days borrowing and exchanging labour were possible because, although the tasks had to be carried out quickly on individual farms, they could be staggered throughout the village. But now the irrigation timetable requires that the same tasks be completed throughout a large area in a short space of time, and so the peak demands for labour are much more intense. In the old days nobody hired labour, but now many people hire themselves out at transplanting and harvesting time for the equivalent of about M$38 per hectare of work. Many elderly people who no longer farm, or women or young men who do not own padi land, hire themselves out at these times, as do poorer farmers who otherwise would find it difficult to meet the expense of purchasing inputs. The owners of larger padi farms now usually work only on their own land.

Monoculture and markets

Rice-land can be cropped extremely intensively, producing higher total outputs than any other type of grain-land. In a commune in Central

China a rotation of two crops of rice followed by one of wheat produced a total of 20 t/ha (Wertheim and Stiefel 1982: 28); in the central islands of Indonesia it is also common to grow two crops of rice followed by some other crop, and the annual output of rice may reach 8 to 10 t/ha (e.g. Gerdin 1982: 66). The output of rice has been enhanced by recent improvements in technology, but the intensive use of rice-land is nothing new. A late seventeenth-century Chinese work, *New Descriptions of Guangdong Province*, says:

[The inhabitants of Southern Guangdong and Annam] produce more grain than they can eat, so they carry it in great wains to the fairs of Hengzhou [modern Nanning, on the border of Guangxi and Vietnam], where it is bought by merchants who ship it down the Wu, Man and Tan rivers to Canton . . . The reason for the abundance of grain is that the climate in these southern regions is so warm that the land produces three crops in a single year . . . They grow two crops of rice in the early fields and then plant brassicas to make oil or indigo for dyeing, or grow turmeric or barley, rape or sweet potatoes. Once the main-field crops have been harvested they soak the straw in sea-water and burn it for the salt. On flat hills and ridges reeds, sugar cane, cotton, hemp, beans, aromatic herbs, fruits and melons are grown in profusion. The people are all extremely industrious and devote themselves so diligently to their farming that truly no patch of land is wasted and no hands are ever idle. (*Guangdong xinyu*: 371, tr. Bray 1984: 509)

But despite its great potential productivity, too heavy a dependence upon rice cultivation alone is not advisable. Expounding his concept of 'agricultural involution', based on a historical study of Indonesia, Geertz (1963) suggested that it was possible to absorb extra labour generated by population growth through the intensification of rice cultivation, thus providing the whole community with a small, if often inadequate, livelihood. In fact, despite its potential for responding positively to increases in labour inputs, the intensification of rice monoculture is a far less efficacious way of absorbing labour and generating extra income than is economic diversification.[4] There are a number of possible improvements which eliminate bottlenecks and spread the labour requirements for rice cultivation more evenly over the year (figure 4.2), yet underemployment in areas of rice monoculture tends to be high (table 4.2) even though there may still be acute labour shortages at peak periods (e.g. Shand and Mohd. Ariff 1983: 102). While it is possible to relieve such shortages through mechanisation, this only exacerbates the problem of overall employment in rice cultivation, and tends to cause economic inequalities by depriving the poorer farmers and the landless of opportunities to hire out their labour.[5] Only where circumstances are particularly favourable to rice-farmers, for example in postwar Japan

Rice and the wider economy

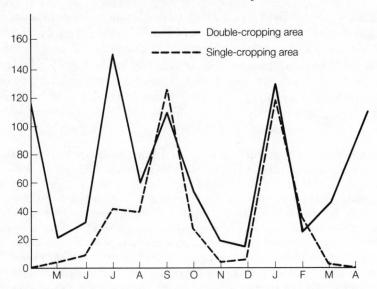

Figure 4.2   Labour inputs in single- and double-cropping areas in Province Wellesley,
Malaysia
(after Purcal 1972: 22, 71)

Table 4.2   Underemployment in single- and double-cropping rice areas in
Province Wellesley, Malaysia

Months:	M (%)	J (%)	J (%)	A (%)	S (%)	O (%)	N (%)	D (%)	J (%)	F (%)	M (%)	A (%)	Average (%)
Double-cropping area	52	38	2	23	35	27	33	44	7	52	43	43	33
Single-cropping area	64	40	8	8	24	36	37	45	−3	50	60	61	36

Source: Purcal 1972: 26, 76

where rice prices have been high and input costs low, is specialisation in
rice monoculture profitable and relatively secure from fluctuations in
world grain and oil prices. Where rice monoculture is imposed upon
farmers despite relatively unfavourable conditions, acute problems
frequently result.

Grain markets depend upon adequate means of bulk transport, and
especially of water transport. In the Mediterranean, where every city had

easy access to the sea, control of the grain trade had become the key to political power by the time of the Greeks and Phoenicians. The vast land-mass of East Asia, with its tangles of mountain ranges, is not so easy of access; even today one of the chief obstacles to China's economic development remains the lack of adequate transport networks. If Asian states have always taken such an active interest in encouraging agricultural production within their territories, this must be due in part to the difficulties of supplementing local food supplies from abroad.

By the tenth or eleventh century Song China already had a huge volume of inter-regional trade in rice, concentrated mainly along the Grand Canal, the Yangzi and other large southern rivers, and the east coast.[6] Private grain-ships plying the Grand Canal could often carry 1,000 piculs (approximately 7,000 hectolitres), while certain ocean-going junks had double that capacity (Shiba 1970: 73). The main centres of the regional rice-trade were the great Yangzi river-ports, Hangzhou, Nanjing and Wuchang. Rice was commercially produced in almost every southern province of China, and was sold not only to the cities but also to rural areas which had difficulty in meeting their own needs, either because they were unsuited to rice production, or because of a poor harvest, or because they had turned to the production of more lucrative commercial crops. In the twelfth century the mountainous district of Huizhou in Fujian sold tea, lacquer, paper and wood to the Yangzi Delta in exchange for rice. The Song long-distance rice-trade was extensive, and was an important factor in encouraging the expansion of rice production in many areas such as the Canton region, which by the thirteenth century was exporting rice to Champa and other foreign parts (ibid.: 63).

But this lively response to markets was only possible where water transport was available, and Shiba makes the point that 'at the periphery of the commercialised system, there remained a number of localised, discrete and self-sufficient marketing systems' (ibid.: 67). This has been true of China throughout her history. Rawski's (1972) study of Fujian and Hunan in the sixteenth to eighteenth centuries clearly demonstrates the ready response of Chinese farmers to market stimuli such as price rises, but this was conditional on access to transport, so that it was not uncommon, as indeed it still is not today, to find flourishing trade centres separated from self-sufficient backwaters by a single ridge of mountains.

It has often been said that the growth of commerce, and of the rice-trade, in Tokugawa Japan was largely due to the *sankin kōtai* system 'whereby feudal lords were required to spend six months of every year in the capital and the other six months in their fiefs. The passage of the lords and their many retainers from distant parts of the country led to improvements in the road system and to the development of commercial facilities for them along the way, while keeping the more remote parts of the country in communication with the capital and other urban centres' (Francks 1983: 50).

But easy access to transport and markets often tempted farmers into more profitable ventures than rice production, to the disapproval of officials concerned with forestalling food shortages. A thirteenth-century Chinese official, Fang Dazong, complained that certain districts in Fujian had almost given up cultivating ordinary rice in favour of sugar-cane or glutinous rice for wine-making, whereas in the most productive regions of the province '[the authorities] have forbidden the cultivation of glutinous rice, the manufacture of wine from it, the growing of oranges, and the excavation of ponds for the rearing of fish. The reason for this ban is the desire that no inch of land should be uncultivated, and no grain of rice uneaten. If regions which produce a surplus of rice take such precautions, how much more should those whose harvests cannot supply half their needs' (Shiba 1970: 54).

Governments were not easily able to restrict a farmer's choice, however, even by obliging him to pay taxes in kind. Even in Song China many farmers chose or found it necessary to purchase rice in order to pay their taxes (ibid.: 56).

The principal rice-producing region of China in Song times was Jiangsu in the Yangzi Delta, but by the 1720s it had become a net importer of rice, buying it not only from the provinces of the Central Yangzi but also from Shandong and Taiwan. By that time the Canton region too had switched from exporting rice abroad to importing it from the neighbouring province of Guangxi (Chuan and Kraus 1975: 59, 65, 71). Areas of intensive rice cultivation tended, if they had access to other markets, to diversify into the production of more profitable commodities, while hitherto underdeveloped areas found an incentive to step up their rice production in order to fill the gap.

In a stimulating article on the indirect effects of colonial capitalism on monsoon Asia, Baker (1981) describes the resulting shift in inter-regional economic links. At first it was the long-settled, densely populated areas of intensive agriculture which supplied food to the new areas of colonial industrial or semi-industrial production, most of which were in sparsely populated regions where there were few obstacles to claiming land and establishing plantations or factories:

The planters moved into the hills of central Ceylon, upper Malaya, outer Indonesia and Annam, and spread out estates of tea, rubber, coffee, and spices. The peasants were pushed out into the hitherto relatively vacant parts of India,

Malaya, and Indochina to grow cotton, sugar, indigo, tobacco, and oilseeds, and onto the marginal lands of Java in order to accommodate sugar . . . Initially [the demand for food] was satisfied by the established agricultural systems in the long-settled densely populated areas. Tonkin sent food into Annam; India exported rice to Ceylon and to the Straits; Java exported to the Outer Islands. But before the end of the nineteenth century, this situation had substantially changed. The west also helped to open up new areas of food production within the southeast Asian region . . . the most important and spectacular expansion came through the opening up of the lower reaches of the Irrawaddy, Chao Phraya, and Mekong river basins . . . Roughly fourteen million acres were newly planted with rice in mainland southeast Asia in little over half a century. (Baker 1981: 332)

The colonial powers played an important role in providing infrastructure for the opening up of new land, constructing canals which served the dual purpose of draining marshy areas so that they became cultivable and providing easy access by water so that the produce could be shipped out. But much of the labour force for this expansion of food production came from the 'ancient' areas (East India, South China, Tonkin, Java), as did the technical skills and a great deal of the capital. In return the 'ancient' areas received an inflow of remittance money and, eventually, large quantities of grain. 'In the late 1920s, Burma, Thailand, and Indochina were producing about 9.4 million metric tons of cleaned rice (or equivalent) a year, and exporting about 5.4 million tons of this total. Indonesia, Malaya, and Ceylon together produced 3.9 million tons and imported another 1.6 million, while China and India were importing about a million tons apiece' (ibid.: 338).

These new areas of rice monoculture were, however, extremely vulnerable, as were the rice regions of Taiwan and Korea developed by the Japanese in the early decades of this century to supply their home market with cheap rice. Farmers in such areas had not developed any alternative sources of income. When the Depression hit Asia and the demand for rice suddenly contracted, in Southeast Asia the resulting surpluses of rice made for a devastating fall in prices, severe impoverishment, communal strife, and a stagnation of the rural economy which in Burma and Thailand lasted until well into the 1950s (ibid.: 341, 346). Japan had made a particular effort to step up rice production in her colonies as well as in Japan after the urban Rice Riots of 1918, but unfortunately the rise in production coincided with the Depression and a consequent decline in per capita rice consumption in Japan. In 1931 exports to Japan accounted for about half the total rice production in both Korea and Taiwan, and for 15% of Japan's total consumption, but from 1933 Japan introduced strict import controls (Ogura 1980: 167).

However the situation of Taiwanese and Korean rice-farmers soon picked up as Japan launched into full-scale war (Wade 1982: 25).

The problems associated with over-reliance on rice monoculture were amply demonstrated in China during the 1960s and early 1970s, when everyone was urged to 'take grain as the key link'. To encourage self-sufficiency government grain supplies to areas which had formerly specialised in cash crops such as cotton were cut off. Not only did this policy have a drastic effect on the output of non-cereal crops, but the use of unsuitable land for the intensive production of irrigated rice and other grains was often quite counterproductive (Lardy 1984a). The recent trends towards agricultural specialisation and renewed government efforts to redistribute grain between provinces have led both to increases in grain yields and to improved levels of consumption (Lardy 1984b).

In Malaysia too the government has in effect forced rice monoculture on farmers in certain areas, most notably in the Kemubu and Muda regions. The construction and extension of irrigation networks in these areas, together with the introduction of double-cropping, is part of an effort to achieve national self-sufficiency in rice. But new patterns of land use and the more intensive labour requirements of double-cropping have effectively precluded economic diversification in these regions. In 1974–5 Malaysia succeeded in supplying 93% of its national rice requirements (Mokhtar 1978: 119), but the demand for rice is relatively inelastic, particularly as many better-off Malaysians are now turning to wheat products, and so a rice-farmer's potential for increasing his income by selling more rice is limited.

Considering the Muda region, traditionally a monoculture area, where holdings are relatively large, mechanisation is advanced and the labour force is fully commercialised, Bell (1978) saw few opportunities for improving rice-farmers' incomes. The intense economic specialisation of the region meant that there were few opportunities for off-farm employment, and the technical demands imposed by the irrigation scheme allowed no possibility of switching from rice to high-value crops. Recent increases in government support prices have benefited large farmers more than small, for profit elasticity is very high with respect to land, for which the factor coefficient is nearly 1.0 (Mokhtar 1978: 125). The outcome foreseen by Bell was a rural exodus and the concentration of landholding accompanied by increasing mechanisation of rice production, and more recent evidence tends to support his predictions (Muhd. Ikmal 1985).

The situation in the Kemubu region is somewhat different, for Kelantan has a long tradition of economic diversification (table 4.3). Rice-farmers supplemented their incomes by growing vegetables,

Table 4.3   Non-padi income as proportion of net padi income in
KADA and MADA (1979/80)

Tenurial group	Full tenants (%)	Part tenants (%)	Owner-operators (%)
KADA	144	77	60
MADA	49	25	26

Source: From official sources.

tobacco, rubber or coconuts, by local and long-distance trade and, of especial importance, by seasonal migration. The transformation of much good dry-crop land into mediocre irrigated land has considerably restricted opportunities for non-rice cropping. Since the income from dry land is frequently double or triple that from double-cropped rice-land, the prices of the remaining dry land have shot up and much wooded land has recently been cleared for vegetable gardens or orchards (Bray and Robertson 1980: 237). Perhaps more serious than the encroachment of irrigated on dry land are the new patterns of labour inputs demanded by double-cropping, which often require a farmer to make a choice between growing rice and supplementing his income through other activities. Shand and Mohd. Ariff (1983: 171) suggest that in Kelantan the introduction of double-cropping has restricted the freedom of farmers and their families to take up sustained off-farm employment, while its positive impact on agricultural underemployment has been modest, since this still amounts to over 25%. While Shand and Ariff (ibid.: 253) see mechanisation as a possible solution enabling farmers to earn more off-farm income while still producing padi for sale, other official sources point out that the labour absorption consequent upon the introduction of double-cropping in Kemubu, although low, is still higher than it has been in Muda; they say that for reasons of equity further mechanisation in Kelantan would be very undesirable. At the same time they severely criticise the emphasis on monoculture, blaming the Malaysian government for sacrificing Kelantan's regional needs to national objectives.

Economic diversification

The possibilities for increasing employment and incomes and for generating wealth lie not so much in maximising the production of rice as in using intensive rice cultivation as a basis for economic diversification. The resource and management requirements of rice cultivation generally mesh extremely well both with commercial cropping and with small-scale manufacturing activities.

Rice lends itself to productive combinations, such as the centuries-old system of rice, fish and silk production typical of certain regions of East China and South Japan, which is in fact a self-sustaining ecosystem (Fei 1939; Ishikawa 1981: 46): mulberry trees are grown on high land, often along the banks of the rice-fields (figure 4.3); silkworm droppings are used as powerful fertilisers for the rice; fish live in the irrigation channels as well as the rice-fields, nibbling away the water-weeds and eating the larvae of insect pests as well as being fed with the silkworm moultings. Often the farmers raise ducks in the rice-fields too, in which case some of the fish will enliven the diet of the ducks rather than that of the farmers.

The importance of vegetable gardens and orchards in the Kelantan rural economy has already been mentioned. Since almost every household, however poor, owns a house-plot, the income from garden produce plays an important role in poorer households, especially those with no other agricultural land to their name. In a study carried out in Java in 1972/3, Stoler (1981) found that poor households cultivated their garden plots far more intensively than households with access to other land, but tended to concentrate on production for their own consumption rather than for sale. Wealthier households had a much more entrepreneurial attitude towards their gardens.

In another Javanese village, Mizuno (1985) found that half of all the farmers and one-third of the labourers were engaged in part-time production of coconut sugar. Even though the adoption of rice double-cropping has increased opportunities for labour hire, many households prefer sugar to rice production: although it requires an initial cash outlay to lease the trees and several hours' labour daily to tap the trees and boil down the sap, sugar production 'has the great advantage of providing a secure daily cash income' (ibid.: 32).

In Java, as in Malaysia, rice cultivation is not in itself a profitable occupation. It provides a degree of security, but all farming households, whether they own land, rent it, or hire out their labour, derive the major part of their income not from rice but from other part-time occupations. This is not entirely surprising in regions where the pressure on land is so acute that very few households have large enough rice-farms even to supply their domestic needs. Since the population in Java averages 660 per sq. km,[7] this is true of the majority of Javanese households (Mizuno 1985: 1, 34), and almost all of them resort to what White (1976: 280)

Figure 4.3   Picking mulberry leaves to feed silkworms, illustrated in the Song work
Gengzhi tu
(Agriculture and sericulture illustrated) (Qing edition of 1886)

calls 'occupational multiplicity' simply to survive (see also, for example, Mantra 1981; Montgomery 1981).

Even in more prosperous economies it is rare to find that rice production is profitable in itself (see chapter 5); nevertheless it still serves as a basis for more profitable diversification. Taiwanese rice-farmers realise little or no profit on double-cropped rice, yet they continue to cultivate their rice-land, apparently because: '(1) "it is a resource that must be used", (2) it [is] a source of food, specifically rice, (3) taxes levied on it [have] to be paid, and (4) additional taxes [are] imposed if it [is] not cultivated' (Gallin and Gallin 1982: 218). Interviews with part-time farmers in Northeast Japan indicated that their refusal to give up rice cultivation stemmed from (1) a sense of responsibility, both spiritual and proprietorial, (2) their emotional attachment to the land, and (3) a need for security. As a consequence the men often took full-time work in the vicinity but left the farm in charge of the women, who diversified their incomes by growing fruit and vegetables, and especially a highly profitable species of mushroom, as well as rice (Shimpo 1976: 45, 72).

Petty commodity production and rural industrialisation

In the 'skill-oriented' technology of wet-rice cultivation increases in agricultural production are generally achieved through an intensification of land productivity rather than an expansion of the cultivated area, and it is the skilled application of large amounts of labour that counts rather than capital investment or the introduction of machinery. The required equipment is simple, and labour is most frequently supplied by the household or community involved. The technical requirements of wet-rice cultivation have consistently placed a high premium on the application of skilled labour, and given only low returns on investment in capital equipment or the expansion of production units (see chapter 5).

Wet-rice agriculture can support higher population densities than most other agricultural systems, and this has been extremely important in shaping more general patterns of economic development. Before the Industrial Revolution such countries as China could be considered technically and economically in advance of Europe. Boserup points out that for reasons of transport facilities, markets, access to labour and so on, it was only in densely populated areas that commercialisation and manufactures were feasible at that time, and 'the main advantage of a dense population, i.e., the better possibilities to create infrastructure, seems to have outbalanced the disadvantage of a less favourable ratio between population and natural resources' (1981: 129). Changes in the medieval Yangzi Delta (see appendix B) show clearly how density of population and economic advance may go hand in hand. Nevertheless, the generalised economic growth of medieval China did not lead to capitalism and industrialisation as in Europe, partly because the demands of intensive rice cultivation and multi-cropping placed heavy constraints on the availability of labour.

In industrialising Northern Europe (see appendix A) agricultural development led to a polarisation of rural society into large farmers and a landless labour force. Although much manufacturing in the early stages was rural- rather than urban-based, even those who combined the occupations, eking out their agricultural wages with Smith's famous 'pin-money', belonged to a potentially mobile labour force, for as labourers rather than tenants they had no direct stake in the land they farmed. If higher wages could be had elsewhere, or in another form of employment, then there was nothing to tie them to the land. It was the existence of this type of labour force that provided a basis for increasing occupational specialisation, the development of more concentrated production and eventually the large-scale mechanisation of industry. On the other hand the experience of medieval China, as of early modern Japan (see appendices B and C), strongly suggests a link between the intensification of wet-rice production and the growth and entrenchment of part-time petty commodity production, which continues to flourish even today.

The organisation of resources typical of a 'skill-oriented' technology such as intensive rice-farming dovetails very neatly with petty commodity production, which requires very little capital to set up a family enterprise, and absorbs surplus labour without depriving the farm of workers at times of peak demand. It can be expanded, diversified or contracted to meet market demands, but the combination with the rice-farm guarantees the family's subsistence. The products can be conveniently conveyed to local or national markets by merchants, who pay the villagers for their labour and often provide raw materials as well as information on the state of the market. Since the owners of the enterprise also supply the labour, rural manufactures of this type sometimes prove more competitive than larger urban industries: the case of the silk industry in eighteenth-century Japan comes to mind. Japanese entrepreneurs turned increasingly to the countryside for cheap labour, and highly developed putting-out systems were evolved, taking advantage of household labour that was only partly absorbed by the demands of agriculture. By the late Tokugawa period a large proportion of households in the more advanced regions of Japan were engaged in some form of commercial manufacturing (Francks 1983: 51).

In Song and Ming China, as in Tokugawa and early Meiji Japan, there was almost no centrally organised, large-scale, capital-intensive industry. The market was supplied by petty commodity producers, and visitors from early capitalist Europe were generally impressed by the high levels of consumption that they found at all social levels. But the successful and durable system of intensive rice-farming combined with petty commodity production effectively inhibited indigenous technical and social changes of the type prerequisite for mechanisation and industrialisation.

As capitalist industry flourished in the West, it rapidly outstripped the manufactures of Asia in efficiency and levels of production. Most Asian nations, as soon as the opportunity arose, endeavoured to develop their own capitalist industries; Japan is the first and to date the most successful example. Yet it is striking how deeply Japanese industry has been and remains rooted in the countryside. The improvements in rice agriculture during the Meiji period spread labour requirements more evenly over the year and thus did not prevent younger sons or daughters from taking up by-employment or working at home (Francks 1983: 57). In 1884, 77% of Japanese factories were situated in rural areas, and more than half in 1892 (Umemura 1970). Much of the rural industrial labour force consisted of village women, often young girls on short-term contracts of three or four years, whose families received their wages while they themselves were given only board and lodging and a little pocket-money (Boserup 1981: 167). While the chemical and machine industries were concentrated in the towns, textile and ceramics manufactures and metal-working factories were mostly to be found in rural areas, and the majority of these establishments employed fewer than 20 people (Francks 1983: 53, table 3.1).

In Japan today, centralised capitalist industry still relies heavily on the putting-out system, and many farming families are involved in the production of components for large companies such as Mitsubishi or Sony. Although they may need to use high-cost and sophisticated equipment, and although the product is an element in capitalist industry, the workers are still part-time farmers who control their own labour, not industrial proletarians. Of course an increasing number of rural Japanese now work full-time in industrial jobs, but they still belong to households whose patterns of economic organisation are determined to a large extent by the family farm (Shimpo 1976).

In Southeast Asia, where recent development policies have resulted in a widespread intensification of rice production, again rural petty commodity production has accompanied the expansion and commer- cialisation of agriculture. The nature of such enterprises varies widely, but usually reflects the prevailing level of national prosperity. The goods produced may require almost no investment of skills, material or technology, or (as in the case of Japan) they may be almost as sophisticated as urban manufactures. In Central Luzon village women weave straw hats for sale (Takahashi 1970), and in Sumatra men produce iron hoes and other tools for the national market while their wives run the rice-farms and work as dress-makers (Kahn 1980).

In the Sumatran village studied by Kahn, the villagers produced rice only for consumption and relied on the sale of cash-crops and locally produced goods for all their other needs. Their village speciality was steelware, sold locally to pedlars and small merchants who redistributed it throughout the province. The small steel workshops relied entirely for raw materials on scrap steel, and the more expensive equipment like anvils was usually purchased second-hand. Most workshop-owners employed two, or sometimes three, hired labourers. The running costs and profits were divided into equal shares, one going to each worker and one to the workshop. The owner of the workshop thus extracted a small surplus from his workers (Kahn 1980: ch. 5).

Kahn demonstrates clearly the symbiotic relationship between petty commodity production and rice cultivation in Indonesia. While the economic enterprises typical of rural commodity production in monsoon Asia cannot be classed as capitalist, they are highly dependent on fluctuations in the world as well as in the national economy. Thus increased demand for peasant-produced commodities during Indonesia's period of economic isolation from 1958 to 1965 led to a rapid expansion of steel-smithing: enterprises increased both in number and in scale. But the subsequent opening up of the economy and the crippling inflation of the mid-1960s, epitomised in rocketing rice prices (600 *rupiahs* for 10 litres in Jakarta in 1963, 48,000 *rupiahs* in 1966), led to the temporary collapse of rural manufacturing enterprises. Farmers stopped engaging in commodity production and turned back to cultivating their rice-land in order to secure their subsistence. When the economy began to recover, petty commodity production expanded again, and since it was so much more profitable than rice-farming, many farmers no longer cared to produce enough rice even for their own subsistence (ibid.: 195–8).

At a higher level of economic reward, the spectacular expansion of rural-based industry in Taiwan over the last two decades is based in large part on family enterprises: in 1971 three-quarters of the industrial and commercial establishments located in the rural areas of Taiwan were small family businesses with fewer than ten workers (Gallin and Gallin 1982). Again the development of rural industries has been closely meshed with rice cultivation. In 1956 the only factory in the village of Xin

Xing studied by the Gallins was a brickworks. Most of the farmers devoted themselves principally to intensive rice cultivation. The lack of agricultural machinery and of rural industries meant that there were very few opportunities for local off-farm employment, and those who succumbed to the lure of higher manufacturing wages (some 15% of the local population) were obliged to migrate to distant cities. 95% of local incomes came from farming and agricultural labour.

By 1979 the situation had completely changed. Farmers had been able to adopt new technology enabling them to overcome labour shortages and change their patterns of land use. They either diversified into profitable cash-crops or worked part-time in remunerative off-farm activities, although they did not give up cultivating their rice fields. Over 30 labour-intensive manufactures had been established locally, ranging in size from large textile or furniture factories to family workshops doing piece-work. 85% of local incomes was now derived from off-farm activities, although about 83% of the local households still farmed. Significantly the growth of local industry had led a number of former migrants to return.

In Taiwan in the 1960s and 1970s large numbers of industries moved to the countryside in search of cheaper labour and raw materials. By 1971, 50% of industrial and commercial establishments and 55% of manufacturing establishments were located in rural areas. As a result, between 1952 and 1972 the average real income of farming households doubled, although remaining significantly lower than urban incomes (Gallin and Gallin 1982: 239).

In China a significant increase in rural incomes has been achieved since 1978 through the simple expedient of raising agricultural prices (see chapter 5), and the introduction of the 'responsibility system' led to a spurt in overall agricultural production. But many economists doubt that there is much potential for further growth in agricultural output (e.g. Lardy 1984b: 864). The fostering of rural manufactures, even at the level of petty commodity production, seems vital if differentials between urban and rural incomes are to be reduced, as present economic policies recognise:

[The] historical 'scissors' gap between agricultural and industrial prices cannot be closed overnight and its existence has provided a way of concentrating agricultural accumulation in the hands of the state. The major mechanism has been the high profit made on light industrial products manufactured using agricultural raw materials. (Dong Furen 1982, quoted Watson 1984: 86)

Since about two-thirds of China's light industrial products are sold in rural areas (Watson 1984: 86), it is only by involving the rural labour force in their production that the 'scissors' effect can be counteracted. Although many brigades set up small factories in the 1960s and 1970s, it was acknowledged that there were serious problems involved in management, providing incentives, responding to market needs, acquiring plant and raw materials, and distributing the goods efficiently. The new economic policies expressly encourage economic diversification and decentralisation, but as yet figures on public and private investment in rural-based industries, their production levels and profits, are hard to come by. In an initial burst of post-Maoist euphoria, the authorities in Chen Village in Guangdong simply parcelled out all the brigade factories to the highest bidders, regardless of their antecedents or qualifications (Chan et al. 1984: 273). If such excesses and carelessness can be avoided in the future, given the abundance of labour and raw materials and the new levels of rural accumulation, there seems no reason why local industrialisation should not go hand-in-hand with overall rural growth in China as it has in Taiwan and Japan.

5

Development

'Development' is a subject so complex that it has generated its own branches of economics and sociology. This chapter is not intended to provide comprehensive treatment, descriptive or prescriptive, of development in Asia's rice economies.[1] Instead, after raising some of the general issues likely to affect rural development in these economies, it concentrates on the technical means by which growth may be promoted (institutional means such as land reform and collectivisation will be dealt with in chapter 6). In the past growth in Asia's rice economies has followed a very different pattern from agricultural development in the West, particularly where the balance between labour and capital is concerned. The highly specific characteristics and tolerances of wet-rice cultivation are factors which should be borne in mind by development planners.

It has often been asserted that traditional patterns of agriculture in Asia have been brutally disrupted, first by the impact, whether direct or indirect, of capitalism and world markets, and then, directly, by modernisation programmes, and in particular by the so-called Green Revolution with its associated package of New Technology. The intrusion of capital, the necessity to purchase inputs and to sell grain for cash, especially in areas of subsistence economy, were expected to offset the benefits resulting from increased output by causing profound changes in the relations of production, enriching wealthy farmers and emmiserating the poor. It is certainly true that the Green Revolution, with its heavy reliance on such capital inputs as chemical fertilisers, irrigation infrastructure and farm machinery, has highlighted many of the problems involved in developing the means of production. Questions of both equity and efficiency have arisen, and the social or technical desirability of differing degrees of agricultural mechanisation, the possible emergence of capitalist farming and differentiation of Asian peasantries, are intricately linked to the roles of capital and labour in producing technical change. It must be recognised that the capital requirements of the New Technology and of participation in national and international markets, like the unprecedented degree of centralised planning and grass-roots level intervention which are typical of the Green Revolution, have marked a new era in Asian rice-farming. Yet it would be rash to say that they have caused a complete rupture and brought about a radical transformation in the nature of Asian rice technology. The heritage of centuries is not so easily overcome.

Some basic issues

The stated aim of almost all development programmes is 'growth'. In the case of agriculture, 'growth' may mean increasing overall agricultural output, increasing its value and/or increasing rural incomes. Considerations of equity, the redistribution of wealth and the eradication of poverty have to be balanced against requirements for absolute increases in output and rapid rates of growth, investments in capital goods and international expertise must be weighed against investments in education or the encouragement of local enterprise.

These days agricultural development in Asia is usually seen as a major economic priority to be tackled at national level. Most Asian states have an explicitly formulated agricultural development programme, for which they rely heavily on international expertise and finance. Centralised planning has played an increasingly important role in development of late, but although the Five-Year Plan as such is a twentieth-century phenonenon, development planning and government intervention in economic activities, and especially in agriculture, have a long pedigree in East and certain parts of Southeast Asia. Where the state derives the bulk of its income directly from agricultural production it has a clear interest in agricultural development.

As appendix B shows, in eleventh-century Song China the state put into action a well-coordinated programme of agricultural development: it introduced new varieties, popularised double-cropping through the distribution of new seeds and of leaflets on cultivation techniques, invested heavily in water control and provided peasant farmers with financial aid. Nor was this period unique. One of the most influential agricultural works ever published in China was the *Complete Treatise on Agricultural Administration* (*Nongzheng quanshu*) of 1639, written by the statesman and one-time Prime Minister Xu Guangqi; this contained lengthy sections on systems of colonisation, land distribution, water rights and credit as well as famine relief, all based on Xu's long experience as a high-ranking official and on a vast range of earlier writings on agricultural administration and improvement (Bray 1984: 64). Xu was one of a long line of Chinese administrators who attempted to popularise wet-rice cultivation in China's northern provinces (Brook 1982; on famine relief see Will 1980).

Vietnamese rulers too invested in water control and land reclamation projects, and provided peasant farmers with financial aid. The medieval empires of Angkor and Ceylon constructed huge irrigation systems dependent on centralised management. While the rulers of Tokugawa Japan largely confined their intervention to issuing exhortatory edicts, it was recognised that agriculture was the foundation of the economy; the urgent attention subsequently paid to industrialisation has never blinded Japanese statesmen to the economic (and of course political) importance of agriculture, and ever since 1870 Japan has made systematic efforts to achieve balanced sectoral development.

Until recently modern development plans all too frequently excluded the possibility of including the farmers themselves among the planners, but the innumerable difficulties encountered in imposing change from above have lately made many development experts sensitive to the importance of whole-hearted grass-roots participation. Historical examples show clearly how important the contribution of farmers has been to sustaining or even initiating growth. In China since 1949 this has been an ideological tenet: the active participation of farmers in advancing agricultural technology was for many years declared to be even more crucial to success than scientific research and development; more recently, rural demands have been instrumental in effecting a complete reshaping of rural institutions, and indeed of national economic policy. Such attitudes are perhaps to be expected in a socialist country, but a stress on popular participation and greater decentralisation is becoming current now in many other Asian countries (e.g. Afifuddin 1977; Tamaki 1977).

Today planned development has reached unprecedented levels of sophistication and expenditure, and frequently transcends national boundaries. A programme to increase rice production may depend on technical expertise from IRRI, chemical fertilisers and machinery supplied by multi-national conglomerates, oil at prices dictated by OPEC, and credit – and consequently strongly worded advice – extended by the World Bank. All this, together with conflicts of interest between political parties, rich landowners and poor peasants, town and country, the industrial and the agricultural sector, is bound to affect not simply the nature of development programmes but even perceptions of the issues involved. To cite one well-known instance, the problems of rural Java were perceived by Sukarno's administration as an agrarian question; land reform was believed to be the answer, but since it was clearly going to be a slow and difficult process, and since Sukarno had repudiated foreign aid, immediate efforts were concentrated on rural extension work. In 1964/5, despite shortages of fertiliser, the short-lived Demas (Mass Demonstration) Project resulted in yield increases of between 40% and 140% (Palmer 1977: 26). After the political turmoil of 1965, however, Indonesia was welcomed back into the international economic fold. Anxious to impress its foreign creditors, Suharto's government reassessed the rural problem as primarily one of backward technology, and it brought in multi-national corporations to raise rice yields with advanced technology. This proved very profitable to the corporations but less so to Javanese farmers: fertiliser imports rose from $34.6 million in 1964 to $290.5 million in January–June 1974, while yields on the farms which had adopted the new Bimas (Mass Guidance) technology, although higher than on the non-Bimas controls, seldom surpassed the levels achieved on the Demas farms in 1964/5 (Palmer 1977: 192, 104).

Everyone agrees that rural Asia faces severe problems, but not everyone agrees on their precise nature. Even overpopulation is a relative concept (Grigg 1980). Mao maintained that China would benefit from population growth because labour could be substituted for capital; China's population policy was subsequently completely reversed, but the reorganisation of management under the 'responsibility system' seems likely to produce demands for a further reconsideration. Most of Asia's other rice regions also have extremely high population densities (table 5.1), average farm sizes are very small, and in most regions rural underemployment is common and the marginal productivity of labour very low.

Rural poverty is recognised as probably the most pressing problem Asia faces, but again interpretations vary. Poverty can be absolute or relative. For a majority of Asian farmers it is absolute: their basic needs are not met, their incomes are tiny (table 5.2) and indebtedness is high (ILO 1977). Whether their lot has been improving or not as a result of recent development programmes can again be disputed: in a recent conversation between two economists, both experts on current events in Indonesia, one maintained that the poorest Javanese peasants had experienced a steady increase in real income over the last five years, the other that in fact even in absolute terms their incomes had fallen significantly. And then there is the gap between rich and poor farmers: does the introduction of new technology and increased commoditisation

Table 5.1   Population densities in Asia

China (PRC)	1968/70[a]	763 persons/km^2 arable land
C. and S. Chinese communes	1979[b]	1,666 persons/km^2 arable land
Vietnamese communes	1980[c]	1,400–2,000 households/ km^2 wet-rice land
Japan	1968/70[a]	1,887 persons/km^2 arable land
S. Korea	1968/70[a]	1,408 persons/km^2 arable land
Indonesia	1975[d]	731 persons/km^2 arable land
Java and Madura	1977[e]	660 persons/km^2 arable land
C. Java	1977[e]	1,090 persons/km^2 arable land
Lombok	1930[f]	1,200 persons/km^2 wet-rice land
	1971[f]	2,500 persons/km^2 wet-rice land
Malaysia	1975[d]	202 persons/km^2 arable land
Thailand	1975[d]	268 persons/km^2 arable land
Philippines	1975[d]	563 persons/km^2 arable land

Sources:
[a] Ban et al. 1980: 17
[b] Wertheim and Stiefel 1982
[c] Fforde 1984
[d] Taylor 1981: 6
[e] Mizuno 1985
[f] Gerdin 1982: 63

Table 5.2   Income shares of decile groups in Asia

	Entire economy		Rural areas	
	Poorest 40%	Richest 20%	Poorest 40%	Richest 20%
Malaysia 1970	11.6	56.0	12.4	45.7
Philippines 1971	11.6	53.8	13.3	51.0
Sri Lanka 1973	15.1	45.9	17.0	42.7
Bangladesh 1963/4	18.0	44.5	18.5	43.0

Source: IRRI 1977: 20

widen or narrow it? It is well established that wealthy farmers almost always do better out of technological change than the poor or landless, if only because they have access to credit on more favourable terms. But obviously much depends on previous agrarian conditions, on the nature of the new technology and on the way in which it is introduced. The case of Japan is poles apart from that of Java.

The gap between rural and urban incomes is an acute problem in Asia. According to one estimate, '415 million people or about 40 per cent of the total population representing the developing market economies of Asia lived in conditions of absolute poverty in 1969 and about 355 million (85 per cent) of these were found in rural areas'; despite overall economic growth in a number of these countries, the Asian Development Bank felt that the problem had worsened considerably during the 1970s (ADB 1977: 61, 63). South Korea has been a notable exception: there government pricing policies and technical advances brought agricultural incomes to just above urban levels in 1975, though this was a short-lived achievement (Ensor 1985: 69).[2] In Korea the rapid expansion of the industrial sector has permitted the absorption of a large quantity of surplus rural labour and contributed significantly to maintaining rural living standards; the rural population fell from 58% of the total population in 1959 to 38% in 1975 (Lee 1979: 57). In other Asian countries such as Thailand, Malaysia and the Philippines there has also been a high rate of out-migration from the countryside, but there the rate of industrial and economic growth has not been sufficient to provide jobs for the majority of the rural poor, and landlessness and underemployment are widespread (ILO 1977).

Some progress has been made in narrowing the urban-rural gap where it has been possible to diversify rural production and integrate rural labour into the national economy through agricultural diversification, the production of commercial crops and, above all, the expansion of rural manufactures and industries. Japan and Taiwan are the outstanding examples (e.g. Shimpo 1976; Gallin and Gallin 1982), and China is making increasingly successful efforts in that direction. But the success of such policies presupposes the existence of well-developed consumer markets, at home or abroad, as well as the provision of transport facilities and the availability of equipment and raw materials. Off-farm incomes in poor countries like Indonesia, and even in high-growth economies like Malaysia, are seldom sufficient to raise farmers above the poverty-line (e.g. Kahn 1980; Shand and Mohd. Ariff 1983: 248).

Rice-farming today is not generally a profitable occupation in itself, particularly if expensive commercial inputs are used. Part of the reason is that staple food cereals, and indeed agricultural products in general, suffer from severe underpricing relative to industrial goods, including such essential inputs as chemical fertilisers. Governments bent on industrialisation are usually more than willing to subsidise this process by keeping domestic food-prices low, and the now common institution of the Guaranteed Minimum Price (GMP) may well leave the double-cropping rice-farmer little better off than if he had spent half the year idle. A government study conducted in Taiwan in 1971/2 showed that a rice-farmer could make US$50–70 per hectare on his first crop, but suffered a net loss on the second (Huang 1981: 115). In response to increasing rural discontent and illegal migration to the cities, China recently decided to shift the urban-rural economic balance by drastic repricing: between 1978 and 1982 average procurement prices for all agricultural products rose by 41.6%, and grain procurement prices rose by 48.9%; this raised annual grain production over the same period from 304 to 353 million tonnes (OECD 1985: 45, 16), an increase which can only have been welcome given China's demographic conditions.

In Japan, on the other hand, a politically powerful rice-farmers' lobby has ensured that rice cultivation has been kept profitable through costly government subsidies. But one undesirable result of subsidies familiar to anyone from the EEC is overproduction: in contrast to the situation in China, the Japanese population is not growing, and furthermore wheat products are becoming increasingly popular. While rice prices before the Second World War were based on calculations of the costs of production, since 1946 support prices have been designed to reduce the gap between industrial and agricultural incomes, and the government has calculated family labour costs not on the basis of agricultural labourers' wages but on the average wages of manufacturing workers. This has resulted in heavy financial loss to the government as well as high levels of overproduction (Ogura 1980: 208). Japan now has a mountain of rice so expensive that it is quite uncompetitive on world markets, selling at double the price of imported grain (ibid.: 219). Some *saké* brewers now import Japanese varieties of rice grown in the USA. Far from encouraging further increases in rice production, Japanese policy-makers' prime concern is how to persuade rice-farmers to switch to other crops (e.g. Ogura 1980), not an easy task given the traditional reverence for rice and the technical difficulties of transforming rice-fields.

In Malaysia higher rice prices have failed to stimulate production. Despite an increase in the GMP of 36% in 1981, there was a 35% drop in rice production in the KADA region that year (Shand and Mohd. Ariff 1983: 177). Young Malaysians refuse to become rice-farmers; they would rather leave the land they inherit idle and find jobs in the towns. The rural poor of countries like Thailand, Java and the Philippines are usually less fortunate: non-agricultural jobs are scarce and the struggle to gain access to farm-land, even as a labourer, is becoming increasingly acute (Hart and Huq 1982).

A further drawback to price manipulations as a means of increasing rural incomes is that they often increase inequalities *between* farmers, since farmers with larger marketable surpluses will benefit more from higher prices than those who are obliged to use most of the rice they produce for their own consumption. Even in the case of South Korea, conspicuous for its lack of inequality between farmers, it has been argued that high agricultural support prices 'tended to have a regressive influence on income distribution' (Lee 1979: 43, quoting Hasan 1976: 53).

Equity and increased production frequently impose conflicting demands on development planners, and problems of production are usually easier to solve, both technically and politically. The Malaysian government has repeatedly stated its commitment to combating rural poverty, particularly among rice-farmers (most of whom are Malays). But at the same time it is aiming to achieve self-sufficiency in rice, a need the more urgently felt after a world shortage in the early 1970s when cheap imports from Thailand were for a while virtually unobtainable. It seems unlikely that Malaysia will ever achieve complete self-sufficiency in rice, but through heavy investment in double-cropping and irrigation, particularly in MADA and KADA, domestic production had come to fulfil 85% of national requirements by 1980 (Min. of Finance 1980: 105). The criticism has been made by several economists, however, that by forcing farmers into rice monoculture so as to maximise national production the government has increased their economic vulnerability and reduced their real incomes, in effect sacrificing regional development to national objectives (e.g. Bell 1978; Taylor 1981: 186).

Labour and capital

The first three chapters discussed trends in the technical development of the basic resources, or factors of production, in wet-rice cultivation: the biological adaptation and improvement of the plant itself; the development of the productivity of the land upon which it is grown; and the perfection of control over the water supply. Here the relative potential of labour and capital for bringing about such improvements will be explored.

There are of course considerable problems inherent in the use of the term 'capital', which can take on a range of meanings that not only denote financial assets, equipment and infrastructure, but can also be extended to include a labour force and its quality, as for example when a nation's educational system is described as contributing to its human capital. Since I am concerned here with historical as well as contemporary situations, including both subsistence and commercialised economies and the transition to capitalised farming, in order to avoid confusion I shall define my terms as follows.

The term *capital* is used to denote financial assets which can be accumulated or invested in expanding the means of production. *Capital goods* are durables acquired through the investment of capital and include, for example, draft animals and farm machinery or equipment which is purchased rather than home-made. *Capital inputs*, as well as capital goods, would also include commercial fertilisers, purchased seed-stock, cash rents, land tax and irrigation fees, as well as the *hiring* of labour. Rents in kind, the use of family or exchange labour, and taxes paid in labour or in kind would not come under this heading. *Technical infrastructure* includes such constructions as irrigation works, terraced fields or transport networks, which may be achieved either through capital investment or simply through the organisation of labour. In the former case the necessary raw materials will be purchased and the labour force (usually) paid for its work; in the latter, materials may be locally available free or they may be contributed by a benefactor or by the beneficiaries of the work, and the labour will be levied or donated. It seems to me particularly important to draw these distinctions given recent trends towards centralised agricultural development planning in both the socialist and the capitalist nations of Asia. In the capitalist nations development strategies have been principally based on the investment of large amounts of capital in infrastructural projects and in the dissemination of new technology, whereas socialist governments have not infrequently preferred to substitute labour for capital where possible, especially in the construction of infrastructure.

Given the importance of central economic planning in Asian economic development today, it is crucial to pay close attention to the relative efficacy of labour and of capital under different circumstances. The amounts of both labour and capital available for use in agriculture are not independent variables: agricultural production cannot be isolated from the national economy as a whole, especially when labour supplies and levels of capital accumulation are to be taken into account. But here for the sake of clarity agriculture will be treated independently of other sectors of the economy.

The historical experience: the predominance of labour and the 'Japanese model'

It would hardly be accurate to characterise Asian rice-based economies, even before the advent of Western capitalism, as subsistence economies in which capital played little or no role. Many were commercialised, some (such as medieval China and Tokugawa Japan) to quite a high degree. Nevertheless, the nature of the inputs required to raise output in wet-rice cultivation was such that capital played a subordinate role to labour in developing the forces of production.

The historical material shows clearly how over time Asian systems of wet-rice cultivation became progressively more intensive in their use of labour, while relying on relatively low levels of capital investment. In large part this is because the general trend in technical development has been towards the concentration of resources on raising the productivity of land. Although total labour requirements vary from region to region, depending upon soils, climate, water supply and so on, it can be shown that broadly speaking yields of wet rice correlate positively with labour inputs (Ishikawa 1981: 2, 22) (table 5.3).

Table 5.3   Rice yields and labour inputs

	Yields (t/ha)	Human labour inputs (man-days/ha)
Japan 1950	4.25	255
1956	5.07	229
1962	5.79	190
S. Korea 1960	3.27	139
Taiwan 1926	2.11	96
1967	5.1	113
1972	5.7	125
E. China 1921–5	2.56	146
Java 1969–70	3.5	360
Thailand (Nong Sarai) 1972	2.0	83
Philippines C. Luzon 1966	2.2	60
1970	2.7	71
1974	2.2	82
Laguna 1966	2.5	88
1975	3.5	105
India Madras 1956	2.25	216
W. Bengal (Hoogly) 1956	1.80	133
(24-Parganas) 1956	1.54	103

Sources: Ishikawa 1981: 3; Taylor 1981: 89

Rice yields are also directly related to the efficacy of management of the water supply, and until very recently this imposed restrictions on the size of wet-rice fields and was an important barrier to mechanical rationalisation of the European type. Given the large investment in labour and time required to develop a productive rice-field, there was instead a strong incentive to evolve land-saving skills, skills which were both technical and managerial. Effective supervision of such skilled work is highly demanding, and as rice cultivation systems became more productive there was a marked tendency for units of management to become smaller rather than larger, usually taking the form of family farms supplying the bulk of their own labour.

The Asian wet-rice economies were often characterised by a high level of investment in the form of such technical infrastructure as irrigation works, but at least until the colonial period these used only a small proportion of liquid capital, relying instead on voluntary or enforced labour contributions and the donation by state or local beneficiaries of construction materials.

As to capital inputs, many of the new inputs characteristic of early periods of development in Asian rice agriculture were *divisible*, that is to say, extra labour, new seed or improved fertilisers could be bought in any quantity according to the farmer's needs, inclination or financial situation. Often organisational improvements or a more careful carrying out of operations would make important contributions to increasing output while requiring no increase in capital outlay at all. Innovation was thus within the scope of farmers of all income groups.

An early example of divisible inputs is to be found in the case of medieval China. The expansion of agricultural output in medieval South China was brought about by the introduction of quick-ripening and drought-resistant rice varieties, permitting the development of multiple cropping and an increase in the rice-growing area; by the development of local irrigation and water control facilities; by an increase in the application of fertilisers, mainly industrial by-products such as bean-cake; and by the spread of improved rice cultivation techniques, described in such works as the *Chen Fu nongshu* (1149) and *Wang Zhen nongshu* (1313). These are all what Ishikawa (1981: 36) calls 'labour-using technological factors', that is to say, higher yields are obtained through a new technology requiring increased labour inputs. Describing similar developments in Tokugawa Japan, Smith says of commercial fertilisers:

Insofar as they replaced natural fertilisers they saved an enormous amount of labour. They drastically reduced and might entirely eliminate the work of cutting and hauling grass from the mountainside, then trampling it into the ploughed and flooded fields; moreover, this labour was saved at the planting when the work load reached its annual peak and time and human energy were most precious. How great was the potential for saving at this season may be judged from the fact that in the seventeenth century about ten man-days per *tan* [bushel] of paddy were spent in cutting grass and composting fields prior to planting. But this is only part of the story. Multiple-cropping was a common result – indeed often the chief aim – of the adoption of commercial fertilisers; and insofar as it was, the new fertilisers added more labour to farming than they saved, though it should be noted that the addition came mostly at a time when employment was otherwise slack. (1959: 101)

In fact, as Smith points out later (1959: 142 ff), there were four principal technical elements in Tokugawa agriculture, namely commercial fertilisers, a new type of thresher (the *semba-koki*), multiple cropping and crop diversification (in response to market demands) which, while increasing a farmer's total labour requirements, spread them out evenly over the year (figure 5.1). The steady reduction in the gap between the size of large and small farms, which by the late Tokugawa period were approaching uniform family size, is also significant in this context.

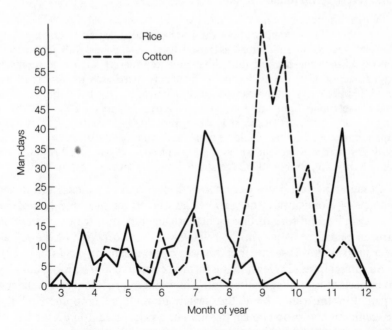

Figure 5.1   Labour demands on a holding in Shinshū in 1823
(from Smith 1959: 143)

One might be tempted to attribute this type of technological development, in the case of medieval China at least, to historical necessity: the lack of capital for investment in, or the lack of scientific knowledge for production of, labour-saving devices such as farm machinery or chemical herbicides. But it is in fact intrinsic to the technical trends in wet-rice cultivation examined in previous chapters. The new inputs which made possible the surge in agricultural productivity in Song China and Tokugawa Japan form a very similar package to that being promoted in Asia today under various Green Revolution policies. The 'New Technology' is frequently seen as a package requiring heavy and unaccustomed capital investment on the part of traditional farmers, forcing a shift towards the commercialisation of agriculture and a consequent emmiseration of poor peasants who must borrow in order to obtain the necessary capital (e.g. de Koninck 1978). As mentioned above, such capital inputs as commercial fertilisers had in fact been a crucial factor in agricultural improvement in both medieval China and Tokugawa Japan. Problems of transport and distribution meant that their cost was a significant item even then in a peasant farmer's accounts, especially since prices were not infrequently fixed at high levels by merchant monopolies:

Although farm income was highly variable costs were relatively rigid. The prices of the commodities the peasant bought were controlled, within certain limits, by powerful merchant guilds that exercised local monopolies with government sanction. Since the peasant sold either in a free market, or in one positively rigged against him and in favour of monopoly merchants to whom he was required by law to sell, he was periodically caught in a cost-price squeeze. The squeeze was more frequent and tighter moreover by virtue of the fact that a single item, fertiliser, accounted for a very high percentage of his cash expenditures; for one item could be more easily controlled than several, and this particular item was one for which the peasant could not reduce his purchases without suffering an immediate and sharp decline in income. (Smith 1959: 159)

Commercial fertilisers were a very heavy item of expenditure in the budgets of Tokugawa farmers. They accounted for over one-half of the total cash expenditure of one eighteenth-century mixed rice and cotton farm in Settsu province (in the relatively advanced region of the Kinai, near Ōsaka), and it seems that this was by no means atypical (ibid.: 82).

So capital inputs, at least in the form of commercial fertilisers, did play an important part in agricultural development in pre-modern China and Japan. On the other hand the switch to multiple cropping and the diversification of crop choice, though largely dependent upon the use of commercial fertilisers (and also new, improved crop varieties), necessitated no increase in capital inputs unless it became necessary to hire labour.

While there definitely was a growth in the free agricultural labour market in Tokugawa Japan (as opposed to various sorts of bonded labour), it was mainly hired by larger holdings to help with such commercial activities as silkworm-breeding or brewing (Smith 1959: ch. 8; Nakamura 1959). Slow demographic growth and a steady expansion of trade and industry in both urban and rural areas not only pushed up wages but also, by the eighteenth century, brought about severe labour shortages in agriculture which the central and provincial governments attempted in vain to curb.[3] High wages must have been a contributing factor in maintaining the majority of holdings in Tokugawa Japan at the size of a family farm, where the bottlenecks of transplanting and harvesting could be overcome through exchanging labour with neigh-bouring families. However the lack of any major labour-saving inventions or innovations in agriculture (apart from the thresher mentioned earlier), even on large farms where labour costs were a considerable drain on the budget, sustains the point that the investment of skilled labour was more profitable in wet-rice agriculture than that of labour-saving capital goods.

The value that was placed on the quality rather than the quantity of labour can be seen in the following passage, in which a seventeenth-century Chinese landowner exhorts his heirs to choose their tenants with care:

There is a proverb which says, 'It is better to have good tenants than good land', and this is a very accurate statement . . . There are three advantages in having good tenants, namely that they are on time with ploughing and sowing, they are energetic in fertilising, and they are resourceful in conserving every drop of water. The men of old used to say: 'The most important thing in agriculture is doing everything at the proper season.' . . . With diligence like this, one *mou* may yield the produce of two. Without the land being extended or the acreage increased, the tenant will have a surplus and the landlord too will profit by it. In the conservation and use of water, everything depends on speed and timing. Damming up the waters, waiting, and then releasing them, all have to be done at the proper time. Only good and experienced farmers know about this. (*Hengchan suoyan* by Zhang Ying, tr. Beattie 1979: 146)

Zhang Ying goes on to stress the crucial importance of adequate irrigation networks in producing good rice crops and maintaining an income from rents, and urges his descendants: 'When it comes to constructing ponds and building dykes, you must supervise the matter in person' (ibid.: 148): clearly the tenants themselves were expected to provide both tools and materials (tamped earth, shovels and baskets in the main) as well as the labour force.[4] Improvements in water control were one of the most important contributory factors in the growth of agricultural production in pre-modern China and Japan. Here, capital investment was at a minimum, while the initial labour requirements were very high, and skills and knowledge were thereafter required in order to profit fully by these infrastructural improvements.

Although accurate cost-accounting for farm management in pre-modern China and Japan is no easy matter,[5] it is fair to assume that the purchase of new seeds and fertilisers, the construction of water control systems, and so on, yielded reasonable economic returns in the majority of cases, given the remarkable and rapid expansion of the economy as a whole. Just as important, one can deduce that although many of the improvements were 'labour-using', nevertheless labour productivity in rice agriculture did not fall: the spread of agricultural specialisation and of multiple cropping, and the growth of rural manufactures and other income-generating activities, in conjunction with slow demographic increase,[6] show that labour productivity in agriculture must have risen quite significantly; and while the improvements in rice cultivation absorbed larger amounts of labour, they did not cause insuperable bottlenecks, nor did they preclude the possibility of combining rice cultivation with other economic activities.

In an important essay on labour absorption in Asian agriculture, Ishikawa (1981: 1–149) maintains that increased labour inputs are essential to combat underemployment and raise incomes in rural Asia. The historical case of Japan is particularly important in this context, especially as it is the only Asian country for which accurate calculations of long-term changes in labour inputs can be given.[7] From the early Tokugawa period (*c*.1600) up until the commencement of agricultural mechanisation in the late 1950s both rice yields and per hectare labour inputs increased steadily (table 5.4). Since many South and Southeast

Table 5.4   Rice yields and labour inputs in Japan

	Rice yields (t/ha)	Rice labour inputs (man-days/ha)	Total labour inputs (man-days/ha)
1874	2.36	278	353
1880	2.53	275	375
1890	3.04	271	393
1900	2.87	267	397
1910	3.08	251	398
1920	3.94	235	384
1930	3.92	211	357
1940	3.74	206	359
1950	4.13	256	394
1960	4.99	214	345
1970	5.75	146	235

Source: Ishikawa 1981: 42

Asian agricultural systems, at least prior to the innovations of the Green Revolution, were at a level of technological organisation and development of resources comparable to that obtaining in Japan before the Meiji reforms of the 1870s and 1880s, the possibility of following a 'Japanese model' of agricultural development has of late gained quite wide popularity among economists and planning agencies. Perhaps the clearest exposition of the model is presented by Ogura (1967; see also Ishikawa 1967: 59).

The 'Japanese model' differs from most Western-derived development strategies in that it is based on improvement in the application of human skills rather than the substitution of machinery for labour, and requires a low level of capital investment. The three principal features derived from Japan's historical experience are: (i) the intensification of land use relying on such inputs as fertilisers, improved varieties and better techniques; (ii) the modest level of capital required; and (iii) the small scale and easily divisible nature of the improvements, appropriate to the prevailing levels of technical development and patterns of agricultural organisation.

As Ishikawa points out, however, there are two levels of success which may be achieved by increasing labour inputs. The first, typified by China up to 1954, Korea up to the same period, and by India and other Asian countries today, shows a marked increase in yields but a diminution in farm size and almost no improvement in farm income (1967: 78): in this case technical improvement perpetuates subsistence-level agriculture, and while this allows for demographic growth it cannot improve rural living standards, nor can it contribute to the general development of the national economy. But in the case of Meiji Japan a higher level of improvement was achieved, where farm incomes and the *productivity of labour* increased. Ogura and other economists suggest that this was what allowed Japanese agriculture not only to finance its own development but also to accumulate capital which contributed to the growth of the industrial sector (see also Geertz 1963; Ishikawa 1967: ch. 4). As Ishikawa (1981) repeatedly stresses, if the economies of the poorer Asian countries are to improve, it is crucial not simply to increase agricultural output through an increase in labour and other inputs, but also to maintain, and preferably increase, the marginal productivity of labour. There are some inputs which are more likely to achieve this effect than others (1981: 40).

Choice of technological inputs

One can make a clear distinction between two types of technology in rice agriculture: (i) *biochemical* technology, which denotes improved rice varieties, fertilisers and pesticides; these can be considered land substitutes since they increase yields; and (ii) *mechanical* technology which substitutes for labour. Some inputs may save both land and labour, for example chemical herbicides or mechanical pump-sets. Usually a rational choice can be made as to which type of input should be invested in to produce the greatest improvements under particular circumstances.

The higher a country's latitude, the shorter the growing season for rice. In the Yangzi valley the season is about 120 days, and a single crop of rice alternated with wheat or barley had been standard cropping practice for centuries. As from 1956 quicker-ripening rice varieties were disseminated and efforts were made to double-crop rice over an area of 2.3 million ha in Central China. But in the absence of mechanisation acute labour shortages were experienced during the busy season, and results on the whole were poor. The lack of pump-sets for irrigation was one of the chief problems; another was the overlap between harvesting and threshing the first rice crop and tilling the fields and transplanting the second. From the mid-1960s a major effort was made to mechanise these processes, and the double-cropping of rice then became feasible (Ishikawa 1981: 52, 107).

In lower latitudes the growing season is longer. In Taiwan at the turn of the century, when the Japanese decided to develop rice production, the major constraint on the introduction of double-cropping was not the short growing period or the lack of mechanisation but insufficient water. Under Japanese rule the Taiwanese irrigation network was greatly expanded and improved, and the process was only discontinued in 1933 when rice prices in Japan fell sharply. After the Second World War there was less investment in the expansion of the irrigation network, but this was compensated for by improvements in water conservation and management (ibid.: 62). The cultivation of two crops of rice followed by a third crop of maize, potatoes, soy, tobacco or vegetables is now widespread in Taiwan (Food and Fertiliser Centre 1974).

Where water supplies are inadequate rice yields will always be low. At this stage the improvement of water supplies will in itself increase yields more than the introduction of improved varieties and fertilisers, since adequate water is a prerequisite for the efficient use of biochemical inputs. The development of water control facilities not only stabilises and raises rice yields but also permits greater cropping frequency. The efficiency of large-scale irrigation projects as opposed to various types of low-level improvement has to be considered in such cases (e.g. Taylor 1981: 121–75; Ishikawa 1967: 131–53).

Improvements in water control nowadays require considerable capital investment, but the biochemical inputs typical of the Green Revolution package, namely HYVs, fertilisers and pesticides, are, like the innovations of Tokugawa and Meiji Japan, both divisible and labour-using, and so they are likely to prove accessible and beneficial to farmers at all income levels. Mechanical inputs tend to be indivisible or 'lumpy': either one buys a whole thresher or no thresher at all. But the costs can be split if they are purchased by groups or cooperatives, or hired. And when it enables farmers to intensify their cropping practices then mechanical technology, like biochemical inputs, can absorb rather than displace agricultural labour: this is characteristic of such items as pump-sets, threshers and drying machines, but not always of tillers and tractors (Ishikawa 1981: 70).

It seems to be especially difficult to raise the marginal productivity of agriculture without resorting to mechanisation in cases where labour use is already intensive and skills highly developed. A survey carried out in North Arcot (Tamil Nadu, India) by IRRI (1975) showed that in 1981 of the extra labour necessitated by the cultivation of high-yielding as opposed to traditional varieties (232 as opposed to 175 days), 60% was required for extra weeding and plant protection and 40% for harvesting and processing; at the same time the new varieties yielded 4.0 t/ha as opposed to 2.9 t/ha. Here, then, labour inputs rose by 33% and yields by 38%, showing a slight increase in labour productivity. But in Sidoarjo (East Java), the same survey showed that while labour inputs rose by 8%, from 256 to 276 man-days/ha, yields rose by only 6%, from 4.5 to 4.8 t/ha. On the other hand, in Subang (West Java), where the introduction of the new varieties led to the replacement of the reaping-knife by the sickle, yields rose by 30%, from 3.0 to 3.9 t/ha, and labour inputs fell by over 9%, from 170 to 154 man-days/ha, a rise in labour productivity which might seem to denote a signal improvement for the peasants. But while the replacement of the reaping-knife by the sickle may hardly strike the reader as a radical shift to advanced technology, the reallocation of labour involved has had considerable social repercussions, mainly due to the inequalities in access to land and in labour opportunities prevailing in Javanese society (Palmer 1977: 145; Collier 1981). Similar disruptions have resulted from the mechanisation of farming in the Muda region in Malaysia, and more especially from the introduction, not of sickles, but of combine-harvesters (Lim et al. 1980: 65; de Koninck 1981: 12). Indeed they are typical of regions where opportunities for off-farm employment are scarce, and this includes even relatively affluent rice regions where monoculture prevails, for in such cases the labour productivity of a few farmers can be increased only at the cost of unemployment to others.

Capital investment

The dissemination of the 'New Technology', with its heavy reliance on capital inputs such as chemical fertilisers and new pressures on traditional forms of labour organisation, has marked an important shift in the balance between labour and capital. Capital investment by the state has increased enormously, as has that made by the private sector and by farmers themselves. Let us first look at the ways in which the state may invest in rice agriculture so as to encourage increased output and, to a greater or lesser extent, relieve the financial burden on the farmers themselves.

The state has several areas in which it may invest to foster agricultural growth. The first is technical infrastructure: land reclamation; the provision of transport facilities; and most importantly water control, an essential prerequisite for the efficient development of rice cultivation. As we saw in chapter 3, Asian states traditionally met most of the costs of constructing large-scale water control networks with conscripted labour, but under the pressures of colonialism and the expansion of world rice markets hired labour was increasingly substituted in a number of regions from the mid-nineteenth century. Now that reclamation and irrigation schemes are designed by professional engineers, and specialised plant is available which can carry out such work much more quickly and effectively than coolies with shovels, and expensive equipment like sluice-dams and central pumping-stations are part of the designs, hydraulic projects have become extremely capital-intensive. At 1979 prices it was projected that the future costs of irrigation development in Asia as a whole would be between $3,055 and $3,975 per hectare, and already the cost of constructing new projects in parts of Malaysia was as high as $5,465 per hectare (Taylor 1981: 180).

Malaysia is perhaps an extreme case, where the state has undertaken sole responsibility for investment in infrastructural construction, relying entirely upon capital investment to achieve it. China on the other hand has continued to use labour in the process of capital formation, keeping cash costs to a minimum. Up to 1957 state-organised labour used outside the community mobilised 5 to 10 million peasants a year; from 1957 responsibility for their wages fell upon their commune. 'According to the latest data, nowadays 17 million people, or about 5% of China's total agricultural labour force, work all-year-round in regular agricultural capital construction teams under the [prefecture] or commune' (Vermeer 1977: 63). The PLA played an important role in large projects, for example undertaking 49% of the earth-work and 73% of the concrete-work on the Jinjiang (Middle Yangzi) Project (ibid.: 105). Most labour and capital for local-level projects was provided not by the central government but by the province, prefecture or commune. It is interesting that since 1979 state investment in hydraulic works has fallen from 3,496 million *yuan* (1979) to 1,774 million *yuan* (1982), but to compensate the government is trying to negotiate contracts with households or work-teams which stipulate the contribution of a certain number of unpaid work-days for capital investment in agricultural projects (OECD 1985: 48, 50).

It is not only the socialist regimes of Asia which require local-level participation in the provision of technical infrastructure. Ever since the Meiji period the Japanese government has required both the prefectures and the benefiting farmers to meet a substantial proportion of the costs, often as much as 25% each (Ishikawa 1967: 143). Under such arrangements new projects would require the approval of at least two-thirds of the landowners involved, which often proved a consider-able obstacle to innovation (Shimpo 1976: 18). (In Japan, as elsewhere, the irrigation fees paid by farmers are intended to meet some of the running costs rather than to recoup initial expenditure.)

In South Korea many small-scale infrastructural projects have been organised locally under the New Community Movement (*Saemaul Undong*), launched by President Park in 1971. Over the first decade, 'approximately 70% of the total resources required for these projects was contributed by rural people in the form of donations of labour, land, and recently even cash. In this respect, the managerial capabilities of the Saemaul leaders must be given special credit' (Whang 1981: 15). Or, to put it another way, 'local self-help projects require considerable uncompensated labour and often the contribution of other scarce resources by villagers, while in many cases benefits are intangible or deferred for many months or even years' (Brandt 1980: 277).

When it comes to capital inputs, especially fertilisers, and capital goods such as tilling, harvesting and processing machinery, state investment or subsidy can take a number of forms. The government can establish national industries to supply these products, it can import them, or it can rely on the private sector to import or produce them. Generally imported products cost more than locally produced goods, and the private sector charges more than the public. If it is left to the private sector to supply the capital inputs, the cost to the farmer will be high unless state subsidies are applied at various levels. Let us take fertilisers and tractors as illustrations.

In Indonesia after 1966 the value of fertiliser imports rose steeply, from $34.6 million in 1964 to $290.5 million in January–June 1974; meanwhile government subsidies on fertilisers rose from 1,000 million *rupiahs* in 1964 to 5,700 million *rupiahs* in 1967–8, but then fell to 2,250 million *rupiahs* in 1969 and to 714 million *rupiahs* in 1970 (Palmer 1977: 172, 192). The original subsidy level was set so that the price of 1 kg of urea would be equal to that of 1 kg of milled rice, but the balance was soon upset since the oil crisis sent fertiliser prices up at a time when the government was keeping rice prices low (ibid.: 54).[8] Despite the financial difficulties facing the farmers, however, the application of chemical fertilisers increased from 3.5 kg/ha in 1960/1 to 26.3 kg/ha in 1973/4 (ADB 1978: 416), largely because government regulations obliged farmers to grow the new HYVs which, unlike traditional varieties, cannot be grown without chemical fertilisers (Loekman 1982).

In China green manures, nightsoil and other organic fertilisers have continued to play an important role in maintaining soil fertility; although the amounts used are impossible to quantify, they have been described as 'enormous' (American Delegation 1977: 200), but the proportion of chemical fertilisers used has been growing continuously. Organic manures are usually locally produced and distributed. Until about 1958 most chemical fertilisers were imported, but domestic production began to take off in the late 1950s, helped by the setting-up of innumerable small-scale local plants producing mainly urea; this development was possible thanks to the wide distribution of coal deposits in China (ibid.: 154). While fertiliser imports stayed at between 1 and 2 million tonnes between 1969 and 1979, domestic production shot up from 1.4 million to over 12.3 million tonnes over the same period (Stone 1982: 236). In 1973 small-scale plants accounted for 60% of national production. Since 1980 the Ministry for the Chemical Industry has been reorganising and amalgamating small plants, and state investment has dropped (OECD 1985: 52).

Under the commune system the costs of fertilisers, as of all other production expenses, were met by the production team or brigade, which derived its income from selling its produce and products to the state (e.g. Aziz 1978: 57). Under the 'responsibility system' there are several ways in which production may be organised.[9] Probably the most widespread is 'contracting everything to the household' (*baogan daohu*), under which arrangement the household is responsible for all investment in production, as it also is under 'contracting output to the household' (*baochan daohu*); under specialised contracting for grain production the contracting unit is a work-group and fertilisers and other inputs are purchased with internal credit coupons issued at the beginning of each year to the group, to the cash value of its output target (Walker 1984: 787; Watson 1984: 95, 93).

Turning to the case of tractors, two government projects in Malaysia offer an interesting contrast. On the Muda scheme (MADA) in Kedah the mechanisation of ploughing developed rapidly through the 1960s. 40% of ploughing was mechanised by 1966 and 94% by 1970; double-cropping of rice was introduced in 1969. MADA is a relatively prosperous rice region, and in the late 1960s some farmers began to invest in power-tillers and even in four-wheel tractors; a majority, however, hired large tractors from private contractors to plough their fields. The contracting industry was extremely competitive; average ploughing costs fell from M$77–87 per ha in 1965 to M$65 (for two passes) in 1970. Contracting was entirely in private hands; the Farmers' Associations did not provide tractor hire as one of their services. Some 300 to 400 private business contractors were in operation in MADA in the mid-1970s. But after the introduction of double-cropping, farmers with larger than average holdings (regardless of their tenurial status) invested in power-tillers, the number of which rose from 580 in 1970 to about 3,500 in 1976; the mean farm size of tiller-owners was 3.15 ha, compared to the average MADA farm of 1.6 ha. Not only did the purchasers use their tillers on their own farms, they also undertook contract ploughing (on an average of 18 ha per season in 1976), thus competing with the businessmen who owned the large tractors and eventually ousting many from the market (MADA 1980).

In contrast, on the Kemubu scheme (KADA) in Kelantan, a region characterised by generalised poverty, there are a few commercial firms which provide tractor-hire services, but almost no tillage machines are owned by farmers. The overwhelming majority of tractors (over 100 large tractors in 1982) are owned by KADA and hired out through the local Farmers' Associations. By keeping hire prices extremely low (at only M$26 per hour in 1982) KADA effectively cuts out any competition from the private sector (Abdullah Hussein, pers. comm. 1982). Even so, many farmers still rely on buffalo ploughs, largely for financial reasons (Bray 1985). In 1980/1, 21% used animals for all or part of the tillage of their fields, and in 1981/2 the figure rose to 35% (Shand and Mohd. Ariff 1983: 119). The overall degree of mechanisation is thus much lower than on the Muda scheme, despite the state subsidies.

Another area in which the state can invest in order to encourage agricultural growth is the provision of credit facilities. Formerly if farmers needed cash they would turn to their landlords or to money-lenders, pledging their next harvest or their land as collateral. Many Asian states have legislated against such transactions, which all too frequently plunged families into irredeemable misery. It is not easy to eradicate money-lending, however: a poor peasant who has urgent need of cash and little chance of persuading the local bank that he is credit-worthy may well turn to a money-lender in desperation. But Asian governments have made conscientious efforts to supply credit on favourable terms and on a reasonably egalitarian basis for investment in agriculture, and to foster organisations which count the provision of credit facilities among their functions. Agricultural banks, cooperatives and Farmers' Associations are all willing to provide loans and savings facilities to farmers, but there are certain drawbacks for both sides. Poor farmers often find it difficult or impossible to obtain credit from official sources, from banks because they have little security, and from cooperatives or FAs because these are frequently dominated by the wealthier farmers who tend to monopolise credit facilities (e.g. ILO 1977). On the other side, farmers feel much less obligation towards impersonal institutions than towards known individuals, and of course it is more difficult for such institutions to enforce repayment than for a landlord or money-lender, for governments are honour-bound not to foreclose on mortgages and expel farmers from their land. Malaysian officials frequently complained to me of the high levels of default on debts; in the Philippines farmers repay money-lenders, but not the government which is helping them to buy their land (Mangahas et al. 1976).

While Asian governments are investing heavily in promoting agricultural production, the rice-farmers' cash disbursements are also increasing. Whereas formerly many subsistence farmers were obliged to enter the market to obtain cash to pay their taxes (see chapter 6), now they also need cash to purchase inputs. In theory it is possible to remain aloof from such pressures, cultivating old-fashioned varieties by traditional methods. But even where governments do not impose regulations enforcing the adoption of new technology, as was the case recently in Java (Loekman 1982) or earlier this century in Japan and its colonies (Dore 1969: 104; Ban et al. 1980: 164), the systemic nature of change in rice cultivation systems exerts heavy pressure to conform. A farmer whose land is incorporated into an irrigation scheme designed to permit double-cropping, for instance, will no longer be able to plant traditional slow-ripening varieties in his fields (Bray and Robertson 1980). He is therefore obliged, at the very least, to purchase improved seeds and fertilisers. In areas where cropping frequency increases, old patterns of labour input will change: the hiring or purchase of machinery may become necessary, and labour exchange gives way to labour hire. Farmers who are struggling to break even, especially tenant farmers, will seek to minimise their costs by using only family labour on their own farm, but will be anxious to supplement their income by hiring out their labour to others (e.g. Takahashi 1970: 105), while farmers with capital to invest may prefer to lease or purchase machines rather than hire labour. Overall, the introduction of the New Technology has brought a fall in the proportion of total labour inputs supplied by household rather than hired labour (table 5.5).

Table 5.5   Proportion of hired labour used in rice production

	Total labour (man-days/ha)	Family labour (%)	Hired labour (%)
Indonesia			
Java 1969/70	360	22	78
Philippines			
Laguna 1966	88	42	58
1975	106	20	80
C. Luzon 1970	71	39	61
1974	82	33	67
C. Taiwan 1967	113	69	31
1972	125	62	38

Source: Taylor 1981: 89

Productivity of labour and capital

In the past it appears that increases in rice yields in Asia were always dependent upon an increase in labour-inputs, but were considerably enhanced by the improvement of techniques and by the use of better varieties and of more fertilisers. When such improved inputs were used, as in medieval China and in Tokugawa and Meiji Japan, labour productivity rose as well as the productivity of land, and generalised economic growth was possible; when they were not, as in colonial Tonkin and Java, labour productivity fell and emmiseration resulted. To what extent has this pattern been modified by recent changes in technology, and how has the increased importance of capital inputs affected the productivity of capital and of labour?

In recent years rice yields have risen throughout Asia. This has in the main been attributed to the dissemination of the New Technology, and in particular of 'land-saving' biochemical technology. The divisible nature of biochemical technology has allowed its almost universal adoption, indeed in certain places an inverse ratio has been found between farm size and the adoption rate of biochemical inputs (Fujimoto 1983: 126; Palmer 1977: 82). On small farms biochemical inputs are in general the principal capital outlay, and household labour is very intensively used; hired labour, and even the hiring of machinery, is kept to a minimum.[10] This reduction in capital investment does not reduce yields – on the contrary, rice yields per hectare often increase as the size of farm decreases (Gibbons et al. 1980: 128) – but it does have an adverse effect on profits and on the productivity of household labour.

To take the case of China, where for many years it was contended that labour could and should be widely substituted for capital: between 1957 and 1975 the productivity of agricultural labour, reckoned in output-value per man-day, fell by between 15% and 36% (T. Rawski 1979: 119; see also Watson 1984: 87, table 1). The fall occurred despite considerable improvements in water control and fertiliser use over the period. These technical improvements in fact raised production costs steeply, since agricultural prices remained low while industrial prices were high. The gross income from agricultural production over this period grew by only 80%, and production costs increased by 130%; thus returns to capital investment in agriculture also declined (Watson 1984: 85). But this was largely a result of pricing policies: in terms of absolute output, labour productivity did at least remain more or less stable, for while the total agricultural labour force grew by 50% between 1957 and 1975, so too did grain output (ibid.: 88).

To remedy the stagnation in labour productivity and stimulate agricultural growth, China's economists at first advocated a policy of mechanisation. But from the outset doubts were expressed in many quarters as to the wisdom of displacing agricultural labour when rural underemployment was such a serious problem. Large-scale agricultural mechanisation has been confined to a few regions like the Manchurian provinces; elsewhere investment in mechanisation has been aimed principally at eliminating bottlenecks so as to permit increased cropping intensity and the diversification of economic activities (see chapter 2). It is noteworthy, however, that the spectacular gains in output since the adoption of the 'responsibility system' are apparently due mainly to the renewed energy which Chinese farmers are pouring into their land. Yields of all crops have increased significantly, and rice yields went from a national average of 4.0 t/ha in 1978 to 5.1 t/ha in 1983, up by over 25%; during the same time output per head of total population in the rich rice-growing central and eastern regions increased by 16% and 25% respectively (Watson 1984: 805, 808). How much of this is due to improved management and longer hours, and how much to greater investment in improved inputs, is difficult to say, for now that management and accounting have been decentralised, figures for levels of household investment will not be easy to estimate. Nevertheless, the overall pace of agricultural growth and the rapid diversification into commercial and industrial crops as well as other economic activities indicates that, as in medieval China and Tokugawa Japan, the productivity of labour must also be rising at a good pace.

Under certain circumstances Chinese farmers are now even allowed to hire labour, though only in limited amounts, to supplement that which the household alone can supply. Although the hiring of labour represents an additional production cost, the size of farm is an important determinant of the profitability of rice-farming, so that labour hire can be a very worthwhile investment if sufficient land is available. A study undertaken in 1977/8 in Province Wellesley, Malaysia, showed that the factor coefficients of increase in income for land, total labour and fertilisers were 0.54, 0.26 and 0.16 respectively, so that an increase of 10% in the land farmed would theoretically result in an increase of over 5% in income, an increase in 10% of fertiliser use in under 2% (Fujimoto 1983: 141). (In the Muda region the factor coefficient for land was in the order of 1.0 [Mokhtar 1978: 125].) Although returns to total labour are seen, at least in this case, to be at an intermediate level between land and fertiliser, it is the hiring of labour which enables a farmer to cultivate larger areas and so make larger profits. The division of a given area of land into very small farms will produce higher yields and a greater total output, but also higher total consumption and much lower profits for the farmers. In Province Wellesley, where almost equal amounts of household and hired labour are used by rice-farmers, the level of profits was such that household labour earnings were slightly above the average for casual labour, but in the poorer and more densely populated state of Kelantan, where farms are smaller and almost all labour is provided by the household, household labour earnings are in fact negative.[11] This is indeed the vicious circle of subsistence production deplored by Ishikawa.

Even in countries like Japan, where yields are high, technology is advanced and farmers enjoy relatively high incomes, rice-farming itself is an unprofitable occupation; it is the complementary activities from which Japanese rice-farmers derive their comfortable incomes. In 1979 only 15% made a profit from rice-farming as such, namely those who cultivated over 1 ha of rice-land (Matsuda 1982: 449), and this despite the extremely high rice support prices and low cost of fertilisers in Japan.[12] In part the low profits may be ascribed to overinvestment in machinery. Labour hire has been uncommon, expensive, and limited by legal restrictions in Japan since the land reforms (Ogura 1980: 465), and every stage of rice cultivation has now been effectively mechanised. But while land productivity (measured in terms of output per hectare) has increased steadily, if quite slowly, at a rate of 0.97% per annum between

1965 and 1977, and labour productivity has increased spectacularly at 6.5% per annum, returns to capital invested in machinery have dropped steeply by 9.8% per annum; meanwhile returns to capital invested in fertiliser have increased by 0.77% per annum (Matsuda 1982: 441).

While the rapid increase in labour productivity is highly desirable, it could have been achieved at much lower capital costs if farmers had been willing to share or hire machinery rather than buy it outright. The overinvestment in labour-substituting rather than land-substituting mechanisation has led to discrepancies in profitability between small and large farms, i.e. the appearance of scale economies, which were absent in Japan in the prewar period, when most increases in production were effected with scale-neutral improvements such as water control and biochemical technology (ibid.: 443). That sizeable increases in labour productivity as well as output can be achieved without resorting to wide-scale mechanisation can be seen from the example of South Korea, where the mechanisation of rice-farming has been later and much slower than in Japan[13] (table 5.6). One of the important if non-quantifiable factors contributing to the rapid development of Korean agriculture has been a marked improvement in expertise, both in the education level of farmers and in the quality of extension services (Ban et al. 1980: 111).

Table 5.6   Mechanisation in Korea and Japan

| | Korea | | | | Japan | | |
| | 1964 | 1979 | | 1962 | | 1978 | |
		A	B	A	B	A	B
Power tillers	653	236,000	9.2	1,414,000	4.1	3,168,000	1.5
Tractors	376,000 HP	2,000	—	11,000	—	1,096,000	4.3
Transplanters	—	2,400	—	—	—	1,601,000	3.0
Threshers	14,610						
Harvesters		12,500	—	—	—	2,450,000	1.9

A: Total number
B: Number of households per machine

Sources: Hou and Yu 1982: 198; Ban et al. 1980: 75

Expertise and participation

In the case of a crop like rice, the intensification of production is a systemic process and is therefore heavily dependent upon the skills, experience and active involvement of the broad mass of rice-farmers. Successful scientific research and development (R & D) should therefore aim to integrate the ideas and suggestions of the farmers themselves with the results from experimental stations, encouraging the active participation of the farmers in agricultural improvement.

R & D is frequently regarded as a process by which the results of specialised scientific research are popularised through extension work, and the potential contribution of the target farmers may well be underrated. Yet such research activites as crop breeding were practised by peasant farmers for millennia before falling into the hands of the scientists. The high-yielding varieties of rice developed in Meiji Japan were bred by farmers. The most famous and widely adopted was called *Shinriki* (power of the gods), and was bred in Hyōgo, near Ōsaka, by a local farmer in 1877. Its appearance coincided with a growth in official extension services which greatly improved communications between agricultural regions, permitting its rapid adoption in most of Southern Honshū (Francks 1983: 61). At the same period Japanese farmers were also trying to develop improved farm equipment and machinery, working in active cooperation with local manufacturers (Ishikawa 1981: 164). Many of the technological advances of the period were in fact due to research and experiments carried out by the farmers themselves. The same is true of modern China. Wertheim and Stiefel report a not untypical case of individual initiative from Northern Hubei, where a commune director was determined to develop the double-cropping of rice in a region where it had never previously been practised for climatic reasons. Experimenting through the 1960s and 1970s, he and his colleagues succeeded in breeding appropriate rice varieties, and rice double-cropping subsequently became common throughout the district, with the addition of a winter crop of wheat or rapeseed; in 1978 an experimental plot gave a total yield of 20 t/ha (1982: 28).

Just as important as incorporating grass-roots contributions into R & D is engaging popular support for innovation. The extent of popular participation in agricultural development depends to a large extent on how innovation is advocated or imposed, and by whom. Not surprisingly, farmers tend to be suspicious of official intervention and respond more positively to the example of successful peers. One thinks of the centuries-old Chinese policy of using 'master farmers' as disseminators of improved techniques. Many rice-growing cultures have a long tradition of village officers meeting regularly to decide on technical matters such as the distribution of scarce resources like water and labour, and the technical cohesion imposed by the requirements of intensive rice cultivation often helps to smooth the path of innovation. The extension of technical information through the help of cultivating landlords in Meiji Japan is described in appendix C.

Wertheim and Stiefel maintain that successes in both production and distribution in China have depended in large part upon the rate of true popular participation, fostered by emphasis on the 'mass line' (1982: 135, 87). This permitted all levels of planners, administrators, experts and farmers to contribute to the gradual formulation of appropriate development strategies through a process of feed-back. Perhaps the most dramatic example of popular contribution to the economy in China is the official adoption of the various forms of the 'responsibility system' in Document 75, issued in 1980, in which the government was obliged to recognise a *fait accompli* and incorporate the complexities of a system evolved by the masses themselves into official economic policy (Watson 1984: 90).

The New Community Movement (*Saemaul Undong*) launched in Korea in 1971 has depended for its success on a number of elements familiar from earlier Chinese experience, including (as well as the charismatic leadership provided by President Park himself) mass participation under the leadership of educated and dedicated members of the local community (e.g. Whang 1981). Again a key feature has been the integration of local experience with centralised expertise: 'detailed information about the reasons for success or failure in the case of specific projects does in fact flow back up through bureaucratic channels, and problems are discussed and solutions proposed at every level of the hierarchy' (Brandt 1980: 278).

The crucial importance of popular involvement in running water control systems effectively has already been mentioned in chapter 3. Lack of active support can prove disastrous, as in Central Luzon, where the villagers will hardly participate at all in maintaining irrigation systems; they leave it entirely to the irrigation authority and take water from the system whenever it suits them, cheerfully disregarding their neighbours' needs; 'a sort of anarchy prevails' (Takahashi 1970: 52). But the cohesive nature of rice farming technology requires cooperation, not anarchy, if decent yields are to be achieved: one farmer flouting the water regulations can damage the crops of all the farmers in the same irrigation block.

The potential contribution of popular participation is well illustrated by the case of the Demas (Mass Demonstration) programme carried out in Java in 1964/5. At this time there were few funds available for subsidising new technology; instead the programme relied almost exclusively on extension work carried out by young and dedicated officers living in the villages and working in close consultation with the farmers. Despite prevailing shortages of fertilisers, yield increases of between 40% and 140% were achieved. Such levels were seldom attained by farmers under the later Bimas (Mass Guidance) programme, which was imposed upon the farmers through government regulations; the new extension officers did not feel the need to fraternise with the farmers, and their advice was not always enthusiastically received (Palmer 1977: 192, 104; Loekman 1982).

In rice-cultivating societies technical choices and management decisions are in the hands not of a few landlords but of vast numbers of family farmers. The higher the levels of rural education and training, the more likely farmers are to be receptive to advanced techniques, as the examples of the East Asian nations show. Whatever the excellence of existing extension services, active grass-roots support is more likely to emerge where the farmers feel they have some personal control over what is happening, and where innovation by individuals is the result not of half-hearted submission to remote authority but of an active and informed commitment to change.

6

Peasant, landlord and state: changes in relations of production

Asian rural societies have usually been characterised, at least until very recently, as 'peasant societies'. If we accept the loose definition of peasants as rural producers with a degree of independent control over their resources, who produce for their own consumption and sometimes also for sale, relying principally if not exclusively upon household labour,[1] then the rice economies studied here certainly developed over time into peasant economies. The progressive development of Asian wet-rice technology was linked with the intensification of skilled labour inputs and a reduction in farm size. This tended to improve the position of the farmer vis-à-vis landowners, although intensive rice agriculture was rarely unassociated with tenancy. The potential for economic diversification, using household labour and low levels of capital investment, gave farmers further scope for individualistic entrepreneurial activity. Yet there was an inherent tension in rice-growing societies between individualism and the spirit of communality required to keep irrigation networks functioning smoothly.

Conflict, cooperation and control

In order to ensure access to water and labour, even the most privileged members of rice-growing societies have traditionally been obliged to cooperate closely with their fellow-farmers. On the other hand where essential resources are in short supply — labour and land for instance — conflicts inevitably arise. To some extent such organisations as irrigation societies and labour exchange groups have the effect of reducing social inequalities and promoting communal harmony; nevertheless, social and economic hierarchies are to be found in all village societies where there is pressure on resources.

Lê (1955: 225) refers to the institutionalised hierarchy which existed within the traditional Vietnamese commune. Communal land was distributed regularly by the village notables (mandarins, officials, examiners and old men) among the members of the commune, but not on an egalitarian basis: each member's allotment corresponded to his status, determined by his social rank, titles and seniority. Despite constant legislation during the eighteenth-century Trịnh dynasty to ensure their equitable distribution, communal lands were in fact largely concentrated in the hands of the notables. In 1860 the Nguyên rulers of Tonkin again attempted to reform the inequalities of the commune: all rich landlords were ordered to give one-third of their property to the village as communal land, and the sale and pawning of communal land was forbidden. It was to be redistributed equally between all villagers every three years. But in spite of this legislation the notables retained their power: the poorer peasants were either kept in ignorance of the reforms or were afraid to incur the enmity of the notables. Central government had little direct control over the notables' administration of the villages, and the growing problems of inequality, exacerbated by overpopulation and frequent natural disasters, resulted in frequent popular uprisings, which government attempts at repression and administrative reform were powerless to quell (ibid.: 360).

Once feudal relations began to decline in Tokugawa Japan (see appendix C), village hierarchies became somewhat less marked in that the traditional elites lived elsewhere and did not participate directly in village life (Kelly 1982b: 27). But as the economy grew, differences between rich and poor peasants, landlords and tenants, became more apparent. In Shiwa village in the twentieth century, the rich owned the land near the main irrigation canal: this land had higher yields and lower labour requirements, as well as privileged access to water in times of shortage (Shimpo 1976: 12). Not surprisingly these rich farmers bitterly opposed the construction of a new dam and irrigation network, which threatened to shatter the traditional hierarchy of privilege.

Customary regulations help keep such traditional systems for the allocation of resources working smoothly at village level, but when communities are contending for these resources, especially for water, then a higher authority has to be brought in as arbiter.

Where the wider political structure is undeveloped, communities will often subsist more or less in isolation, relying on kinship and customary law to maintain order. The Laotian villages described by Taillard (1972) were limited in size to seventy or eighty members, linked by ties of kinship or friendship, and their irrigation units were never big enough to overlap village boundaries.

In certain cases the size of the community is actually defined by the capacity of the water source. The surface area of the tank in the Ceylonese village of Pul Eliya studied by Leach corresponded exactly to the area of rice-field it could irrigate, in this case about 60 ha (1961: 18). As a social unit Ceylonese villages were very tightly bound: all the members of one village would belong to a single *variga* category, and endogamy within the *variga* was expected (ibid.: 23). The village community was still more closely bound by the necessity to cooperate in production and to decide jointly on the allocation of resources, under the direction of the irrigation headman, the Vel Vidāne, who mediated between villagers and government. Every year a decision had to be taken, in view of the current level of the irrigation tank and the likely rainfall in the coming months, as to what area of fields was to be cultivated. The traditional tenure system was based on the ideal of fair shares for all: 'The *ideal* system is functionally perfect. Everything fits together like a jigsaw puzzle, the technology of irrigation, the technology of rice-growing and the egalitarian ideology of village politics' (ibid.: 177). But although the allocation of individual strips of land theoretically gave every villager equal rights to water, the actual and the ideal arrangements were not identical. However villagers were also engaged in cooperative labour which 'follows a pattern which is antithetic to that of landownership, and the rewarding of labour has the effect of counterbalancing the unequal distribution of primary title' (ibid.: 241).

Tamaki (1979: 24–33) describes a somewhat similar social system in early Japan: the irrigation ponds of the Yamato kingdom in Western Japan (AD 300–710) (see chapter 3) were of a size to irrigate enough land to feed 10 to 20 families, which thus was the size of a typical hamlet. Again, all the households would meet in May to discuss the prospects for rain, and to decide on the area of padi that could be cultivated and the proportion of their fields which each member was entitled to plant with irrigated rice. Any infraction of these rules was punishable by expulsion from the community.

[But] there is a threshold of complexity in irrigation systems at which cooperation must give way to coordination; at which those served by the systems relinquish their decision-making power and their direct role in settling disputes. Authority and responsibility for these vital functions are then transferred to managerial structures of one sort or another. This is not to say that cooperation is then absent, but rather that it is no longer the dominant pattern of operation. The transfer to managerial coordination is not simply dependent on the size of the irrigated area. It is also – and more directly – dependent on the number of farmers drawing water *from a single source*. Where so many farmers are involved that face-to-face relations break down, management of some kind becomes necessary. Otherwise the system may be disrupted by constant conflict, and much of the community may be deprived of water. (Pasternak 1972: 194)

The most voluminous literature on water rights and customs deals with Japan, and there is an admirable analytical summary in Kelly (1982a).[2] Irrigation rights are seen by many Japanese scholars as a natural response to the conflicts which arise between irrigation communities; because they are the product of specific historical and geographical circumstances they are not considered to be rational or widely applicable (ibid.: 19, 21, etc.).

In general, the nearer a farmer's land is to the source of irrigation, the greater his advantage. Farmers with land at the side of the main channel will have better access to water than those with land at the end of a minor channel; those upstream are better off than those downstream. Traditional agreements as to water rights are not infrequently the outcome of bloody disputes, and such apparent improvements as the building of a new dam may completely disrupt the traditional hierarchies; hence the fierce opposition which such projects often encounter (e.g. Shimpo 1976).

There is political power to be gained through mediating conflicts, whether inter-or intra-communal. Within the community, the irrigation headman is usually elected, although sometimes the appointment must be officially ratified by the government. The post usually goes to one of the wealthier members of the community. It may be short-term or permanent, and rarely does the headman receive more than token remuneration, but in terms of prestige and power the rewards are great. The allocation of water rights often served landlords or gentry as a means of protecting their class (or perhaps 'group') interests. This seems to have been the case in Tokugawa Japan, and Furushima (1954: 202; cited Kelly 1982a: 17) argues that even in the 1930s, when former tenants had acquired titles to land, irrigation customs continued to favour the former landlord elite households. But this may have been only a regional phenomenon. Writing of Northeastern Japan in the late Tokugawa period, Kelly (1982b: 192, 212) maintains that there is very little evidence for landlords or domain officials having exercised much direct authority in controlling water use. Waswo (1977) describes how Meiji and Shōwa improvements in water control, often initiated by landlords, had the eventual effect of reducing their influence within village society. And Kitamura (1950; cited Kelly 1982a: 13) actually maintains that irrigation customs were an obstacle to the consolidation of landlord power, since they tended to encourage tenancy on large holdings and did not favour owner-operation on a large scale.

In China too, Morita believes that there was a gradual decline in landlord participation in water control during the Qing dynasty (1644–1911) and subsequent Republican period, and that the irrigation groups were taken over by independent farmers. 'He attributed this to the increasing dispersal of landlord holdings; landlords were thus less knowledgeable about local water-control conditions and arrangements in all the areas of their holdings and more able to avoid levies and assessments for repairs and operation/maintenance' (Kelly 1982a: 62). This view is supported by Hamashima's study of the Yangzi Delta (1980). The evidence suggests, then, that the increase in absentee landlordism favoured the greater autonomy of tenant smallholders.

When it comes to mediating between whole communities in conflict, a higher level of political intervention is necessary, and the rewards are correspondingly greater. Tamaki (1979) describes how the Kamakura feudal state (1185–1392) had its power base in the upland valleys of Japan, watered by small gravity irrigation networks similar to those of Southeast Asia. Such a system could irrigate larger areas than the Yamato ponds mentioned earlier, areas large enough to establish feudal estates (*shōen*). In their constant search for greater power, the warring feudal lords turned in the fifteenth century to the marshy alluvial plains, where they constructed canals and opened up large areas for cultivation. A powerful feudal lord would have control over a whole plain and would covet possession of others as a sure way of increasing his economic and political power. This was the beginning of the so-called Warring States period. Since farmers were obliged to spend much of their time fighting, it is not surprising that levels of agricultural production were low when the Tokugawa shogunate was established in 1600.

Even the most powerful and bureaucratic centralised state can hardly hope to subdue all the rivalries and enmities which arise over competition for water. It is even more tricky than solving the land problem. In Japan (Kelly 1982a: 21) groups of individual farmers, and not landlords, are now the chief antagonists, and conflicts over water distribution remain unsolved all over the country. Recently a new source of tension has become common:

LIDs [Local Irrigation Departments] in most of the major rice-growing areas have been faced in the 1970s with an increasing concentration of water demands in the field preparation/transplanting period, already the period of highest water volume demand. This has been due in part to mechanisation, which shortens considerably the spring work period, and also to the spread of monovariety cultivation . . . It is compounded by the trend toward part-time farming. Spring Sundays are moments of feverish activity in most areas, and the water difficulties often experienced on those days are nicknamed 'Sunday droughts' by the farmers. As a consequence of these factors, LIDs face mounting shortages and strain on network facilities during this spring peak period. (Kelly 1982a: 46)

Vaidyanathan (1983: 76–85) lists the difficulties encountered in running the large state-managed irrigation systems of India, where sheer scale often precludes the flexibility required to deal with local conflicts. In China it seems that the efficiency of water control has increased steadily since 1965 (Gustafsson 1984: 136). The Constitution provides that water areas and water flows be owned by the state (ibid.: 153), and the 150 large irrigation districts of over 20,000 ha, as well as the medium districts of 667 to 20,000 ha, have a professional body of management established by the government. Integrated smaller systems drawing on several different sources, like the Meiquan district in Hubei studied by Nickum (1981) which depended on a combination of small reservoirs and ponds, have the flexibility to cope with drought relying entirely on their own resources. Irrigation systems which share a source such as a medium-size river are more likely to find themselves in competition with other areas, and an increasing problem in China today is the competition for water between the countryside and the cities, and between the industrial and agricultural sectors. The recent introduction of the 'responsibility system', which divides up irrigation tasks and allocations not between production brigades but between individual households, has led to much confusion over water rights (Gustafsson 1984: 140).

Historical changes in relations of production

The contrast between the evolution of wet-rice economies and the Northwest European model of agricultural development is very striking if one considers the social effects of the development of the productive forces.

'Feudal' relations and frontier zones

In rice-growing areas where cultivation techniques were undeveloped and extensive, one often finds relations of production which share certain features with those of feudal Europe. Since the land's productivity and thus its population-carrying capacity are low, control over labour is crucial to the dominant class. The peasant producers have access to land only through establishing tributary relations with a member of this dominant class, and there is no market through which producers might acquire proprietary rights in land.

Discussing conditions in Europe, historians have pointed out that one important characteristic of classic feudalism is that the nature of political relations and of the process of extraction is such as seriously to inhibit development of the factors of production (Kula 1970: Ch. 3; Brenner 1982: 34–40). The economic cake is thus limited, and any gain by one class is necessarily at the expense of another. All European observers remarked that in Malaya peasants were loath to produce any more than their basic subsistence requirements for fear of the rapacity of the rulers. The ultimate rights to all land were vested in the rajas (Clifford 1895: 114; Downs 1967: 117). A peasant had rights of usufruct over all the wet-rice land he was able to keep under cultivation ('living land', *tanah hidup*), but although he could pass these rights on to his heirs he could neither buy nor sell land. To maintain his usufructuary rights he was obliged not only to pay fees in kind on the produce of his land but also to perform corvée labour or *krah* for the local raja. The usual levy on rice-land consisted of a tithe (Ooi 1966: 178), and there were additional levies on fruit-trees and other produce. Some scholars suggest that since access to manpower was such an important asset, the Malay rulers were obliged to refrain from exploiting their subjects so ruthlessly that they fled their territories (Lim 1977: 4), but usually the *krah* system was shamelessly abused to support a whole ruling class:

In theory, apparently, the Krah was an order issued by the Ruler to the people, conveyed on a sealed paper, which must be instantly obeyed, whatever its nature. In practice, however, every relative of the Ruler and every person who can boast a drop of blood of the Rulers, reserves to himself the right to Krah whenever opportunity offers, according to his ability to enforce obedience to his orders, by which means the wants of the upper classes are supplied free of cost by the labour of the country people, who are forever working out some Krah or other ... (Graham 1904: 16)

The peasants in Java were in a still more insecure position, for they did not even benefit from permanent rights of usufruct over their rice-land: each year the village chief redistributed the wet-rice fields among the villagers, so that (as on many medieval European manors) nobody cultivated the same field two years running. Only to dryland fields did usufructuary rules similar to those of Malaya apply (Raffles 1817: I, 151).

Although the institutions of the Angkorian empire were bureaucratic rather than feudal in character, many officials were rewarded for their services with fiefs 'provided with fields and cultivators', and it has been suggested that the cultivators had a status similar to that of European serfs (see Sahai 1970: 144).

Tenurial relations in early Tokugawa Japan also strongly resembled

Western feudalism; peasant farmers acquired improved tenurial status and greater independence as agricultural methods improved and the economy expanded and diversified (appendix C).

As a general rule, given the importance of individual skills and experience in developed rice technology, it seems improbable that serfdom was ever compatible with intensive rice cultivation (Erkes 1953). In his discussion of the concept of 'hydraulic societies' Eberhard argues that 'there was a clear correlation between irrigation and tenancy' (1965: 87). Little is known of tenurial conditions in China's rice-growing regions before the Song, but although many Japanese scholars maintain that the large estates amassed during that period were feudal in nature,[3] others such as Lewin (1973) affirm that there is no evidence whatsoever for the existence of feudal institutions in the Song. By far the largest category of landholders registered in the early Song were independent smallholders, followed by the category known as 'farmers tilling land half their own', *ban zi geng nong*, that is, farmers who leased in extra land to make ends meet: such farmers clearly could not have been serfs (Bray 1984: 605).

It is likely, however, that conditions in China's frontier regions were less favourable. Wherever the population was sparse it was possible for rich men to lay claim to huge tracts of land, unhampered by official intervention. Labour was in short supply, but as economic alternatives were non-existent, the unfortunate farmers working on these estates found themselves with few privileges and a great many obligations (Golas 1980: 305). However when Fujianese migrants opened up land in Taiwan in the eighteenth century, constructing irrigation networks in order to grow rice intensively, there was no question of feudal relations between landowners and their tenants; in fact Taiwan's tenurial system was directly evolved from the system of three-level ownership (see appendix B) then prevailing in Fujian (Meskill 1979: 47).

In nineteenth-century Indochina and Siam we find a contrast between the traditional population centres, where intensive wet-rice production was practised, and the technically underdeveloped frontier zones of Cochinchina and the Chao Phraya Delta, or Bangkok Plain, then in a phase of rapid expansion. In the regions of intensive rice cultivation the relations between landlord and tenant did not include labour services or other forms of control over personal freedom. But in the frontier zones, where land was plentiful but labour scarce, migrant farmers reverted to relatively primitive, land-extensive techniques (Tanabe 1978: 42); furthermore the forms of appropriation in these areas presented many similarities to those of feudal Europe. Although Scott (1976: 67) has described the colonisation of Indochina as an example of the growth of capitalist labour relations (in contrast to the situation in Tonkin and Annam), 'capitalist' seems an inappropriate label for a situation where the landless poor worked small individual plots on the estates of large landowners to whom they owed labour dues, political allegiance and a variety of demeaning services (Brocheux 1971; Popkin 1979: 181).

One of the reasons why peasants in frontier zones are so vulnerable to feudal-type exploitation is their inability to participate directly in markets. They are obliged to rely on rice monoculture and have little or no opportunity to diversify their economic activities or even to sell their rice directly. This ensures their economic subjugation to the owners of the land. In Cochinchina the powerful landowners exerted their rule in opposition to state policy, but during the early stages of the reclamation of the Bangkok Plain in the 1860s and 1870s, the Siamese kings institutionalised a system of 'feudal' relations such as by then had disintegrated further inland: large grants of land were made to financially distressed members of the royal family and noble officials, the labour to be largely supplied by corvée peasants, *bao phrai*, or by debt slaves (Tanabe 1978: 55). The intention behind this policy was to expand rice production in the Delta to supply the growing demand for rice in China and other Asian countries. But the government was soon obliged to recognise that the large noble estates were not in fact as productive as peasant smallholdings. In 1877 a new policy was introduced which encouraged landless peasant migrants from the crowded north to reclaim unoccupied rice-land along the newly excavated canals of the Delta and to work it independently, in return for the payment of land-tax and irrigations dues directly to the state (ibid.: 62).

The Siamese rulers were not alone in recognising the pernicious effects on productivity of 'feudal' relations of production and the relative advantages of independent peasant farming. Raffles roundly blamed the extortions of the Javanese chiefs for the poor state of the country's agriculture (1817: I, 151), and during their brief occupation in 1811–16 the British governors abolished feudal dues and land allotments in many regions, redistributing land among the villagers and commuting all former dues into a land-tax based on a proportion of the average produce of the field (ibid.: 158). Immediate improvements were reported both in the industry of the Javanese peasants and in the crime rate. It is not clear whether these early nineteenth-century modifications in tenurial relations were directly responsible for the subsequent intensification of Javanese rice cultivation, or whether they merely facilitated an inevitable response to the reduction in the wet-rice area imposed by the Dutch introduction of the Culture System. Geertz (1963) argues that the obligation to cultivate sugar on part of their rice-land forced Javanese peasants to adopt more intensive rice-cultivation techniques in order to survive. But Elson (1978) has pointed out that in fact rice cultivation techniques were more advanced and productive in the areas where little sugar was grown and thus more resources could be devoted to the rice crop. It was the non-sugar regions, Elson says, which produced surpluses of rice which were sold to those rice-farmers who also worked as wage-labourers on the sugar estates. In Elson's view, then, the intensification of rice cultivation in the non-sugar areas can be seen as a response to market demands.

Smallholder economies: expansion and stagnation

Wet-rice cultivation is not, like the farming system of Northwest Europe, subject to economies of scale, nor does it respond positively to the centralisation of management. It is therefore not surprising to find that in both medieval China and Tokugawa Japan, as new techniques were applied and land productivity rose, the position of tenants vis-à-vis their landlords improved: they acquired more managerial and economic independence, and tenurial contracts were modified in their favour (appendices B and C). The development of intensive rice production gave rise to long-term economic expansion and diversification, and although the ownership of land was concentrated in relatively few hands, the household rather than the estate was the basic unit of both agricultural and commodity production.

In China and Japan it seems that technological development gradually led to modifications in tenurial relations, whereas in the cases of Siam and Java the state took an active role in imposing tenurial change expressly to favour increased production. In the Malay States the British introduced a system of land registration which protected peasant rights, and in Kelantan the acreage under padi rose from 66,000 acres in 1911 to 207,000 in 1925 (Bishop 1912: iv; Shaw 1926: xiii). As the Malayan population grew and the supply of new arable land diminished, tenancy rates increased, but the relations between landlord and tenant were usually of a redistributive rather than of an exploitative nature; they generally remain so today despite the increased commercialisation of agriculture (Bray and Robertson 1980; Horii 1981; Fujimoto 1983). On the East Coast sharecropping contracts prevail, while cash rents are more common on the West Coast, but most contracts are between kin, indeed often between parents and children, and they are flexible and relatively generous. The landlords are frequently older people, sometimes too poor or ill to farm the land themselves, more often older relatives of their tenants, renting them land as a way of starting them out on the ladder towards ownership. Pure tenants are most commonly young people who as yet have acquired no land of their own.[4] Owner-tenants are older householders with growing families. Tenancy is a means of matching land and labour within a community so that resources are not wasted.

Initially the transition from subsistence to commercial production in wet-rice economies appears to increase the value of skilled labour and to sustain a general expansion of the economy, as in medieval China and Tokugawa Japan. But eventually a point of crisis may be reached. Once the population grows beyond certain limits, pressure on land reaches a point where returns to labour begin to diminish, and the rural population becomes increasingly impoverished. The competition for land enables landlords to impose heavier burdens on their tenants, and in addition, as more and more mouths have to be fed off the same area of land, rents which once seemed fair become extortionate.

The difficulties faced by the poorer peasants are especially acute where rice monoculture prevails and there are few opportunities for profitable alternative employment. In several instances the policies of colonial governments, anxious to extract agricultural taxes from their new subjects but loath to invest in the colonies, led to a rapid degradation of rural conditions. Geertz's account of what happened in Java is well known. The small island of Lombok, off the tip of Bali, also suffered severely.[5] Lombok was taken over by the Dutch from the Balinese in 1894. Although Balinese rule had not been especially lenient rice exports had flourished then. They continued to grow under the Dutch, but peasants were now obliged to sell much of their produce in order to pay cash taxes on irrigated land which amounted to 20% of the crop in 1914–20, over 15% in 1930–40 and over 25% in 1940–50. The Dutch government made little or no attempt to develop local industries or to promote the cultivation of alternative crops; however it did invest in irrigation improvements (though the farmers themselves also had to contribute to these, being liable for up to one month a year in corvée duties).

During the colonial period the population increased steadily at a rate of between 1.3% and 2% per annum; the extension of the cultivated area did not keep pace. 'The decline in the total ration of *sawah* [rice-land] per capita during the colonial period is to some extent counterbalanced by the extension of permanent irrigation facilities, which allow for a more stable and therefore higher output. The impact of irrigation extension should not be overestimated, however, since the best irrigation opportunities were probably exploited before the Dutch takeover.'

Although the irrigated land per capita doubled from 0.047 ha in 1900 to 0.086 ha in 1940, the total of irrigated plus rain-fed rice-land dropped from 0.131 ha to 0.123 ha in the same period, and had fallen as low as 0.066 ha by 1971; in the most productive region, Western Lombok, the total fell from 0.083 ha in 1930 to 0.040 ha in 1971 (Gerdin 1982: 63).

The Dutch government introduced a system of land registration which gave peasants legal possession, rather than inalienable usufructuary rights, to the land they cultivated. This meant they were also registered as tax-payers, and land could now be freely bought, pawned or sold. Although certain forms of tenancy and wage-labour had existed in pre-colonial times, in the 1890s most peasants still had hereditary rights of production. Even in the 1970s, peasants still regarded ownership of rice-land as the primary economic resource, but official statistics showed that by now one-third of the population of Lombok owned no land at all, and 67% of all holdings (owned, not cultivated) were under 1 ha in size; in certain areas the figures for landlessness reached over 70% (Gerdin 1982: 84–5). This is not to say that none of the landless had access to land as tenants, but the landowners' positions had been considerably strengthened: rents were 50% higher than in the 1940s, preference was given as tenants to those who had land of their own, the length of tenancies had decreased and various forms of wage-labour were replacing tenancy (ibid.: 92).

Similar disruptions were caused by the French colonial government in Tonkin and Annam. Before the advent of the French 'the great mass of peasant households cultivated their own plots, which they held either as private land, or as part of the allocation of communal land; the role of landlordism was insignificant, and the largest landowner in the commune was usually the commune itself' (Fforde 1983: 24). French researchers of the 1920s and 1930s believed that tenancy and wage-labour in the pre-colonial period were almost unknown (Henry 1932: 113; Gourou 1936: 360). Rice production was the basis of the economy: trade and commodity production were not highly developed, and were not regarded as profitable (Fforde 1983: 41, 104). The introduction of monetary taxes by the French (who also turned a blind eye to corruption for private ends of the communal system of land allocation) brought about significant changes: 'Higher and monetised taxes forced peasants to borrow funds from their patrons in the communes. *In the absence of resources with which to increase commodity output* this was the only way in which average producers in wet-rice areas facing demographic saturation could obtain the necessary funds' (ibid.: 9; my emphasis). There was a rapid change from 'a rural social structure . . . based primarily upon small peasant cultivators of their "own" land, to one based upon a mixture of heavily indebted and rackrented tenants and a poverty-stricken landless rural proletariat' (ibid.: 45).

Egalitarianism or differentiation: the impact of capitalism

There are two principal schools of thought as to what happens to peasant economies under the impact of developing capitalism. The first is that increasing commoditisation and commercialisation lead to the gradual disappearance of family farming and the differentiation of the peasantry into a small class of capitalist farmers (or an agrarian bourgeoisie) and a large class of landless agricultural labourers.[6] The second is that the peasant economy survives, in articulation with the capitalist mode of production, largely because peasants are able to supply goods more cheaply than capitalist producers.[7] To say that there is disagreement as to the precise definition of capitalist farming is an understatement. The question has not yet been resolved for Europe (e.g. Cooper 1978; see also Brenner 1982), let alone for Asia.[8] Perhaps the most useful definition is that a capitalist farm is one that relies principally upon wage-labour and accumulates surplus value by this means (see, e.g., Sen 1975: ch. 7).

The introduction of money taxes to Asia's rice regions had effects which were anything but benign. But significantly, even though landlessness increased under such conditions, the transition to capitalist relations of production, whereby landowners evict their tenants in order to run large, consolidated farms using cheap wage-labour, did not generally occur. This seems surprising, especially in the case of Java where export crops like sugar and coffee were grown on capitalist plantations alongside the rice-fields,[9] until we remember the considerable technical obstacles to such a transformation. In the Philippines also, the two systems of capitalist and smallholding farming co-existed: the Spanish government made large grants of land to religious foundations and wealthy entrepreneurs, and the *haciendas* which produced export crops were run with hired labour, but those which grew rice were operated either through direct leaseholdings to peasant farmers, or through the *inquilinato* system, by which an agent leased the land and sub-let it in small parcels to sharecroppers (Ofreneo 1980: 10). In nineteenth-century Siam too, capitalist commercial plantations co-existed with smallholder rice-farming (Tanabe 1978: 42).

One cannot account for this by pleading the absence of international markets or of commercial inputs, as chapters 4 and 5 have shown. Even today, wet-rice economies still prove remarkably resistant to the transition to capitalist farming.

The egalitarian, redistributive aspects of Asian rice economies have been highlighted in a number of studies. Leach (1961) describes how the *ideal*, if not the real, allocation of land and water in a Ceylonese tank village is based on the principle of fair shares for all; Fujimoto's study (1983) of economic relations between Malaysian rice-farmers leads him to conclude that they are not intended to maximise the personal gains of the landowner but permit a more equitable sharing of income among kinsfolk and friends. Perhaps the most influential spokesmen for the redistributive nature of wet-rice economies have been Geertz (1963) and Scott (1976), with their concepts of 'shared poverty' and 'moral economy'.

In his study of the Javanese colonial economy Geertz put forward the view that social and economic differences in village society were kept to a minimum by a variety of redistributive means such as labour-sharing, tenancy relations, public feasts and so on, so that even the poorest were assured of survival through the largesse of those somewhat richer than themselves. These practices had the effect of inhibiting economic differentiation, reinforcing existing relations of production. Geertz's concept of 'shared poverty' has been criticised on a number of grounds. Alexander and Alexander (1982) say that it obscures important elements of social stratification in colonial Java, for instance ignoring the large number of landless already noted by Raffles; furthermore, they say, 'redistributive' practices such as group harvesting actually contribute to economic differentials, since kin and neighbours are rewarded at a much higher rate than landless peasants or outsiders. The Alexanders feel that accepting the concept of 'shared poverty' leads to a misinterpretation of the Green Revolution, since the New Technology does not in fact require a rejection of traditional attitudes towards wealth and profit, but rather has changed the balance of economic advantage. Elson (1978) too criticises Geertz for attributing an exaggerated homogeneity to traditional Javanese society. Other studies suggest that redistributive work-spreading today does not operate throughout the economic strata of Javanese rural society but is most common among poor farmers who have no cash to hire labour (Gerdin 1982: 68).

Scott's argument, based on his studies of late colonial Vietnam and Burma, is not that economic differentiation and exploitation were largely absent from village life, but that there was a general consensus among rich and poor alike that everyone had a right to survival. Poor tenants and other clients of rich landowners would seldom have the opportunity to cross the poverty line, for normally high rents and rates of interest would claim most of their income; but what remained would be sufficient for subsistence under normal conditions, and it was accepted by landlords as well as tenants that in case of a poor harvest or some other crisis rents would be lowered or even abolished, loans would be made, and the charity of the rich would ensure the survival of the poorest. Since the poor were concerned with subsistence rather than with profits, social stability could be maintained over long periods. However if once the poor suspected that their minimal requirements for survival were threatened, they became ripe for rebellion.

This view of class and economic relations between Southeast Asian peasants was quickly countered by Popkin (1979) in another study of Vietnam. Popkin argues that Scott's view of rural institutions is over-romanticised and that Asian peasants are primarily motivated by individual economic and political gain. Benevolence towards others comes not so much from principles of equity as from the controls imposed by other members of society, and significant inequalities are to be found between individuals within a community.

Both Scott and Popkin have been criticised for over-generalisation (e.g. Peletz 1983). It has been pointed out that Scott's area of study in Northern Vietnam had a long history of high population density, so that one might naturally expect social constraints on economic behaviour to be well developed there, while Popkin's material comes mainly from the frontier zone of Cochinchina, where social norms had not yet been established which might curb rampant individualism.

The debate as to the existence of a 'moral economy' is in many ways paralleled by interpretations of the Chinese lineage or clan. While an eleventh-century document on the administration of the Fan clan estate in the Yangzi Delta expressly forbids the land to be rented out to members of the clan (Twitchett 1960: 11), in the frontier zones of the south single-lineage villages were in the majority, and the leasing of land to members of the lineage was thus inevitable. Here the lineages were powerful solidarity groups, which fiercely protected the rights of their members against outsiders. Freedman (1958, 1966) believes that lineages developed in China's frontier zones in response to competition for land and water; in unity lay strength, and a cohesive lineage group could more easily undertake irrigation works for rice cultivation and protect its assets against other lineages than could communities of individuals without such strong ties. Freedman argues that a significant reason for the greater strength of lineages in South China than in the north or centre was the need for cooperation to establish irrigated rice cultivation.[10] But cooperation did not lead to egalitarianism. There was a considerable status gap between the highest and lowest members of a lineage, although '... the contrast between high and low status reinforced the integrity of the lineage. It may be that in a popular sense the poor were exploited by the rich, but even as they were exploited they enjoyed privileges important enough to make their continued residence worthwhile' (1958: 127). It was better to be a minor member of a strong lineage than a slightly more important member of a weak one which had fewer resources at its disposal.

Land and landlessness

It was believed by many that the recent exposure to capitalist markets and the introduction of the New Technology would lead to the differentiation of the peasantry into rich managerial farmers and landless labourers. As was mentioned in chapter 5, wealthier farmers do have better access to credit and to other inputs which should allow them to make more efficient use of their resources, and it was felt that many poorer farmers, especially tenants, becoming indebted through the necessity to purchase costly modern inputs, would eventually have to sell their land and work as hired labourers. But despite the commercialisation consequent on the recent widespread adoption of the New Technology, and the increase in the number of landless, capitalist relations of production have seldom emerged: large farmer-operators are the exception, and the basic unit of production remains the family farm.

One rare example of what might be called capitalist farming is to be found in the Muda region of Malaysia, where holdings were traditionally rather large, and where environmental conditions have favoured large-scale mechanisation of rice-farming (see chapter 2). A number (as yet very small, and not necessarily increasing) of Malay and Chinese entrepreneurs operate holdings of 7.5 to 30 ha (Muhd. Ikmal 1985: 28). This has led to the displacement of agricultural labourers by machines, and to a consequent fall in agricultural wages and the marginalisation of small farmers, suggesting to many (e.g. de Koninck 1981; Lim et al. 1981) that this is a case of incipient capitalist farming. But it is a new phenomenon and little studied; as yet the number of large farms seems to be insignificant: 28 farms out of perhaps 50,000 were found to be larger than 7.5 ha (Muhd. Ikmal 1985). Furthermore it has been suggested (ibid.: 89) that the capitalist interpretation fails to take account of the relationship between the farm unit and the family life-cycle, for apparently the family is still the basic operational unit even on Muda's largest farms.[11]

Despite the numerous inequalities to be found in rural Asia, the 'skill-oriented' nature of intensive rice cultivation does oblige the upper strata of village societies to give the poorer members direct access to land. Access to land, and direct control of production, whether as owners or tenants, are thus guaranteed to a far greater number of farmers than in a 'mechanical' technology where economies of scale operate. On the other hand there is no doubt that the number of landless in Asia's rice regions has increased in recent years, and that their plight has worsened. To what extent is this a direct result of the introduction of the New Technology, rather than a historical phenomenon exacerbated by demographic increase?

Markets in land are certainly nothing new. While an owner's profits from rice-land may be low, it is nevertheless an excellent long-term security and a source of prestige, hence the lively market in land in most regions where intensive rice cultivation has been practised. Most tenants' dearest ambition is to save enough to buy some rice-land, though how many actually succeed is difficult to say, since most studies are synchronic and do not take into account the domestic cycle, whereby children first work on their parents' farm for nothing, then take on the task as their parents' tenant, inherit a little land on marriage, save enough to buy more, and eventually lend or rent land out to their own children or other tenants.

Since Chayanov's study of the Russian peasantry (1966, first published in Russia in 1925), it has become evident that such cyclical patterns of domestic development are fundamental to an understanding of the structure of rural society (Shanin 1972; Harriss 1982). Their importance, for instance, in determining the nature of tenurial contracts in contemporary Malaysia is clear (Bray and Robertson 1980; Horii 1981). In a village-level study of late Tokugawa Japan, Smith (1977) qualifies the general rise in rural living standards (Hanley and Yamamura 1977) by emphasising that this secular increase is an aggregate of constant fluctuations at the level of intensely competing individual households attempting to match their labour and land resources.

Statistics on landlessness generally are not easy to interpret, since in many cases those classified as landless are actually tenant farmers although they own no land. For instance in Korea in 1945, before the land reform, the number of households without any access to land even as tenants was estimated at less than 3% (Lee 1979: 51); 50% of farming households *owned* no land, but *access* to land was much more evenly distributed. This was also true in China in the 1930s (Buck 1937), as it is today in Malaysia (Shand and Mohd. Ariff 1983: 25).

The constant efforts of the Vietnamese state to set limits to the concentration of land have already been referred to. In China, by maintaining accurate land registers, the government was able to keep track of the growth of large estates and even to impose upper limits on the size of holdings. On several occasions it simply confiscated land above a certain limit and redistributed it to landless peasants. Under the Public Fields Law (*Gongtian fa*) of 1260, for example, the state compulsorily purchased one-third of the land of all families owning over 100 *mu* in the six prefectures around Taihu Lake in the Yangzi Delta; an upper limit of 100 *mu* (about 6 ha), even in such a rich and productive region, hardly seems excessive. But in any case large estates seldom survived for long in China's economically advanced areas, where the risks and rewards of entrepreneurial activity ensured a rapid turnover (Bray 1984: 607).

Such situations, where entrepreneurial opportunities (even on a modest scale) abound, provide the means for many smallholders to grow rich and buy land; conversely, they invariably produce a number of poor, marginalised and landless peasants. Landlessness occurred not only in medieval China but in Tokugawa Japan as the rural economy expanded and diversified (Smith 1959). Once the Japanese invaders had been repulsed in 1597, a reform of the land-tax laws in Korea allowed for rapid advances in agricultural technology (in particular the expansion of irrigation and the spread of double-cropping of rice and wheat), agricultural diversification (tobacco and ginseng became important exports to China) and the growth of a class of rich peasants. Inevitably, it also resulted in the dispossession of many other peasants (Lee 1984: 227). One may then consider that marginalisation and landlessness are not simply a product of capitalism, but a historical phenomenon, though the introduction of the New Technology has probably resulted in the dispossession of a higher proportion of the rural population.

There is no doubt that landlessness is an increasingly severe problem in such rice-growing regions as Java, Bali and Lombok, where the population is extremely dense. In Java now most landless are in fact obliged to seek employment outside agriculture, for small and medium landholders are preferred as labourers to the landless or to migrants on account of their reliability and skills; this despite the fact that landholders command wages up to 30% higher (Hart and Huq 1982). But despite the increasing marginalisation of the landless, Java is a striking example of the tenacity of smallholder farming in rice agriculture. It is a moot point as to whether increasing landlessness in Java should be attributed principally to the adoption of the New Technology, for it is clear that since the early nineteenth century there has been a steady and long-term growth in landlessness, due largely to population increase. Certainly demographic growth rather than technological change was the key factor in the increasing rates of tenancy in Java from 1900 on (Palmer 1977: 131).

There can be no doubt, however, that where pressure on land is acute those working as wage-labourers, whether full- or part-time, have been dealt a heavy blow by the introduction of farm machinery, motorised rice-mills, chemical herbicides and other labour-saving devices, although it must be said that the effect has been compounded by population growth. On the Indonesian island of Lombok the introduction of new HYVs has resulted in a doubling of the labour productivity of cultivators, partly because yields are higher, but also because there has been no corresponding rise in agricultural wages, so that the cultivators can retain a higher proportion of the crop. Landless labourers have fewer opportunities for agricultural employment and now find it almost impossible to get access to land through tenancy, partly as a result of tenants' recent efforts to avoid undue exploitation by landlords in the face of technological changes. Fixed rent tenancy, *majeg* (payable in kind after the harvest), had in any case been in steady decline throughout this century, while landowners' use of wage-labour increased, but Gerdin believes that the New Technology has dealt the final blow:

During 1975–76, there was uncertainty as to how to handle *majeg* agreements. The tenants refrained from cultivating HYVs during the wet season so that the land-owners would not demand higher deliveries of rice [rent was only paid on the main crop, the off-season crop being retained by the tenant]. However, tenants sometimes grew a secondary crop of HYV, since they would get all of this crop. In 1978, there were virtually no *majeg* agreements in the area. If landowners rent their land nowadays, they usually do so on agreements for cultivation during one season (around four months) only. Land rent usually has to be paid in cash beforehand, which makes it more than likely that land is leased to well-to-do peasants rather than to landless workers. (1982: 136)

Yet in Kelantan, Malaysia, the introduction of the New Technology occasioned renegotiations of rental contracts which were not infrequently to the benefit of tenants rather than landlords (Bray and Robertson 1980). But Kelantan is a region of labour shortage rather than labour surplus, and the growth of the Malaysian national economy still provides plenty of alternatives to agricultural work. In Lombok, as in Java and Bali, not only is there no expanding sector of the economy to absorb the surplus labour, but traditional petty commodity production is declining rapidly, faced with competition from cheap imports (Gerdin 1982: 137). In Java too it is notorious that the introduction of the New Technology has led to discriminatory wages and fewer opportunities of profitable employment for the poor, thus increasing rural differentiation

(White 1976). To some extent this is the result of the political changes which took place after the fall of Sukarno in 1965, which deprived the poorer members of Indonesian society of most of their participatory rights.

In chapter 5 it was shown that although small farms can often outdo larger farms in terms of absolute land productivity, profit margins are usually in direct relation to farm size. Access to land is just as important as its ownership; in fact ownership may actually be an economic liability (Fujimoto 1983: 129). The system of 'three owners of a single plot', *yitian sanzhu*, was introduced to Taiwan by Fujianese colonists in the early eighteenth century. The chief owner, *dazu*, paid taxes to the government and received rent from the minor owner, *xiaozu*. During the eighteenth century the minor owner acquired most of the attributes of full ownership, notably the right to sell the land or to sub-let it to tenants, *dianren*, who were often poor migrants. 'The parcels available were often quite large (5 *jia*[12] was a standard size in portions of the Upper Valley [in Central Taiwan]) and came with houses, sheds, stables, seedbeds, gardens, bamboo palisades, and tools. Three-year leases were customary and could be had for a small rent deposit and a rent of about half the crop' (Meskill 1979: 49). The *xioazu* cleared about 10 to 20 taels of silver per *jia* of land rented out, but the after-tax income of the actual owner of the land, the *dazu*, was only 5 taels per *jia* (ibid.).

In his study of Malaysia in the 1970s Fujimoto says: 'From the static economic point of view, it was clearly shown that tenancy *per se* did not harm but improved the cost-return relations on individual farms. In other words, tenancy appeared to provide access to one of the most important production factors, land, at lower cost than the ownership of land' (1983: 220).

Where the economy has been successfully diversified, rice prices are low in relation to other products and the profits to be made through rice cultivation are less than those made through commercial cropping, petty commodity production or other non-agricultural work (as is the case in most of East Asia today); in such a case farmers do not regard the acquisition of extra rice-land as a priority once they have enough for their own subsistence, nor are they prepared to invest heavily in improving their rice-farms if easier profits can be made elsewhere (see chapter 4). Nakamura believes that in the Meiji period most savings from the Japanese agricultural sector were not reinvested in agriculture but were transferred to more profitable sectors (1966: 137). Mizuno points out that while the better-off peasants in Java today owe their prosperity to the Green Revolution improvements in and commercialisation of rice-farming, they invest the surplus thus accumulated in non-agricultural activities. Well-to-do Malaysian farmers often invest in profitable equipment such as rice-mills (pers. obs.). In Korea, the initial government emphasis on investing so as to increase basic agricultural productivity has now shifted towards the promotion of higher incomes through diversification (Brandt 1980: 277). In China the new economic policies allow farmers to choose how they will use the rest of their land once they have fulfilled the grain quota, and it seems that the area devoted to grain has fallen significantly, despite its increased price both for quota and on the free market; this, the eminent economist Chen Yun declared at a special meeting of the Chinese Communist Party in September 1985, could result in grain shortages leading to social disorder (*Guardian*, 24 September 1985).

In areas such as Java and the Muda region of Malaysia, where the chief profits are to be made through rice-farming, it seems that those who have no access to land at all are becoming more numerous and find themselves in an increasingly difficult position because of the new technology. They rely entirely on wage-labour for their living, and the advance of mechanisation has reduced opportunities for labouring and consequently brought down wages; furthermore farmers often prefer to hire other farmers as labourers, since this guarantees a certain degree of skill and experience. In fact what seems to be happening in areas like Muda and Java is that the truly landless are being displaced from agriculture, while larger farmers draw their (part-time) labour force from those with farms which have dwindled to below subsistence size because of increased competition for land. This development is largely a result of pre-existing institutional inequalities, not in land ownership, but in access to land. 'Under the economic and institutional conditions prevailing in [Northwest Malaysia and Northern Sumatra], the possibility to reproduce and increase capital is a direct function of a farmer's capacity to hire labour which, in turn, is largely a function of his farm size and tenure. However ... the farm benefits, although distributed very unequally, are still such that they do not allow for a caricatural classification of tenurial groups nor for a clear distinction of operators versus landless labourers' (Gibbons et al. 1980: 21).

'Land to the tiller'

The examples of Japan, Taiwan and Korea demonstrate even more clearly the desirability of reducing institutional inequalities. They also show that the intensification of rice production and general expansion of the rural economy are in no way incompatible with the predominance of family smallholdings, even in a capitalist national economy. In rice-growing societies family farms do not simply survive the competition with capitalist farms, as Kautsky predicted (Banaji 1980), for it seems that capitalist rice-farming is unlikely to develop at all, even in such an advanced economy as Japan.[13] This makes a strong case in favour of populist land reform of the 'land-to-the-tiller' type as a prerequisite for rural growth in the rice regions.

In Japan and Taiwan land reforms had immediate positive effects, rapidly reducing tenancy to very low levels, increasing farmers' incomes and freeing them from the necessity to produce enough rice for the payment of rent, and thus encouraging saving and reinvestment in agriculture as well as the diversification of agricultural production (see appendix C on Japan, Mao [1982] on Taiwan). In Korea the process was more confused and the impact somewhat delayed:

The politics of Korea's land reform efforts in the 1945–52 period is as complex and confusing as most of what was going on in that period. American combat officers with no prior experience in Korea understandably made less than ideal administrators during the first years of Liberation from Japanese rule. Koreans, with no recent experience in running their own government, weren't much of an improvement. (Ban et al. 1980: 283)

Yet, partly through government intervention, partly through private negotiations between landowners and their tenants, the percentage of full tenancy fell from 49% in 1945 to 5% in 1964 (ibid.:286). Nevertheless, agricultural growth was slow during this period, for reasons which are not entirely clear. In Korea, although to a slighter extent than in Japan and Taiwan, there has been a gradual convergence of farm size to the 0.5–2.0 ha range (Ban et al. 1980: 295; appendix C; Mao 1982: 737), accompanied by diversification of the sources of farm income and a marked increase in rural prosperity.

Institutional inequalities in access to land are recognised throughout Southeast Asia as a significant obstacle to rural development. In Malaysia the desirability of land reform has been much debated (e.g. Gibbons et al. 1980; Fujimoto 1983), but no concrete legislation has ever been proposed. In Indonesia agrarian laws were passed in 1960 and 1961 which set upper limits both on ownership and on the leasing-in of land, but implementation proved extremely difficult and led to considerable unrest. 'The change in government in 1966 was a special setback for land reform since agitation for reform had come to be regarded as within the province of communist politics ... Today land reform has been largely forgotten under an avalanche of rice intensification programmes which scarcely touch upon the topics of farm size and ownership' (Palmer 1977: 135). In the Philippines the mildest of land reforms were proposed, but again implementation proved almost impossible because of the fierce opposition of landowners (Mangahas et al. 1976; Wurfel 1977; Tadem 1978):

Philippine agrarian reform has already produced an increase in rural conflict since 1973. That conflict will escalate as reform moves into small landholdings (that is, below 24 ha), because landlord resistance will rise, and will spread most rapidly if the reform slows . . . because of tenant frustration. Some of the recent literature has warned that the Philippine agrarian scene is inherently explosive. (Wurfel 1977: 39)

An additional threat to Philippine peasants is the government's recent policy of granting huge areas of land to contractors to set up 'corporate farms', run with wage-labour. Although export crops occupy the larger part of many such farms, the contractors are also encouraged to devote part of their land to rice production. One such farm, established in Davao del Norte in 1977, was 549 ha in size, and the 34 peasant farmers who had originally opened up the land for cultivation were evicted and gaoled when the title-holder took possession (Tadem 1978: 56). The corporate farming programme was initiated in 1974. By late 1977, 84 such farms had been set up, requiring heavy capital investment in land development and equipment; efficiency and productive levels were low, even by Philippine standards (ibid.). Another government approach was to encourage group rice-farming, 'voluntary groupings of small individually cultivated farms of approximately equal productive capacities into larger units, the aggregate area treated and operated as a single farm' (Ofreneo 1980: 72). Production of rice on such farms was reported as being 75% above average, but as of 1980 very few groups had been formed.

Even in Japan, Taiwan and Korea it is doubtful if land reform could have been successfully carried out except with the backing of outside forces. In Japan before the Second World War the landlord class had effectively blocked all attempts at legislation to help tenants, and it was the Americans who instigated land reform in 1945 (see Dore 1959; appendix C). In Korea too the American occupation forces played an important role; furthermore the defeat of the Japanese colonial government, and the weakening of the political power of Korean landlords, many of whom had been collaborators with the Japanese, reduced the potential opposition to reforms (Ban et al. 1980: 288). In Taiwan the government which initiated land reform consisted of mainlanders who had no loyalty to the traditional Taiwanese landlord class, and who based their legislation on Sun Yat-sen's Principle of Equalisation of Land Rights (Mao 1982: 724).

Group farming

It must be said that rapid rural development in these three countries has still not been successful in eliminating the gap between rural and urban incomes. The lag in agricultural profits is not infrequently attributed to diseconomies in management which the rigidity of the present land laws makes it difficult to transcend, and it is not rare to find the persistence of smallholding deplored as backward and an obstacle to further growth (Moon 1982: 205). In Taiwan amendments are in fact being made to the land laws so as to 'promote land use efficiency' (Mao 1982: 751).

In all three countries various forms of group and cooperative farming are to be found, some still at the experimental stage, and some more successful than others. In Korea cooperation between farmers is largely confined to the traditional practice of group transplanting, but in the late 1960s the government introduced a Joint Rice Farming programme, under which 5 to 10 ha were to be farmed by the 10 to 15 cultivators who owned the land. The idea was that operations would be carried out jointly, but private ownership would be retained, and each farmer would receive the harvest from his own plot (Reed 1979: 29) The programme has not been a great success, for it seems that 'whatever benefits might accrue to joint farm members, they are not seen by the majority of farmers as great enough to offset their perceived costs of participation' (ibid.: 33); the persistence of joint farming in Korea is completely dependent on constant official supervision.

One reason for the lack of success of joint farming in Korea so far must be the relatively low levels of mechanisation. In Taiwan the mechanisation of rice-farming is more advanced, and in 1975 71% of farms were under 1 ha in size (Hong 1979: 52). The Joint Commission for Rural Reconstruction started a pilot programme for joint rice-farming in 1964, whereby blocks of 12–15 ha of rice-land were farmed as a single unit. The programme has proved especially successful among farmers in their thirties and forties, mostly full-time farmers. In 1971, 617 working units were organised to farm 11,290 ha of rice-land, with the participation of 15,345 farmers; by 1976 the figures had risen to 4,306 units, 107,392 ha and 144,336 farmers; during this period yields were 10% to 14% higher than in control areas, production costs were 10% to 15% lower and profits from rice-farming 20% to 45% higher (ibid.: 62). Hong felt that joint cultivation, appropriate as it was to present social and technical conditions in rural Taiwan, might be only a temporary phenomenon, if farm incomes rose and the price of farm machinery declined; but he felt that in such a case, a return to individual farming might well prove a long-term obstacle to rural development (ibid.: 64).

Various types of joint farming are also found in Japan, including organisations for the joint use of machinery (the most common), group cultivation organisations, cooperatives and contract farming organisations (Kubo 1979; appendix C). Some Japanese agricultural specialists believe that group farming is only a transient phenomenon and predict that it will eventually be replaced either by independently viable family farms or by capitalist large-scale farming. Others (Ogura 1980; appendix C) see sophisticated forms of group farming as the main hope of Japanese agriculture.

Socialist land reform

The socialisation of Chinese agriculture was a gradual process, conducted with the active support of the majority of farmers:

Chinese peasants were not expected to exhibit self-sacrificing altruism in their embrace of socialism. Nor were they expected to shed very quickly their age-old preoccupations and beliefs in favour of ideological attachment to Marxism-Leninism. They were, on the contrary, expected to be willing to cooperate with social and economic change insofar, and only insofar, as they were convinced that change might benefit themselves. (Shue 1980: 326)

Mutual Aid Teams and cooperatives were not totally alien concepts to most Chinese peasants, for in several respects they were 'intrinsically very much akin to the traditional rural cooperative practices which had widespread existence in many parts of China [and especially in the rice regions] long before the advent of Communism' (Wong 1979b: 99). The course of land reform in China, the rise and fall of the communes and the recent rise of the 'responsibility system' are briefly described in appendix B.

In Vietnam, traditional communal institutions, retained even during the colonial period, resumed much of their former significance as the Vietminh established their political dominance, even before the formal passing of the Land Reform Law in December 1953 (Fforde 1983: 46; Moise 1983). In fact in the rural areas under Vietminh control, a large proportion of land was reallocated before the Land Reform Law was passed, between 1945 and 1953 (Fforde 1984: 10).

Cooperativisation occurred in 1959–60. It appears that coercion was generally absent, and the rapid movement of peasants into 'lower-level' producer cooperatives resulted from perceptions of the balance of material benefits and costs. The steady trends from then until the 1970s were for, first, a transition from 'lower-level' to 'higher-level' cooperatives (this was largely completed by the late 1960s) and, second, an amalgamation of cooperatives. Whereas the earliest cooperatives were well below commune level, with an average membership of ca. 50 families, by the late 1970s the clear target was to have cooperatives coterminous with communes. By that time a typical commune would possess around 250–350 ha of wet-rice land and ca. 5,000 families. Agriculture remained dominated by rice monoculture. Such strikingly high population densities were permitted by the adoption of double rice-cropping and the growing of a third crop of non-rice staples where and when possible. (ibid.: 11)

But as in China collective agriculture on the commune scale presented numerous problems, and it seems that by the mid-1970s, despite a reaffirmation by the central government of its commitment to the collectivist principle, most communes' Management Committees were largely non-functional. Such collective economic activity as there was, was controlled by the work brigades (ibid.: 14). By the late 1970s it was clear that the communes were performing well below expectation, and at the 6th Plenum of August 1979 a fundamental change in policy took place. Agricultural production was to be organised through 'output contracts' signed between cooperatives and their member households, a system similar in almost every respect to the Chinese 'responsibility system' which emerged at almost the same time:

[The output contracts] effectively gave an area of land to the [cooperator] in return for a fixed delivery of output to the cooperative. Collective control was maintained by the stipulation that certain parts of the production process (water supply, pest control, etc.) should be the responsibility of the cooperative. The rest, including most importantly the harvest, were to be carried out by the cooperator. (ibid.: 17)

In Vietnam, as in China, the new policy seems to be a *post facto* official recognition of a grass-roots movement. In both countries there has been a striking increase in agricultural output as a result of the reorganisation of production.

In his 1967 analysis of the economics of Asian agriculture, Ishikawa made what seems at first sight a paradoxical suggestion that one should

treat collective farm agriculture as a variant of peasant agriculture. This is because the present form of collective farm in Mainland China is still substantially a cooperative of individual peasant farms, and the technical foundation of these collective farms does not seem to have changed fundamentally from that in the peasant farm agriculture. (1967: 19)

Recent events bear out Ishikawa's view; nevertheless the role of communal organisation in such aspects of rice production as water control and the use of machinery remains essential. It may be that the current emphasis on the farming household as the basic production unit will shift back to higher levels of organisation in the future, as the balance shifts towards economic diversification, with consequent pressures (as in Japan and Taiwan) to increase the productivity of labour in rice-farming.

Once rice cultivation techniques reach a certain level of intensification, the family farm comes to predominate as the basic unit of production. It shows a remarkable historical resilience: in China family rice-farms gradually ousted other forms of organisation in medieval times, served as a basis for a flourishing and diverse economy for several centuries, and survived not only the demographic pressures and economic deterioration of the period from 1800 to 1949 but also the rise and fall of the People's Communes. In the other countries of monsoon Asia too, the household farm has persisted as the basic unit of agricultural production despite significant changes in other levels of economic and productive relations: the rise of advanced socialism in China and Vietnam, and of advanced capitalism in Japan. The persistence of this form of production in the face of significant historical change can largely be accounted for by the 'skill-oriented' nature of rice-growing technology, but it is not by any means unique to Asia's rice economies. It is a common feature of most agricultural systems where the intensification of labour use is the principal means of increasing output, for instance those of Mediterranean Europe (Duby 1962; Zangheri 1969; Mottura and Pugliese 1980).

At the same time there is in wet-rice agriculture an essential tension, a dialectical relation, between the individual and the community, imposed by the technical requirements of intensive rice cultivation, and the balance between the two is constantly shifting. It seems that the commune is too large for the satisfactory management of rice production, but at the same time the individual family farm is too small to stand alone. Looking at recent development, one might almost speak of a convergence between forms of management in East Asia's socialist and capitalist nations, towards dual-level management.

By combining individual access to land with the sharing of water and of capital resources, the productivity of rice-farming can be increased to levels where it provides a secure basis for economic diversification and rural growth, even where pressure on land is high and average farm sizes small. It is not the ownership of land as such which permits such development, so much as access to land, and the guaranteed right to a fair proportion of its product. Unfortunately political conditions in most of Asia are not such as to allow of appropriate institutional change, nor are demographic trends likely to ease the acute pressure on land. In fact the conditions of tenancy will certainly deteriorate further, and the number of landless will continue to increase, although it is unlikely that capitalist farming and a true differentiation of the peasantry will result. In countries where the vast majority of the population is rural, policies of urban industrialisation can do little to improve the situation. Under such conditions, encouraging the development of rural-based, low-capital industries will not prove such a way to wealth as it has done in East Asia, but in the absence of political solutions it can at least provide more opportunities for marginal farmers and the landless to engage in profitable employment.

APPENDIX A:

The Western model

This commonly accepted model of agricultural development derives from the historical experience of Northwestern Europe (in particular the Netherlands and Britain where 'high farming', scientific methods and mechanisation made especially rapid progress) and of the grain-belts of the New World. In several respects it is a construct or an abstraction – there are those, for instance, who would question the very existence of 'capitalist farming' in Europe (e.g. Cooper 1978) – which amalgamates elements from different historical periods or geographic regions to form a coherent picture of increasing efficiency: the rationalisation of landholdings into large units of management goes hand in hand with the development of farm machinery, a reduction in the labour force and an increase in capital inputs (ranging from drainage systems to chemical fertilisers). Economies of scale are the keynote. The potency of this model's attraction can be seen from the alacrity with which it was adopted by the leaders of socialist states: communisation and tractorisation were accepted as the *sine qua non* of modern agriculture.[1]

If we look more closely at some of the factors which affected agricultural development in Europe, it is apparent that the path followed was closely related to the conditions of production specific to this region. Northern Europe has a short growing season, and the staple cereals, wheat, barley and rye, bear heads with relatively few grains – at best a few dozen, compared with the hundred or more grains in a panicle of rice or millet – and often a single head on each plant. This may seem a trivial point, but it affects yields and means that a much higher proportion of the harvested crop must be kept for seed-grain.[2] The climate of Northern Europe does not permit more intensive cultivation than three grain crops in two years, but even this is a very recent development which depends on the use of fertilisers and scientific crop rotations. Before the seventeenth century the commonest method of fertilising grain-fields was to pasture livestock on the fallows; thus corn could only be grown one year in every two or three.[3] Under these conditions, the farming system of North Europe used land extensively and could not support high population densities. The size of a family subsistence holding was necessarily large: a feudal manse in the ninth century was often as big as 40 hectares (Slicher van Bath 1963: 42; Mukhia 1981: 278).

Livestock played a crucial role in this farming system. First they were the chief source of manure, and the right to fold the village flocks on one's fallow was hotly contested in medieval times.[4] Since yields were so low, draught animals were essential, for it was impossible to till sufficient land for subsistence by manpower alone. Though in some regions plough-teams consisted only of a pair or two of oxen, in heavier soils between eight and a dozen oxen might be needed for a team, and records from the French imperial estates in Carolingian times show that from an early date feudal landholders relied on their villeins to supply not only manpower but also a large proportion of the animal traction necessary for working the demesne (Duby 1962: 206; Slicher van Bath 1963: 67).

In the absence of scientific crop-breeding methods and inorganic fertilisers there was little scope for improving the productivity of land. '[This] could only be achieved in unusually favourable circumstances, namely, when the land could be more heavily manured or more cattle could be kept than was usual on the average farm. If cattle and manure were lacking, the possibility of increased production was practically non-existent' (Slicher van Bath 1963: 18). One way of increasing yields, provided draught animals were available, was simply to bring more land under the plough. A great deal of new land was cleared and brought under cultivation in the eleventh and twelfth centuries as population pressures increased, though it has been suggested that much of it had to be abandoned after a few decades as its fertility was rapidly exhausted (Bloch 1931; Abel 1935; Duby 1962; Neveux 1975). Improved farming techniques, also dependent upon increased use of human and animal labour, were an important factor in raising and maintaining land productivity: several ploughings and careful harrowing could improve germination rates and keep down weeds, contributing to higher yields and permitting the fields to be cropped more frequently. Modifications in both bovine and equine harness, which started to gain currency in Europe in the ninth and tenth centuries (Chaunu 1979), may have contributed to improved farming practice, facilitating, for example, the replacement of the light scratch-plough or ard by the heavy but more efficacious mouldboard plough. It appears that the admittedly slight increase in grain yields between the ninth and thirteenth centuries was largely due to such factors as a more intensive working of the soil (Duby 1962: 193).

Where draught animals and heavy equipment like turn-ploughs and harrows play such a crucial role in agricultural production, it is clear that large farms, which can afford more animals and equipment and can organise their use more efficiently, will have a significant advantage over small holdings. Generally speaking, the larger the farm in medieval Europe, the more likely it was to produce a surplus. Manorial demesnes had varied enormously in size, the area of arable land varying from as little as 5 hectares to as much as 250 hectares (Slicher van Bath 1963: 44). But by the twelfth or thirteenth century urbanisation was providing an expanding market for agricultural produce, and many territorial lords, conscious that large consolidated estates were more profitable and easier to manage than scattered smallholdings, had begun to 'withdraw their demesne land from the village farms, to consolidate, enclose, and cultivate them in separate ownership' (Ernle 1972: 38). The transition to private ownership of land was directly related to the superior economic performance of large farms, for under feudal relations it was extremely difficult for the farmer to increase the quantity of land, or labour, at his disposal. By the twelfth and thirteenth centuries villeinage was dying out in many parts of Northern Europe: the peasants were freed from their feudal obligations but in many cases lost some or all of the land to which they had previously had hereditary rights, and were thus obliged to join the swelling ranks of wage-labourers.

The gulf between subsistence smallholders and successful farmers continued to grow throughout late medieval times. Rises in the price of land were, as one might expect, accompanied by increasing rates of tenancy, and the tenants that landlords preferred were not smallholders but well-to-do farmers who could afford to invest in animals and equipment, 'small capitalists' like the English yeomen, whose profit margins were higher and who could afford to pay decent rents (Duby 1962; Moore 1967). This was a period of land-hunger and widespread enclosures, during which many peasants found themselves unable to survive as independent farmers and were obliged to sell their labour.

Capitalist relations in agriculture were already apparent in many parts of Northwest Europe before the fifteenth century, by which time markets in both land and labour were well developed. Though agricultural technology was still at a primitive stage, the social relations necessary for the foundation of a 'modern', mechanised agriculture already obtained, even though the technical expertise was still lacking. Especially in the Netherlands and Britain, farming methods improved notably in the seventeenth and eighteenth centuries, and land productivity rose accordingly. As effective drainage, scientific crop rotations and other improvements characteristic of 'high farming' were adopted, farmers continued to add to the size of their holdings wherever possible (all the agricultural experts were agreed that only large farms were efficient), and the labour force required on individual farms increased correspondingly.[5]

Throughout its development, the dynamic of the agricultural system of Northwest Europe was the superior performance of large, centrally managed units of production. Under such conditions, an immediate consequence of the expansion of the forces of production was the polarisation of rural society into farmer-managers and wage-labourers. This also had implications for wider patterns of economic development: because very few rural labourers had land of their own, they constituted a relatively mobile labour force, large numbers of whom sought work in the towns, facilitating the development of urban-based industries. Although many of these began as small workshops, run almost like a family enterprise, there were no obstacles to recruiting extra labour and increasing the size of the enterprise, and of course it was in the more sizeable units that mechanisation and the Industrial Revolution had their roots:

Machinery can seldom be used with success to abridge the labour of an individual; more time would be lost on its construction than could be saved by its application. It is only really useful when it acts on great masses, when a single machine can assist the work of thousands . . . It is not called into use by a scarcity of men, but by the facility with which they may be brought to work in masses. (Ravenstone 1824, quoted in Marx 1976: I, 566)

Ever since the beginning of the 'Agricultural Revolution' in the seventeenth century, farmers in Northwest Europe had cherished the hope of substituting machines for at least part of their labour force, which as we mentioned earlier was relatively expensive during this period of conflicting claims for labour. But the agricultural tasks to be performed were complex, and the relatively simple skills of the early engineers were not adequate to the task. Many unsuccessful attempts were made to produce agricultural machines in the seventeenth and eighteenth centuries, and the need for such machines was felt more acutely as time passed. By the early nineteenth century engineers had at their disposal both the specialised materials and the expertise required to develop machines for agriculture (Fussell 1952). The first successful mechanical threshers came on the market in the 1830s, and agricultural labourers rioted all over England as they saw their livelihood threatened on a large scale (Hobsbawm and Rudé 1968). Reapers, combine-harvesters, mechanical drills and horse-hoes followed. By the 1960s the proportion of the British workforce involved in agriculture had dropped from its 1800 figure of over a quarter to nearer 3.5 per cent (Mitchell 1974: 660), and by 1970 it had dropped by a further quarter to 2.7 per cent (Fream 1977: xxxii).

APPENDIX B:

The historical experience of China

The case of Southern China illustrates some of the more general changes in the economy and in relations of production which may accompany the development of rice agriculture. The most striking period of development of Southern Chinese agriculture began in the Song dynasty (960–1279), when the government initiated a series of development policies so sweeping in scope and result that they may well be compared to the so-called 'Green Revolution' of contemporary Asia (Elvin 1973; Bray 1979). The economic centre of China had first begun to shift from the northern plains (where dry grains, millets and wheat, were the main crops) down to the Yangzi rice-growing region during the eighth and ninth centuries. Fear of the Khitan and other nomadic invaders drove thousands of peasants to abandon their land in the north, and by the Song dynasty the greater part of the population lived in the southern provinces.[1] The Chinese government was faced with the double problem of feeding an increased population on a greatly reduced area, and of maintaining large armies to protect its borders.[2]

It was clearly necessary to increase agricultural production in the southern provinces, and the government undertook a series of measures to improve farming methods and yields. One of the most famous was the introduction to the Yangzi Delta in 1012 of new varieties of quick-ripening rices from Champa in Vietnam (see chapter 1). This transformed production patterns, allowing double-cropping of rice or the alternation of summer rice and winter wheat. Seeds of the new varieties were distributed to farmers through the district *yamens*, and written instructions on their cultivation methods were circulated. These were presumably intended not for the peasants themselves, most of whom would be illiterate,[3] but for the Song equivalent of an agricultural extension officer: 'master farmers', *nong shi*, were local farmers chosen for their skill and experience to fill a minor official post which carried the duty of improving agricultural techniques in their village. They were to instruct their peers not only in new techniques such as improved sowing and fertilising methods or crop choices, but also in the organisation of mutual aid and so on. It was presumably these 'master farmers' who channelled to ordinary peasants the information contained in the agricultural books commissioned and printed on government order, which contained information on better cropping practices, new tools, machines, fertilisers and irrigation methods (*Wang Zhen nongshu*; Bray 1984: 55 ff). As well as providing information, seeds and often such infrastructural support as new irrigation networks, the Song government introduced financial incentives to invest in agricultural improvement, including loans to farmers at low interest rates, lower levels of taxation and tax rebates on newly reclaimed land (Golas 1980).

While the role of the government was crucial in stimulating agricultural development in Southern China in its initial stages, perhaps its chief success was the degree to which the rural population recognised the merits of the new technology and were willing to experiment and improve on their own initiative. There was some early resistance to innovation: for instance, some peasants objected to double-cropping because they feared the extra work involved would not be justified by the increase in yields, while landlords feared that it would erode the fertility of their soils; as more commercial fertilisers became available and varieties improved, these objections were silenced. Peasants bred locally new and improved varieties of rice and other crops, some of which travelled from hand to hand over vast distances. Landlord and lineage associations reclaimed lakeside marshes, building dyked and poldered fields, while land-hungry peasants opened up hillside terraces or migrated to the wide, fertile plains of the sparsely populated Middle Yangzi, taking with them improved seeds and advanced technology.

The Song 'Green Revolution' had its roots in the most populous, agriculturally and economically advanced areas of China, the Lower Yangzi provinces of Jiangsu and Zhejiang and the coastal province of Fujian. By the fourteenth century the changes had gained momentum and the new technology was spreading to less developed areas, until by the eighteenth century it had reached even such remote provinces as Yunnan in the far southwest.

The innovations brought about a rapid upsurge in agricultural productivity in Song China. Improved yields and the multi-cropping of staple grains produced unprecedented surpluses, and as a result it was possible for commercial cropping and rural industry to develop on a scale hitherto unknown. Rice was exchanged for charcoal, tea, oil, wine and other locally produced goods at the village markets which sprang up all over the country, while a vigorous national trade in these and other commodities permitted intensive regional specialisation (Shiba 1970; Elvin 1973). Suzhou, near Shanghai, had already become a centre of specialised silk production by the twelfth century, and the local farmers devoted themselves entirely to raising silkworms and producing silk thread; rice they bought on the market. Another important commercial crop was sugar, which was especially popular in Fujian, Sichuan and Guangdong; in certain areas of twelfth-century Sichuan as many as 40% of the peasants were engaged in growing sugar-cane (*Tangshuang pu*: 3a). Sugar had totally supplanted rice in several districts of Fujian by the fifteenth century, and was exported not only to other provinces of China but also throughout Southeast Asia (Rawski 1972: 48). Other commercial crops included tea, vegetables, fruit, timber, oil-seeds, dyes and fibre crops, bamboos and (after 1500) tobacco. These were almost invariably produced by peasant farmers, though some landlords did possess large orchards or plantations (Shiba 1970).

There was also a very marked increase in manufacturing, most of which took the form of 'cottage industries'. The farmer's wife had traditionally been responsible for spinning and weaving, not only for her family's use but also to pay that part of the tax dues which was levied in cloth. The silk industry in pre-Song times had been small and predominantly urban-based, under official control, but during the Song it expanded rapidly, especially in the southeastern provinces and Sichuan. Some areas specialised in rearing silkworms or growing mulberry leaves, others in weaving a particular type of silk cloth. Much of the weaving was done in peasant households: brokers provided the silk thread, paid the women for their work and marketed the cloth (Shiba 1970: 111). The cotton industry, which first became important in the fourteenth and fifteenth centuries, was run along similar lines: there was a national market for raw cotton, which peasant women bought from traders at local markets, span and wove, and then sold back again. Other industries included paper-making, the production of lacquer wares, metal goods, charcoal, and comestibles such as wines, spirits, bean-curd, sauces and pickles. Again, almost all production was on a household scale, and most of the producers were farming families.

It has already been pointed out that wet-rice cultivation is not, like the farming system of Northwest Europe, subject to economies of scale, nor does it respond positively to the centralisation of management. It is therefore not surprising to find that as new techniques were applied in China and land productivity rose, the position of tenants vis-à-vis their landlords improved: they acquired more managerial and economic independence, and tenurial contracts were modified in their favour.

There were no legal obstacles to the sale of land in medieval China, and when the Song improvements brought about an increase in the value of land, many wealthy people invested in landed property and large estates were amassed. But these were not the consolidated, centrally managed holdings with which we are familiar from post-feudal Europe: they were almost invariably subdivided into small parcels leased to peasant farmers. Although a few consolidated holdings were established in areas of low population density, even in the early Song widely dispersed estates were typical of areas such as the Yangzi Delta; by the end of the Song few consolidated holdings survived (Golas 1980: 304).

During the Southern Song (1127–1279) all three forms of rental agreement known in later periods, namely sharecropping, fixed rent in kind and fixed rent in cash, are known to have existed. Significantly sharecropping[4] seems already to have been in decline in Southern China: fixed rents paid in grain were common on the large dispersed estates of the Lower Yangzi, where supervision costs on sharecropping would have been disproportionately high (Golas 1980: 308; McDermott 1978: 208). By the fourteenth and fifteenth centuries tenants in Fujian and most other parts of Central and Southern China always paid their rents as a fixed quantity, and the landlord played no part at all, even supervisory, in the process of production (Rawski 1972: 18). As cultivation techniques became more complex and the supervision of tenants more onerous, landlords took less and less direct interest in the way their land was farmed, and tenants acquired rights to greater security of tenure or even, eventually, to permanent tenancy. So secure were the rights of tenants in fifteenth century Fujian that, on payment of a fee called 'manured soil money', *fei tu yin*, the tenant received transferable and negotiable cultivation rights over the topsoil, and could sub-let or sell his rights without the landlord's consent. This system of 'two owners of a single field', *yi tian liang zhu*, was common in many parts of China right up until 1949 (Fei 1939; Rawski 1972: 190). The tenant had very strong customary rights, and often the landlord could only raise rents if the tenant agreed. Permanent tenancy rights were widespread in China even during the poverty-stricken 1930s (Myers 1982: 40).

Through the centuries there were considerable fluctuations in the distribution of landholding in China, but generally the majority of holdings in the economically advanced rice areas were either those of medium landowners, averaging 6 hectares or so (a minute area compared with the advanced farms of eighteenth- or nineteenth-century Britain, or even the size of a feudal manse), or of smallholders or part-tenants. In the eleventh century the latter constituted over 50 per cent of the registered population of Southern China and held a quarter of the land

(Golas 1980: 303). In the seventeenth-century Yangzi Delta really large landowners were rare and probably three-quarters of the land was owned by medium landowners or smallholders (Huang 1974: 158). Though landlessness did occur, and became more frequent as population growth increased the pressure on land, most peasants eventually acquired access to land at least as a tenant, and under the system of fixed rents, skilled tenant farmers could hope to save enough to buy some land of their own (Myers 1982). Fei (1939: 177) reports that even in a crowded twentieth-century village near Shanghai he met no one who had been landless all his life. Thus there was no proletarianisation of labour, and the basic unit of production remained the family smallholding.

The expansion of agricultural production appears to have kept pace with population growth in China until about 1800 when, for a number of reasons, the situation began to deteriorate rapidly. Landlords were affected as well as tenants, who quite commonly withheld payment of rent temporarily or even permanently if harvests were bad. Absentee landlords had few institutional forms of redress against defaulting tenants in China; as a last resort they would hire bands of strongmen to recuperate the rents due to them. Moore (1967: 180) and Ash (1976: 43) see this simply as evidence of the ferocity of landlord exploitation, but it also offers proof of their financial desperation and their relative helplessness in the face of village solidarity.[5]

Significantly, even though landlessness increased under such conditions, the transition to capitalist relations of production, whereby landowners evict their tenants in order to run large, consolidated farms using cheap wage-labour, did not occur in China. In fact it can even be shown that despite the huge growth of the population and the rather small increase in arable land between 1700 and the 1930s, the land tenure situation did not worsen (Myers 1982: 43).

Land reform under the People's Republic first took the form of simple redistribution: land, livestock and other capital assets were taken from the landlords and 'rich peasants' and redistributed among the 'middle' and 'lower peasants'. There were no absolute criteria for these categorisations, but in general 'rich peasants' had more land than they could cultivate with family labour alone and so they hired extra hands, 'middle peasants' worked their land themselves, and poor peasants had little or no land and had to hire out their labour. According to surveys made in the 1930s, full tenancy was not very widespread in the northern provinces, and was most widespread in the rice-growing regions of the centre, east and southeast (Myers 1982: 40). But even in the rice regions poor peasants in fact benefited only marginally from land reform since the amount of resources available for redistribution, that is to say owned by landlords and rich peasants, in fact formed a relatively small proportion of the land and a very small proportion of the other capital assets (Wong 1973). It was only with collectivisation that the gap between poor and middle peasants was closed.

In the twenty years following the formation of the People's Communes in 1958–9, while wheat production rose by 180%, rice production rose by only 107%.[6] Wong argues that while the Mutual Aid Teams (which derived from pre-existing peasants' cooperative organisations and were the first stage in the process of collectivisation) were the optimally sized unit for efficient agricultural production and decision-making, the Agricultural Producers' Cooperatives (the second stage in collectivisation) 'had clearly reached the limit of an optimum size beyond which productivity growth could not be further increased . . . It can thus be seen that the decision to collectivise Chinese agriculture could only be rationalised on macroeconomic and ideological grounds!' (1982: 6). It is perhaps significant that Wong's studies were carried out in Guangdong, a region of rice multi-cropping.

In regions such as Manchuria, the large-scale mechanisation of wheat and maize production permitted by the reorganisation of land use has proved successful. But the chief advantage offered by the reorganisation of agriculture in rice-growing areas lay not so much in land consolidation or mechanisation as in the communal purchase of electric or diesel pumps for water control. One of the advantages is that while these pumps free humans and animals from the concentrated drudgery of irrigation work, they also often increase the frequency of cropping and the area of irrigated land, thus absorbing labour more evenly over the year rather than simply displacing it (T. Rawski 1979: 85).

But this particular advance in irrigation technology corresponds to a rather low level of social organisation, namely , the brigade or commune. Where major irrigation networks are concerned the improvements have often been rather minor, largely because the responsibility for organising water control is decentralised, and competition for the scarce resource between communes, districts and even provinces has continued unabated (Gustaffson 1984: 129). So much for Wittfogel's notions of the all-embracing powers devolving to the centralised, totalitarian state. The latest shift towards decollectivisation under the 'responsibility system' is, not surprisingly, proving particularly advantageous in areas where intensive rice cultivation is combined with the production of commercial crops or livestock (Dumont 1984).

The recent liberalisation of agricultural production under the 'responsibility system', combined with large increases in prices for agricultural products, rapidly led to an impressive increase in crop production (see chapter 5), and to greater diversification into the cultivation of industrial and other economic crops, and rural industrialisation (see chapter 4). There has been a significant and welcome reduction in the gap between urban and rural incomes as a result. A new problem is now surfacing, however. During the sixties and early seventies 'grain was taken as the key link' and regional self-sufficiency was given priority, a policy which often resulted in inefficient use of local resources and reduced yields even of food-grains. Now the low price of food-grains relative to other agricultural products has led many peasants to reduce the proportion of their plots used for grain to the strict minimum required to fulfil the official quota, and there are fears in some quarters that this will eventually lead to national grain shortages. At a special conference of the Chinese Communist Party held in mid-September 1985, the veteran economic planner Chen Yun complained: 'Some peasants are no longer interested in growing grain. They are not even interested in raising pigs and vegetables because in their opinion there can be no prosperity without engaging in industry' (Bonavia and Lee 1985).

APPENDIX C:

The Japanese experience

An interesting example of the way in which a long-established tradition of rice-cultivation can affect economic patterns is to be found in Japan. It has often been claimed that Japan is the unique example of an Asian state which has followed the European path from feudalism to industrial capitalism. As Japan was the first, and for a long time the only Asian nation to threaten Western domination of the world market in manufactured goods, it is not surprising that many people have tried to explain Japan's success in terms of its basic similarity to Europe. It has even been suggested that over the two centuries leading up to Japan's early phase of modernisation, tenurial relations underwent basically similar changes to those which preceded the Industrial Revolution in England (Yamamura 1979), though since farms, that is units of management, became generally larger in England as they became smaller in Japan, one might question exactly where the similarity lies. But many Japanese economists, equally familiar with their own economy and with those of neighbouring East and Southeast Asian countries (which once formed part of the 'Greater Co-Prosperity Sphere' and now are seen as crucial trading partners), see significant parallels not between Japan and Europe but between the rice-growing economies of this region. Agriculture in these countries uses both land and labour intensively, and many of their common problems derive from this fact. In the case of Japan the problems have been encapsulated in the term *shōnōsei*, 'smallholder system', which is regarded by many Japanese today as a burdensome relic of an agrarian past which they believe to have been significantly shaped by the development of irrigated rice cultivation.

Tokugawa Japan underwent an agricultural and economic expansion in many respects similar to that of Song China, indeed many agricultural innovations were probably based on Chinese precedent (Furushima 1963). In an effort to consolidate their power and increase their revenues, the first Tokugawa rulers organised cadastral surveys to tighten their control over the land-tax, and encouraged agricultural development and the expansion of manufacturing. They opened up communications networks and promoted agricultural innovation as well as the development of industry and commerce, promulgating edicts urging the peasants to work harder, drink less, engage in handicrafts and so on. Treatises on improved farming methods were published, such as the *Nōgyō Zensho* of 1697 and the later *Nōgu Benri Ron*; these were based on their authors' wide experience and intensive practical research in Japan itself, though their debt to the great Chinese treatises is immediately apparent. These works were widely read by Japanese farmers, some of who went on to write their own agricultural tracts.

In Japan, before the agricultural improvements and commercial development of the Tokugawa period (1600–1868), rural society consisted of landowning families and various categories of bondsmen. Some (the *genin*) were hereditary or indentured servants who lived with the landowner's family, but the majority were in a category more akin to the serfs of medieval Europe. These serfs had a number of regional names, the most common being *nago* (Smith 1959: ch. 5). The *nago* lived separately from the landowner but depended on him not only for land and loans of tools and animals, but often (since their allotments of land were small and unproductive) for food (Yamamura 1979: 285). The landowner's status vis-à-vis his *nago* was that of 'master', *oyakata*; he guaranteed their survival in return for labour services. *Nago* had only customary rights to their land (the landowner was legally responsible for paying the land-tax, though in fact a *nago* might be obliged to make the payment, in his landlord's name), and were thus not considered to be proper members of the village community. They had no rights to common land or water, and could not hold office or participate in the village assembly (Smith 1959: 10, 25).

But whereas Japanese peasants had previously produced rice chiefly to pay their taxes and feudal dues, and had themselves subsisted on the produce of their dryland fields (buckwheat and barley), the technical improvements under the Tokugawa allowed them to start to extend the cultivation of irrigated crops to produce rice both for their own consumption and for the market. The number of rice varieties increased dramatically; one record gives 177 names for rice in the early seventeenth century and 2,363 by the mid-nineteenth century, while a nineteenth-century agricultural diary states that between 1808 and 1866 the breeding of improved rice varieties permitted an extension of the growing period by 17 days (Smith 1959: 95). New irrigation works were built on official and private initiative, and new tools and fertilisers became widely available. As in Song China, there was a rapid increase in the production of commercial crops. Cotton-farming in the Kinai is perhaps the best-known example, but in the mountains of Honshū sericulture became important, and sugar-cane was widely grown in Kyūshū and the islands (Smith 1959; Furushima 1963; Hauser 1974).

As agriculture progressed in Tokugawa Japan, so too the economy expanded in other spheres. The basic unit of production, as in China, was the individual household, responsible for the management of its landholding and supplementing its income by cottage industries such as the weaving of silk or cotton, wine-brewing, or the manufacture of bean-curd or pickles. The rapid expansion of textile and other commodity production was based largely upon the increased participation of peasant families in manufacturing on a household scale. Some highly specialised industries, such as the silk-brocade manufactures of Kyōto, now found they had serious rivals in the villages, where labour costs were rated on a very different scale. As in medieval China, the scope for direct investment in production was severely restricted, but there were fortunes to be made as merchants or middlemen, providing the link between local producers and the national market. A class of village entrepreneurs emerged, capable of challenging their urban counterparts (Yamamura 1979: 291), but despite the rapid growth of petty commodity production and inter-regional trade there were few instances of what we should recognise as capitalist development either in manufacturing or in agriculture.

The expansion of the rural economy was accompanied by marked changes in relations of production. The social and legal status of the dependent rural classes improved rapidly. The servant classes decreased in number while the lower echelons of the landholding class grew, and tenants who had previously been obliged to provide their landlords with various free labour-services acquired a far greater measure of economic independence. With the expansion of agricultural production and the growth of non-agricultural sources of income, labour became a marketable commodity. Hereditary servants on the large feudal farms gradually acquired greater freedom, until at last the transition to wage labour was complete; under these conditions tenants too demanded payment for any work undertaken on the landlord's farm.

The increase in labour costs made the large holdings of the formerly privileged landowners uneconomic. They could no longer compete effectively with smallholdings for 'since the one type of holding was prone to buy and the other to sell labour, the competitive positions of the two as farming units . . . were drastically altered. Circumstances now favoured the family-size farm and strongly penalised any larger unit'

(Smith 1959: 125). But it was not merely the growth of a market in labour which led to the demise of the old feudal system. As Smith remarks (ibid.: 92), most technological innovations of the period tended to strengthen the solidarity of the household farm. Technical improvements in rice cultivation, being closely related to the intensification of skilled labour inputs, tended to increase the tenants' degree of independence from his landlord.

During the eighteenth century there was a shift from rents paid in kind to fixed cash rents, and throughout the nineteenth century rents actually fell (Yamamura 1979: 297). But despite falling rental shares landlords continued to lease their land to tenants, and their incomes 'tended to rise, because the total value of output was larger when tenant farmers worked the land than when hired labour cultivated commercial crops for the landholders' (ibid.: 298). The gradual improvement of tenant status continued in Japan through the nineteenth and early twentieth centuries, when landlords found to their dismay that their investments in irrigation and other improvements, by increasing their tenants' financial security, brought them not more but less respect and influence in the village (Waswo 1977).

The *shōnōsei* tradition of family farming made many Western innovations in agriculture quite unsuitable for adoption in Japan. In the late nineteenth century, the period of the Meiji Restoration, Western agronomy and agricultural technology were greatly admired in Japan: officials and students were sent abroad to study, and foreigners were hired as advisers by the newly established Ministry of Agriculture. Many Western breeding techniques and some new crop varieties proved successful and were widely adopted, but Western machinery and farming methods often proved quite unsuitable. After 1880 the government decided to emphasise 'improvements within the framework of Japanese agriculture, by developing new strains of traditional crops, and by diffusing more widely the best practices of particular [Japanese] regions' (Dore 1969: 99). It was not simply that peasant farmers were incapable of adapting to the new Western technology, rather, Western technology and centralisation of management, though appropriate to capitalist farming, were fundamentally unsuited to wet-rice production. A number of capitalist entrepreneurs set up as farmers in Japan in the late nineteenth century, and those who ran livestock farms or grew industrial crops often prospered – indeed wealthy farmers producing industrial crops on large farms, using wage-labour drawn from neighbouring rice-farms, were not uncommon even in the eighteenth century (Yamamura 1979: 299) – but capitalist entrepreneurs who set up in rice-farming invariably failed (Dore 1969: 110).

In Meiji Japan the resident, cultivating landlords (*tezukuri jinushi*) were often instrumental in improving the agricultural methods of their tenants. These well-educated farmers were in the vanguard of technological advance (Waswo 1977: 33, 38). Francks argues that one reason for the success of the *tezukuri jinushi* was 'a function of their role as village leaders, hence their contact with the outside world and their participation in and leadership of agricultural societies, discussion groups and so on . . . the need for access to such non-market information sources was characteristic of the new technology of this period' (1983: 66). But their role as village leaders also enabled them to improve their tenants' performance as well as their own:

> It was an accepted part of the landlords' role that they supervise their tenants' farming – as an old saying put it: 'The trail made by landlords [through their tenants' fields] is the best fertiliser yet devised'. Given the authority landlords possessed, simply commanding their tenants to change farming techniques was often sufficient. Where innovations required greater labour or involved some degree of risk, however, economic incentives were important. A landlord in Gifu Prefecture promised to cover all losses if the advice he gave his tenants on ways to increase yields proved unsuccessful. Others gave prizes of money or tools to tenants who produced superior crops. (Waswo 1977: 39)

These landlords were active members of the local community, farming part of their land but renting the rest to tenants with whose methods they were intimately familiar and over whom they exerted both social and economic influence, such tenurial relations being quite typical of intensive rice cultivation. But although their role as instigators of technical change brought them immediate financial rewards in the form of increased rents, in the long run it undermined their position in rural society: the increased security experienced by tenants as a result of the innovations reduced their economic dependence upon their landlords, who thus lost much of their influence (Waswo 1977: 5).

But the Japanese government was ready to take over the responsibility of promoting innovation among small farmers. For this it relied not only on trained extension officers but also sometimes on police enforcement. Farmers in Japan and the Japanese colonies resented what Japanese historians sometimes refer to as (in allusion to Frederick the Great) as 'extension by the sabre method', and clashes with agricultural officials or with the police were frequent, but in general the ingrained respect of peasants for their superiors prevailed: 'the incidence of compliant submission [can] be inferred from the fact that the improvements recommended did in fact become standard practice' (Dore 1969: 104).

An official report of 1910 stated that tenancy in Japan was then on the increase, and that in 1908 full-and part-tenants together constituted

66% of all farmers (Ag. Bureau 1910: 9). Increasing landlordism was in part a response to the Meiji tax reforms of 1870 which fixed land taxes at about 9% of the gross value of the land (Nakamura 1966: 160). While tenants' incomes were largely unaffected, landlords' incomes rose, and their profits were mostly invested outside agriculture in, for example, the national banks or in government bonds.

It had always been felt by Japanese statesmen that fostering agriculture was not only to the economic benefit of the state but also to its political and moral advantage. In the Meiji period these beliefs were encapsulated in the philosophy of *Nōhon shugi* (literally 'agrarian fundamentalism'): 'The principal *Nōhon shugi* beliefs included a faith in agricultural economics, an affirmation of rural communalism, and a conviction that farming was indispensable to those qualities that made the nation unique' (Havens 1974: 8). 'The ethics textbooks used in the national school system after November 1936 conferred official recognition on agrarianism as a major source of civic virtue' (ibid.: 11). In its official, bureaucratic form, *Nōhon shugi* justified a number of government programmes intended to improve agricultural productivity as a necessary part of industrial expansion. These programmes generally kept rice prices low and did not contribute to the well-being of tenants, but they held a great appeal for landowners.

Conditions for tenants and smallholders gradually deteriorated as Japan invested ever more resources in industrialisation, and their plight grew especially serious after the great crash of 1929; popular forms of *Nōhon shugi* took on anti-establishment overtones and led to several political incidents. Throughout the 1920s and 1930s landlord-tenant relations grew steadily worse, but no attempts at legislation to improve the position of tenants could be effective, for the political role of the landlord class was much too strong (Ogura 1967). A successful policy for defusing popular resentment was found in the state-supported schemes for the agricultural colonisation of Manchuria, introduced in the 1930s under the ideological influence of a private schoolmaster, Katō Kanji, whose nationalistic and expansionist ideas managed to fuse popular and bureaucratic *Nōhon shugi* (Havens 1974: 11). The colonisation of Manchuria was a crucial element in Japan's preparations for war.

By the end of the war Japan's economy was in ruins. In 1945, 46% of Japan's farmland was cultivated by tenants, most of whom were then on the brink of starvation. General MacArthur, the chief of the American occupation forces, was determined to reconstruct Japan as a healthy democracy, and the political opposition of the landlord class cut no ice with him. In 1945 the Americans set in motion Japan's First Land Reform. This provided that any farmland exceeding 5 ha leased by a resident landlord, and all farmland leased by an absentee landlord, should be surrendered to the tenants at the latters' request within five years; that the system of rent in kind should be completely replaced with that of rent in cash; and that contracts could not be cancelled without the approval of the Agricultural Land Commission. Adjustments were made in 1946 during the Second Land Reform which went still further: the government was to buy up all absentee landlords' land and all resident landlords' land over 1 ha (4 ha in Hokkaido), which was to be sold to tenant farmers within two years of the promulgation of the law. It is estimated that 80% of tenanted land, totalling 2 million ha, fell under this provision (Ogura 1967: 145). By 1950 tenancy had fallen to 10%, and continued to fall thereafter (ibid.: 70), since the reform relieved former tenants of the heavy burden of rent which had hampered capital accumulation and limited agricultural diversification and the growth of commodity production.

Independent smallholding was thus institutionalised in Japan.[1] Since the 1950s, sustained by heavy government investment in irrigation, R & D and other development programmes, and more particularly by the rice price support policies mentioned in chapter 5, Japanese rice-farming technology has advanced steadily and has now reached the stage of integral mechanisation (see chapter 2). Increased rice yields have provided farmers with the financial basis for the successful diversification of agricultural production, and they have become increasingly prosperous. Although a large part of their income is derived from other economic activities, to the point where many of them have become part-time farmers,[2] they have not abandoned or converted their rice-fields: apart from their deep-rooted emotional attachment to rice-farming (Shimpo 1976: 45), rice production is heavily subsidised and continues to be lucrative, to the farmers, if not to the national economy. In some regions rice-farming is still expanding (ibid.: xxvi).

Compared to most other Asian nations Japan's development of agriculture appears outstandingly successful, and indeed has often been invoked as a model. But it is not without its problems. The economic inefficiencies of over-investment in capital goods, especially machinery, have been mentioned in chapters 2 and 5; rice production is at present only economically viable on farms where the rice area exceeds 1 ha (Matsuda 1982: 449). Given the increasingly heavy dependence of Japanese farmers on expensive machinery, Shimpo (1976: ch. 5) sees as a solution either the concentration of holdings into 'American-style' large, mechanised farms, or the survival of family farms owning machinery in common and working together as 'cooperative villages'.

Farmers' organisations for the joint use of machinery became common in the 1960s and are still in existence today. But the increase in part-time farming has caused organisational problems within these groups, as well as making it difficult for many farms to manage with family labour alone. For instance in the Yamaguchi City area in 1975, of 5,925 farmers all but 520 were part-time (Morio 1982). Such circumstances provide an opportunity for small groups of four or five what one might call 'professional farmers' to offer their services as contract farmers. They jointly hire or purchase larger-scale machinery and contract individually to other farmers for various stages of rice production, hoping eventually to contract for the full process, in which case they will have complete control of management over the land in question. Such organisations are described by Morio as being highly profit-oriented. But although from 1972 to 1976 the number of contract farming groups increased nationwide from 2,481 to 3,493, and in Yamaguchi from 42 to 58, the area of land under full contract was not large: in the organisation studied by Morio the four individual members had full contracts on only 11.0 ha of rice-land by 1978, a figure which had fluctuated continuously over the previous five years (Morio 1982: table 5).

Another serious problem is that heavy subsidies have resulted in overproduction of rice and constitute a heavy financial burden to the government, which is in no position to alienate the farming lobby. Many observers feel that Japanese agriculture faces a bleak future, having reached the limits of development. Many economists believe that the present organisation of rice production should be changed and greater emphasis given to diversification, for example into wheat and animal husbandry. The influential agricultural economist and adviser Ogura sees a reform of the agricultural structure as the only hope for survival, short of the disbanding of smallholder farming through government purchase. In the Japanese tradition, Ogura believes that 'the marriage of man and land is spiritually essential for the existence of a nation' (1980: 587). He feels that the necessary agrarian reforms should have as their objectives not only a higher degree of self-sufficiency in all foods, but also a reduction in the gap between rural and urban incomes, increased social justice and the strengthening of grass-roots organisations. The policies adopted should aim to foster viable family farms and cooperation between them, in part through legal reforms to ensure the inheritance of land by a single person (ibid.: 596–642).

The chief problems of Japanese agriculture today seem largely to be caused through Japanese farmers' reluctance to abandon growing rice. It was through the development of rice that Japan was able to achieve rapid industrialisation and spectacular growth in all sectors. Has rice-farming now outlived its usefulness?

Notes

Chapter 1   The rice-plant: diversity and intensification

1 There are two families of domesticated rice, the African rices (*Oryza glaberrima* L.) and the Asian rices (*Oryza sativa*), but the African rices are not cultivated outside that continent. Although the African and Asian rices are generally supposed to derive from a common ancestor (Chang 1976a), African rices had no influence on the development of the Asian species and so will not be discussed further.

2 In the People's Republic of China in 1977, 45% of the total food-grain production was rice and 14% was wheat (Barker, Sisler and Rose 1982: 166). The total figure also includes coarse grains such as millets, sorghum and barley, pulses, soybeans, tubers and maize, some of which would be used as animal feed rather than directly for human consumption.

3 More detailed treatment is given in Chang (1976a) and Bray (1984: 481–7); Bray (1984: 29–47) discusses the possible causes and processes of plant domestication, especially as they apply to East and Southeast Asia.

4 There are, however, many difficulties associated with these dates (Reed 1977: 911–17; Muhly 1981: 134).

5 The names of rice in the ancient Southern Chinese Wu language (*i'nuân*), in Annamese (*n'êp*), Cham (*ñióp*), Sedang (*ñ'ian*) and Japanese (*ine*) are all closely related phonetically (Sasaki 1971: 288), indicating a common origin. In his study of Austro-Thai words in Chinese, Benedict (1967: 316) notes that they include a number of terms for rice, including cooked rice, as well as words associated with rice cultivation such as plough, pestle and mortar, seed, sow and winnow. Benedict and several other Western scholars suggest that the Thai originally came from the region of the Yangzi Delta and migrated south and west, but Chinese ethnographers believe that they originated in the border region of Yunnan, North Thailand and Burma.

6 The date of transition from the earliest Japanese neolithic culture, the Jōmon, to the Yayoi is usually put at about 300 BC to coincide with a transition in pottery styles. However it has been suggested (Sahara, forthcoming) that a better criterion than pottery styles would be the transition from a hunter-gathering economy to food production.

7 Wild species of rice 'include the 18 wild-growing taxa in the genus *Oryza* which can be considered as valid species . . . Because of human disturbances of their adapted habitats, many wild forms have receded from cultivated sites. Some wild species are rapidly becoming extinct' (Chang 1976b: 5).

8 Grist (1975: 101) describes some of the more useful classification systems based on morphology and other criteria.

9 The process of differentiation between *indica* and *japonica* rices is still not clearly understood; see Oka (1975a: 25), Bray (1984: 488) for an account of the literature.

10 These figures are taken from Grist (1975: 451); Whyte (1974: 38) gives slightly lower figures.

11 But it is interesting to note that while rice consumption is increasing in popularity outside Asia, in many Asian countries wheat products such as bread are now considered higher-status foods and are beginning to replace rice as the staple among well-to-do members of the population.

12 In countries like Japan, China, Taiwan and Korea, where rice-farming methods are very intensive, the gap is even wider; see Ishikawa (1967: 70, table 2–2).

Chapter 2   Paths of technical development

1 The most famous examples are probably the rice-terraces of Bali, the stone-walled terraces of Peru in which the Incas grew irrigated maize, the serried rows of the Ifugao terraces in Northern Luzon in the Philippines, and the terraced rice-fields of Southern China. But agricultural terracing is also to be found throughout Latin America, around the Mediterranean, in the Middle East, the Himalayan kingdoms, hilly regions of South and Southeast Asia, Japan, Korea and many parts of Africa. There are irrigated and dry terraces, terraces for growing rice, maize, millets, potatoes and beans, shallow and steep terraces, stone-buttressed and earth-walled terraces, in fact terraces of every kind.

2 See Bray (1984: 124) for a summary of the major arguments, diffusionist or otherwise.

3 The floating fields of Lake Dal in Kashmir and of the Mexican lakes are generally used for growing vegetables rather than cereals.

4 Chen (1977), referring to Chinese works of the second and third centuries BC, affirms that transplanting in China must have begun even earlier.

Chapter 3   Water control

1 There is a widely held view that Japanese agriculture 'took off' from relatively low levels of production during the Meiji period. Ogura estimates that rice production doubled, from 3.75 million tons to 7.8 million between 1868 and 1912 (1980: 147), while Ohkawa and Rosovsky (1960) calculate that the agricultural growth rate during the same period was as high as 2.3% per annum. However study of the preceding Tokugawa period shows that

between the 1680s and the 1879s rice yields rose from 1.3 to 1.6 *koku/tan* (from about 2.5 to 3 t/ha), i.e. by about 23% (Nakamura 1966: 137), while the early Meiji statistics on land acreage and productivity, compiled for tax puposes, were recognised by the Meiji officials themselves to be underestimated; in fact a growth rate of 0.8–1.2% per annum for the Meiji period seems more realistic (ibid.). Government statistics also show that between 1920 and 1960, while agricultural output did increase significantly in some regions (i.e. by about 30% in Tōhoku), in other areas progress was very slight (nearer 7% in Kinki and Kyūshū) (Tsuchiya 1976: 46–55).

2 The fact that the Chinese national average yield in the 1930s was still only 2.74 t/ha (Ishikawa 1967: 77; see also Amano 1954: 87), and thus had hardly risen since a thousand years previously, does seem to confirm that modern scientifically developed inputs are necessary to raise productivity above the first landmark. However we must bear in mind that (i) considerable regional and temporal fluctuations occurred in China over the period, the Song and early Ming being a period of rather generalised economic expansion, the late Ming one of decline, the nineteenth century one of severe depression; and therefore (ii) agricultural conditions in China in the 1920s and 1930s were not necessarily representative of the highest technical and economic levels achieved.

3 The literature is too vast to attempt to list it fully. One of the earliest and most circumstantial attacks on Wittfogel's equation between irrigation and centralised political control is to be found in Leach (1961). An excellent critique of the Chinese case is in Eberhard (1965: 74 ff). A more recent evaluation of the debate is in Steward (1980).

4 See Stargardt (1983: 196) on Burma under Pagan rule; the rate there increased in times of war. In many important cases such as Angkorian Cambodia, no record of the level of taxation has survived (Sahai 1970: 113 ff). Thirteenth century documents from South India show that there the water-taxes increased progressively for up to three or four years after construction was completed, as productivity gradually rose; thereafter they were reduced, but as they were proportional to the crop harvested, the overall revenue was still augmented (Venkayya 1906).

5 And also very ancient in origin; it is used in the *Lüshi chunqiu*, a Chinese work of political economy dating from 239 BC.

6 The spectacular nature of such works as the Yellow River dykes in the North China Plain, representing centuries of unremitting struggle and a vast expense of human labour and technical resources, has – together with some impressive instances of state-organised irrigation and drainage which we shall discuss below – provided much of the raw material for theories of 'hydraulic bureaucracies' and 'Oriental despotism'.

7 For much more sophisticated and comprehensive treatment of the climatic, topographic, hydrological and other technical factors involved, see such works as Vaidyanathan (1983), Stargardt (1983), or Gustafsson (1984). Spencer (1974) gives a clear and helpful list of the twenty different techniques of water control known to him from Southeast Asia. The usual

Japanese classification distinguished three main forms of irrigation in Japan: 'river irrigation' (gravity-flow branching canals with intakes along rivers), 'pond irrigation' (canal networks from storage ponds typically fed by hillside run-off and/or off-season diversion from rivers), and 'creek irrigation' (networks of improved natural ditches in the few flat deltas of Japan) (Kelly 1982a: 29). Nishiyama (1959) has applied the same three categories to China: 'river irrigation' he says was confined to the Yellow River system in the north, but in Central China 'pond irrigation' was common, while the flat and swampy lands of the Lower Yangzi relied on a system of drainage and irrigation akin to 'creek irrigation'. This classification, however, does not cover various types of irrigation found in South China, nor those typical of Southeast Asia. Ishikawa (1981) proposes an interesting classification of Asian agricultural systems based on water use rather than water control.

8 The following account is based on Groslier (1974, 1979). The Khmers had conquered the Funanese and taken over the northern plains of Cambodia in the late sixth century, but moved their capital to Angkor only in c.800. As we shall see, the form of the Cambodian 'hydraulic city', as well as its siting in the centre of the empire, was of great religious significance.

9 Nakamura (1982) points out, however, that the supplementary water provided by local storage systems is not always sufficient, at least in South India and Sri Lanka, to provide for widespread irrigated cropping, though it does provide a buffer against rainfall deficits.

10 Most of the titles of irrigation officers recorded in the inscriptions of the Javanese kingdoms of Kediri (1078–1222) and Majapahit (1293-c.1520) are non-Sanskritic, which points to very early origins (van Setten 1979: 60 ff).

11 Stargardt (1983: 270, n. 64) points out that epigraphic and manuscript sources provide striking similarities between the respective roles of royal officers and village organisations in South India, Burma and Bali.

12 The leaves of both these trees are used to feed silkworms. Here we have a good example of the diversification possible within an economy based on wet-rice cultivation; the author was writing of the Lower Yangzi during a period of rapid commercialisation and growth.

13 This passage comes from the Chinese work *Huainanzi* of about 120 BC, quoted in Wuhan 1979: 144.

14 But only the small duck-ponds are privately owned by individual households; the irrigation ponds, like irrigation channels, belong to the Irrigation Authority (i.e. the state) which allocates water rights in return for fees calculated on the basis of the amount of land owned (ibid.: 54).

15 In certain parts of Java, however, it seems that the old *mancapat* system has been revived for the purpose of solving problems attendant upon contemporary developments in irrigation (van Setten 1979: 58).

16 A common irrigation device throughout East and Southeast Asia. Their use in Chinese hydraulic works is described in Needham (1971: 293–5).

17 This account is based on a course of seminars given at the Collège de France in 1980–1 by M. Lucien Bernot.

18 The Japanese term; Taylor (1981: 27) calls it 'controlled drainage irrigation'.

19 The Chinese government took an active role in land clearance and reclamation throughout the imperial era. Settlement schemes were usually in border areas or underpopulated regions. Whether military or civilian, they had an important dual function: first, an influx of Chinese settlers into areas whose political allegiance was often uncertain had a stabilising effect; and second, the new agricultural colonies served as overspill areas for refugees and landless peasants from areas of dense population. Land was cleared, irrigation was often provided and colonists were offered food, seed-grain, animals and implements either as outright gifts or on credit, while for several years they were not required to pay taxes. It is notable that agricultural colonies and state farms still play an important role in the People's Republic today (Bray 1984: 95).

20 This account is based principally on the excellent study by Hamashima (1980).

21 This is a problem commonly associated with the commercialisation of subsistence economies in Asia today, and will be discussed further in chapter 4.

22 As well as for other tropical crops like rubber; see Chesneaux (1971) on the range of colonial exploitation in Vietnam.

23 Yields averaged 1.8 t/ha on single-cropped fields and 2.6 t/ha on double-cropped; these figures were in fact marginally higher than those for Tonkin or Annam, where the adverse effects of extreme subdivision of holdings and seasonal water shortages took their toll, even though cultivation methods were much more intensive (Henry and de Visme 1928: 52).

24 The canals provided only drainage, not true irrigation, so that rice cultivation was confined to the wet season; natural disasters, whether flood or drought, reduced average annual yields by about 25% (ibid.: 52).

25 This account is base on Afifuddin (1978: ch. 2).

26 Common in North China, Central Asia, South India and Northeastern Ceylon (Nakamura 1982: 5). Sometimes wells are linked in a very sophisticated fashion to conduct water over long distances from points where water is more easily accessible (Goblot 1979).

27 In Northeast China, where wells were the most usual source of water for irrigation, even cooperative wells provided water for only 25 to 30 *mu* (1.5 to 2 ha) (Gamble 1954: 155). In South India a single well irrigates on average 1.2 ha of rice-land (Bandara 1977: 95).

28 It is not easy to compile statistics on the areas involved, but the number and names of projects undertaken are easier to find, e.g. Furushima (1956: 229) on Japan from 1551 to 1867, and Perkins (1969: 333 ff) on China; the latter also attempts to deduce acreages.

Chapter 4   Rice and the wider economy

1 Contemporary studies in rice-growing regions of Southeast Asia consistently demonstrate that tenant farmers tend to farm more carefully and achieve higher yields than landowners (e.g. Gibbons et al. 1980: 122; Bray and Robertson 1980).

2 This interpretation is given by Elson (1978), who suggests that Geertz's concept of 'involution' requires revision in the light of the complementary nature of nineteenth-century regional economies in Java.

3 What follows is based on the field-notes which I compiled in 1976–7, plus some additional information acquired in interviews and conversations on subsequent visits.

4 In a study of the Green Revolution in Java, Montgomery (1981) affirms that it is improvements in rice cultivation which offer the greatest hopes of profitable labour absorption, but this would require very heavy investments in irrigation and land improvement which the Indonesian government is unlikely to find attractive.

5 On the concepts of agricultural underemployment and 'disguised unemployment' see, for example, Sen (1975), Stewart (1977) and Ishikawa (1981: 90 ff).

6 International exports were banned at this time, for the war against the northern nomads made it vital to ensure adequate supplies for the Chinese army (Shiba 1970: 50).

7 These figures were calculated by Mizuno from the *Statistical Pocketbook of Indonesia* 1977–8.

Chapter 5   Development

1 The recent work by Barker, Herdt and Rose (1985), which unfortunately appeared too late to be made use of here, treats contemporary development in Asia's rice economies in detail.

2 Lee (1979: 32) points out that deficiencies in sampling techniques, etc., throw doubt on this claim, but acknowledges a significant increase in rural incomes in the decade up to 1974, citing for example the IBRD study which estimated that between 1963 and 1972 there was an annual growth of real wages in manufacturing of 7.2%, the corresponding figure for agricultural wages being 6.5%.

3 Mainly by forbidding immigration to Edo or migration from one lord's jurisdiction to another (Smith 1959: 111).

4 See also chapter 3 and Hamashima (1980) on water control projects in the Yangzi Delta.

5 Especially in the case of China; see for example Beattie (1979: 135). Much more material is available for Japan, where farmers' ledgers, accounts and diaries survive, and farm budgets are cited in the reports of Tokugawa administrators (Furushima 1963; Smith 1959: 81; Toya 1949: 59; Yamazaki 1961).

6 Although the Chinese bureaucracy kept records of population figures from very early times their accuracy is often suspect. Among other problems of interpretation, under-registration was common since the population records were the basis of tax registers. However it does seem that during the two-and-a-half mainly peaceful and prosperous centuries of Ming rule (1368–1644) population growth was steady but linear, rather than exponen-

tial as it was to become later (Ho 1959: 23). In the case of Tokugawa Japan, it can be shown that although agricultural output expanded greatly between 1600 and the mid-nineteenth century, between 1720 and 1868 the population was nearly static (Smith 1977: 5).

7 Though even here it is only possible from the 1930s (Ishikawa 1981: 13).

8 An obvious solution would have been for Indonesia to use its own considerable oil resources to produce fertilisers domestically on a large scale. At the ASEAN summit held in Bali in 1976 it was decided to establish a urea plant in North Sumatra as one of four ASEAN industrial projects, and this plant opened in early 1984 (*Asia Yearbook 1984*:108).

9 For some idea of the variation, see Gray and Gray 1983; for a theoretical justification, see Lin Zili 1983.

10 An exception is to be found where labour hire is used among farmers of equally low economic status as a redistributive measure, for example in the *barrios* of Central Luzon studied by Takahashi, where landlords ruthlessly collected their debts out of the tenants' rice crops but did not touch their other income: under these conditions it was understood among tenant farmers that they would all hire labour from each other, minimising the use of household labour; furthermore, when they were obliged to use family labour they would pay themselves wages (1970: 141, 61).

11 Low yields were a significant factor in the low profitability of rice-farming in Kelantan, and Fujimoto suggests that there was clear scope for increasing incomes through a much more intensive use of fertilisers (1983: 147).

12 Fertiliser costs as a proportion of total rice production costs dropped from 29.65 in 1965 to 13.5 in 1979 (Matsuda 1982: 441).

13 In Korea mechanisation of rice-farming was until very recently chiefly restricted to such machinery as pumps, mills and threshers (Ban et al. 1980: 75), which allow the intensification of cropping and can thus be considered as land-substitutes. Even after a government drive to promote mechanisation under the Third Five-Year Plan (1972–6) there was still only 1 power-tiller to 29 families (ibid.: 190).

Chapter 6　Peasant, landlord and state: changes in relations of production

1 The terms 'peasant', 'peasantry' and 'peasant economy' have been defined in a number of ways; the common factors are that peasants are essentially household producers, and that they are subordinate to other classes within the state, to which they generally owe some form of tribute. Whether or not the concept of a specific 'peasant economy' (first formulated by Chayanov) has real analytical usefulness is much debated (e.g. Harriss 1982: 23–6).

2 One reason why Japanese social scientists and historians have devoted so much attention to the subject is that they feel that the small size of Japanese farms entails their high level of dependence upon communal irrigation and increasingly outdated 'irrigation customs', *suiri kankō*, which are regarded as a potent institutional obstacle to change.

3 As they undoubtedly were in Japan until the seventeenth century; see Grove and Esherick (1980) for a summary of the Chinese debate.

4 Men and women both own and inherit land, either in equal shares according to the traditional Malay *adat* laws, or in the proportion of 2 : 1 if Islamic law is followed. Parents usually give their children some of their share on marriage; the rest is inherited on the parent's death.

5 The following account is based on the meticulous account by Gerdin (1982).

6 A list of key texts can be found in Harriss (1982).

7 This is the argument put forward by Kautsky (Banaji 1980), and it applies very well on the whole to labour-intensive forms of agriculture.

8 See for example Muhammad Ikmal (1985: ch. 2) and Kahn (1980).

9 What Boeke (1955) termed a 'dualistic economy'.

10 Potter (1970) also believes that the strongest lineages emerged in rice-producing frontier zones, far from government control, where the only limits to the reclamation and irrigation of rice land were those imposed by competing lineages. However Pasternak (1969; 1972b), citing evidence from Taiwan, says that lineages were only established once the frontier zones had already been opened up; Meskill's (1979) study of the colonisation of Taiwan supports this view.

11 Of course many of the huge mechanised farms of the North American grain belt are also family enterprises.

12 The *jia* was a variable unit, but was standardised by the Japanese in 1895 at 0.9025 ha.

13 Although the postwar land reforms did constitute an obstacle to the large-scale concentration of management for some time, the Japanese government is now anxious to encourage various forms of rationalised and larger-scale farming.

Appendix A   The western model

1 In the USSR the virtues of 'rationalisation' were at first accepted without question, but it has subsequently become widely acknowledged that small private plots are much more productive than the *kolkhoz* (e.g. Wädekin 1975; Kerblay 1980).

2 Seed : yield ratios for wheat, barley and rye in Northern Europe in medieval times averaged 1 : 3 or 1 : 4 (Slicher van Bath 1963: 238); before the twelfth century 1 : 1.6 or 1 : 2 was more common (Mukhia 1981: 297). Although under modern conditions returns for wheat average 1 : 10 or more (Purseglove 1972: 294), at 3 to 4 t/ha the highest yields are still only about half the best yields of 7 t/ha which can be obtained for rice (Grist 1975: 485; Aziz 1978: 36).

3 The Romans had been familiar with green manures and the fertilising power of leguminous crops like vetch and alfalfa, but these did not gain any popularity in Northern Europe until the seventeenth and eighteenth centuries. Edible pulses such as peas and beans, appreciated for their high and reliable yields, first appear in rotations in the thirteenth and fourteenth centuries (Duby 1962: 183).

4 The rights to *vaine pâture* were still under dispute in France at the time of the Revolution (Moore 1967: 71).

5 Many improvements of the so-called Agricultural Revolution, such as scientific rotations (which increased the intensity of cropping) or more careful weeding, were labour-intensive (Chambers 1967: 112; Mingay 1977: 10).

Appendix B   The historical experience of China

1 Song population figures are quoted in numbers of households rather than individuals. The census of 1080, taken before the population had been driven south by nomadic invaders, put the population at 14.5 million households, of which 10 million lived in the southern provinces. By 1173, when Northern China was under foreign rule, the total population of both North and South China was 18.75 million households, of which 12 million lived in the south (Lewin 1973: 45).

2 Golas (1980: 295) estimates that the total area of cultivated land in about 1100 was 7 million *qing* (1 *qing* = approx. 6 ha), while the figure for 755, though probably overestimated, stood at 14 million *qing*, or roughly double the amount.

3 Illiterate, that is, by the standards of the educated elite. The level of functional literacy in pre-modern China, even in the countryside, seems to have been rather high (E. Rawski 1979: 13–17).

4 Often regarded by economists as a contract which minimises risks but stifles entrepreneurial ambitions (see Bray and Robertson 1980).

5 Similarly, while Geertz's description (1963) of the Javanese system as one of 'shared poverty' has been rejected on the grounds that clear divisions existed between village rich and poor, nonetheless landlords as well as tenants suffered reductions in income as the economy declined.

6 Based on the figures from the *Agricultural Yearbook of China 1980* given in Stone (1982: 212–13).

Appendix C   The Japanese experience

1 Between 1908 and 1970 the number of farms remained more or less constant, at just over 5 million, as did the average size. But during this period the number of farms in the middle range of 1.0 to 2.0 ha increased, showing a convergence towards medium-sized farms relying almost exclusively on family labour (Tsuchiya 1976: 85).

2 There has been a marked decentralisation of industry since 1945, providing opportunities for farming families to engage in commodity production: 'Since World War II there have been a number of instances of the formation of production regions in economically retarded farming areas where there had been no ways whereby local farmers could supplement their income. In

these cases, industries were attracted to the regions in question by a number of factors: relative stagnation in the agricultural sector combined with the creation of a labour surplus by mechanisation and rationalisation; the need to obtain cash to purchase farm machinery, agricultural chemicals and fertilisers; discontent of workers with the instability of being a migrant worker on construction projects far from home; and the desire of the local people to have the entire family work together at home' (Yamazaki 1980: 18).

References

ADB (Asian Development Bank) (1978): *Rural Asia: Challenge and Opportunity*, Praeger, New York and London.

Abel, W. (1935): *Agrarkrisen und Agrarkonjunktur in Mitteleuropa vom 13. bis zum 19. Jahrhundert*, Paul Parey, Berlin; tr. as *Agricultural Fluctuations in Europe*, Methuen, London, 1980.

Adas, Michael (1974): *The Burma Delta: Economic Development and Social Change on an Asian Rice Frontier, 1852–1941*, University of Wisconsin Press, Madison.

Afifuddin bin Haji Omar (1977): *Irrigation Structures and Local Peasant Organisation*, MADA, Alor Setar.

—— (1978): 'Peasants, institutions, and development in Malaysia: the political economy of development in the Muda region', MADA Monograph no. 36, Alor Setar (PhD diss., Cornell University).

Agricultural Bureau (1910): *Outlines of Agriculture in Japan*, Dept of Ag. and Commerce, Tokyo.

Alexander, Jennifer and Paul (1982): 'Shared poverty as ideology: agrarian relationships in colonial Java', *Man* 17, 4: 597–619.

Amano Motonosuke (1954): 'Chūgoku nōgyō no tenkai' [The development of Chinese agriculture], part 2 [3rd to 20th centuries], *Ajia Kenkyū* 1954, 2: 68–92.

—— (1979) *Chūgoku nōgyōshi kenkyū* [Researches into Chinese agricultural history], Ryukei Press, Tokyo (1st edn 1962).

American Rural Small-Scale Industry Delegation (1977): *Rural Small-Scale Industry in the People's Republic of China*, University of California Press, Berkeley.

Ash, Robert (1976): *Land Tenure in Pre-Revolutionary China: Kiangsu Province in the 1920s and 1930s*, Research Notes and Studies no. 1, Contemporary China Institute, SOAS, London.

Asia Yearbook 1984, Far Eastern Economic Review, Hong Kong.

Assoc. of the Japanese Agric. Science Societies (1975): *Rice in Asia*, University of Tokyo Press, Tokyo.

Aziz, Sartaj (1978): *Rural Development: Learning from China*, Macmillan, London.

Bacdayan, Albert S. (1980): 'Mountain irrigators in the Philippines', in Coward (1980): 172–85.

Baker, A. C., MCS, British Adviser, Kelantan (1936): *Annual Report on the Social and Economic Progress of the People of Kelantan for the Year 1935*, Cheong Fatt Press, Kelantan.

Baker, C. (1981): 'Economic reorganisation and the slump in South and Southeast Asia', *Comparative Studies in Social and Economic History* 23, 3: 325–49.

Ban, Sung Hwan, Pal Yong Moon and Dwight H. Perkins (1980): *Rural Development*, Studies in the Modernisation of the Republic of Korea: 1945–1975, Harvard University Press, Cambridge, Mass.

Banaji, Janius (1980): 'Summary of selected parts of Kautsky's *The Agrarian Question*', in Howard Newby and Frederick H. Buttel (eds), *The Rural Sociology of the Advanced Societies: Critical Perspectives*, Croom Helm London: 38–82.

Bandara, C. M. Madduma (1977): 'The prospects of recycling subsurface water for supplementary irrigation in the Dry Zone', in S. W. R. de A. Samarasinghe (ed.): *Agriculture in the Peasant Sector of Sri Lanka*, Peradeniya Ceylon Studies Seminar, Colombo: 87–99.

Barker, Randolph (1978): 'Yield and fertiliser input', in IRRI (1978): 35–66.

Barker, Randolph and Robert W. Herdt (1978): 'Equity implication of technology changes', in IRRI (1978): 83–108.

Barker, Randolph, Robert W. Herdt and Beth Rose (1985): *The Rice Economy of Asia*, Resources for the Future, Washington DC.

Barker, Randolph, Radha Sinha and Beth Rose (eds) (1982): *The Chinese Agricultural Economy*, Westview Press, Boulder, Colo; Croom Helm, London.

Barker, Randolph, Daniel G. Sisler and Beth Rose (1982): 'Prospects for growth in grain production', in Barker et al. (1982): 163–81.

Beardsley, R. K., J. W. Hall and R. E. Wade (1959): *Village Japan*, Phoenix Books, U. Chicago Press, Chicago and London; section on irrigation coops. repr. in Coward (1980): 127–52.

Beattie, Hilary J. (1979): *Land and Lineage in China: A Study of T'ung-ch'eng County, Anhwei, in the Ming and Ch'ing Dynasties*, Cambridge University Press, Cambridge.

Bell, Clive (1978): 'The future of rice padi monoculture in Malaysia', paper given in the *Symposium on the Viability of the Village in Contemporary Society*, Amer. Assoc. for the Advancement of Science, Washington, DC.

Benedict, P. K. (1967): 'Austro-Thai Studies, 3: Austro-Thai and Chinese', *Behavior Science Notebooks* 2: 275–336.

Berwick, E. J. H. (1951): 'Wet padi mechanical cultivation experiments, Kelantan, season 1950–51', *Malayan Agric. Journal* 34: 166–84.

Birowo, Achmad T. and Gary E. Hansen (1981): 'Agricultural and rural development: an overview', in Hansen (1981): 1–27.

Bishop, J. E., Acting British Adviser (1912): *Kelantan Administrative Report for the Year 1911*, Government Printing Office, Kuala Lumpur.

Bloch, Marc (1931): *Les caractères originaux de l'histoire rurale française*, Colin, Paris.

Boeke, J. H. (1955): *Economie van Indonesie*, H. D. Tjeek Willink, Haarlem.

Bonavia, David and Mary Lee (1985): 'Chen's last stand', *Far Eastern Economic Review* 3 October: 10–12.

Boserup, E. (1965): *The Conditions of Agricultural Growth: The Economics of Agrarian Change under Population Pressure*, Allen and Unwin, London.

—— (1981): *Population and Technology*, Basil Blackwell, Oxford.

Brandt, Vincent (1980): 'Local government and rural development', in Ban et al.: 260–82.

Bray, F. (1979): 'The Green Revolution: a new perspective', *Modern Asian Studies* 13, 4: 681–8.

—— (1980): 'Agricultural development and agrarian change in Han China', *Early China* 5: 1–13.

—— (1984): *Agriculture*, Vol. VI Part 2 in Joseph Needham, *Science and Civilisation in China*, Cambridge University Press, Cambridge.

—— (1985): 'Evolution in padi farming in Kelantan', in *Ouvrage collectif dédié à Lucien Bernot*, CNRS, Paris.

Bray, F. and A. F. Robertson (1980): 'Sharecropping in Kelantan, Malaysia', in G. Dalton (ed.), *Papers in Economic Anthropology* 3, JAI Press, Greenwich Conn.

Brenner, Robert (1982): 'Agrarian class structure and economic development in pre-industrial Europe: the agrarian roots of European capitalism', *Past and Present* 97: 16–114.

Brocheux, Pierre (1971): 'Les grands diên chu de la Cochinchine occidentale pendant la période coloniale', in Chesneaux et al. (1971): 147–63.

Brohier, R. L. (1934–5): *Ancient Irrigation Works in Ceylon*, 3 vols, Govt Press, Colombo.

Brook, T. (1981): 'The merchant network in 16th century China', *J. Economic and Social History of the Orient* 24, 2: 165–214.

—— (1982): 'The spread of rice cultivation and rice technology into the Hebei region in the Ming and Qing', in Li Guohao et al. (eds), *Explorations in the History of Science and Technology in China*, Chinese Classics Publishing House, Shanghai: 659–90.

Bruneau, Michel (1980): *L'organisation de l'espace dans le Nord de la Thaïlande*, Atelier Réproduction des Thèses, Université de Lille III (PhD diss., Paris IV, 1977).

Buck, J. L. (ed.) (1937): *Land Utilisation in China*, Commercial Press, Shanghai.

Buddenhagen, I. W. and G. J. Persley (eds) (1978): *Rice in Africa*, Academic Press, London.

Chambers, J. D. (1967): 'Enclosure and labour supply in the Industrial Revolution', in E. L. Jones (ed.), *Agriculture and Economic Growth in England 1650–1815*, Methuen, London: 94–127.

Chambers, Robert (1977): 'Challenges for rural research and development', in Farmer (1977): 398–412.

—— (1980): 'Basic concepts in the organisation of irrigation', in Coward (1980): 28–50.

Chan, Anita, Richard Madsen and Jonathan Unger (1984): *Chen Village: The Recent History of a Peasant Community in Mao's China*, University of California Press, Berkeley.

Chang, T. T. (1976a): 'The origin, evolution, cultivation, dissemination and diversification of Asian and African rices', *Euphytica* 25: 425–41.

—— (1976b): *Manual on Genetic Conservation of Rice Germ Plasm for Evaluation and Utilisation*, IRRI, Los Baños.

Charras, Muriel (1982): *De la forêt maléfique à l'herbe divine; la transmigration en Indonésie: les Balinais à Sulawesi*, Maison des Sciences de l'Homme, Paris.

Chaunu, Pierre (1979): *European Expansion in the Later Middle Ages*, North Holland Publishing Company, Amsterdam.

Chayanov, A. V. (1966): *The Theory of Peasant Economy*, Richard M. Irwin, Homewood, Ill. (1st Russian edn 1925).

Chen Fu nongshu [Agricultural Treatise, by Chen Fu], 1st edn 1149; repr. Zhonghua, Beijing, 1956.

Chen Liangzuo (1977): 'Woguo shuidao zaipei di jixiang jishu zhi fazhan ji qi zhongyaoxing' [The development of certain Chinese wet-rice cultivation techniques and their importance], *Shihuo yuekan* 7, 11: 537–46.

Chesneaux, J. (1971): 'L'implantation géographique des intérêts coloniaux au Vietnam et ses rapports avec l'économie traditionelle', in Chesneaux et al. (1971): 74–88.

Chesneaux, Jean, Georges Boudarel and Daniel Hémery (eds) (1971): *Tradition et révolution au Vietnam*, Editions Anthropos, Paris.

Chi, Ch'ao-ting (1936): *Key Economic Areas in Chinese History*, 2nd edn Paragon Reprint Corp., New York, 1963.

Chuan, Han-sheng and Richard A. Kraus (1975): *Mid-Ch'ing Rice Markets: An Essay in Price History*, East Asian Research Center, Harvard University Press, Cambridge, Mass.

Chūgoku Suirishi Kenkyūkai (ed.) (1981): *Chūgoku Suirishi Ronshū* [Collected essays on the history of water control in China], Kokusho Press, Tokyo.

Clifford, Sir Hugh (1895): 'Expedition to Trengganu and Kelantan', *Journal of the Malay Branch of the Royal Asiatic Society*, 34, 1 (May 1961): xi-162.

Coédès, G. (1948): *Les états hindouisés d'Indochine et d'Indonésie*, Brocard, Paris.

Colani, Madeleine (1940): *Emploi de la pierre en des temps reculés: Annam-Indonésie-Assam*, Publ. des Amis du Vieux Hué, Hanoi.

Collier, William L. (1981): 'Agricultural evolution in Java', in Hansen (1981): 147–73.

Condominas, G. and C. Gaudillot (*c*.1960): *Plaine de Vientiane: étude socio-économique*, Rapport d'études, 2 vol., Bureau pour le Développement de la Protection Agricole, Paris.

Cooper, J. P. (1978): 'In search of agrarian capitalism', *Past and Present* 80: 20–65.

Coward, J. Walter, Jr. (ed) (1980): *Irrigation and Agricultural Development in Asia: Perspectives from the Social Sciences*, Cornell University Press, Ithaca, NY.

Dasgupta, Biplab (1977): *Agrarian Change and the New Technology in India*, UNRISD, Geneva.

Davidson, J. (1975): 'Recent archaeological activity in Vietnam', *J. Hong Kong Arch. Society* 6: 80–100.

Delvert, Jean (1961): *Le paysan cambodgien*, Mouton, Paris/The Hague.

Ding Ying (ed.) (1961): *Zhongguo shuidao zaipei xue* [The cultivation of wet rice in China], Agriculture Press, Beijing.

—— (1964): 'Zhongguo shuidao pinzhong di shengtai leixing ji qi yu shengchan fazhan di guanxi' [An ecological classification of Chinese wet-rice varieties and their relation to the development of production], *Zhongguo nongye kexue* [Chinese Agronomy], no. 10.

Dobby, E. H. G. (1957): 'Padi landscapes of Malaya: Kelantan', *Malay J. of Tropical Agriculture* 10: i-42.

Dong Furen (1982): 'Relationship between accumulation and consumption', in Xu Dixin et al., *China's Search for Economic Growth*, New World Press, Beijing.

Donkin, R. A. (1979): *Agricultural Terracing in the Aboriginal New World*, University of Arizona Press, Tucson.

Dore, Ronald (1959): *Land Reform in Japan*, Oxford University Press, London.

—— (1969): 'Agricultural improvement in Japan 1870–1900', in E. L. Jones and S. J. Woolf (eds), *Agricultural Change and Economic Development: The Historical Problems*, Methuen, London.

Downs, Richard (1967): 'A Kelantanese village of Malaya', in Julian H. Steward (ed.), *Contemporary Change in Traditional Societies*, Vol. 2, *Asian Rural Societies*, University of Illinois Press, Urbana: 105–86.

Duby, G. (1962): *L'économie rurale et la vie des campagnes dans l'Occident médiéval*, 2 vols, Aubier, Paris.

Dumont, René (1957): *Types of Rural Economy*, Methuen, London.

—— (1983): *Albanie, Pologne, Nicaragua (Finis les lendemains qui chantent, vol. 1)*, Seuil, Paris.

—— (1984): *La Chine décollectivise (Finis les lendemains qui chantent, vol. 2)*, Seuil, Paris.

Eberhard, W. (1965): *Conquerors and Rulers: Social Forces in Medieval China*, Brill, Leiden.

Elson, R. E. (1978): 'The cultivation system and 'Agricultural Involution'', CSEAS Working Paper no. 14, Monash University.

Elvin, Mark (1973): *The Pattern of the Chinese Past*, Eyre Methuen, London.

—— (1978): 'Chinese cities since the Sung dynasty', in Abrams and Wrigley (eds), *Towns in Societies*, Cambridge University Press, Cambridge: 79–89.

Embree, J. F. (1946): *A Japanese Village: Suye Mura*, Kegan Paul, Trench and Trubner, London.

Ensor, Paul (1985): 'Loneliness is not the farmers' only problem', *Far Eastern Economic Review*, 18 July 1985: 69–71.

Erkes, E. (1953): *Die Entwicklung der chinesischen Gesellschaft von der Urzeit bis zur Gegenwart*, Proceedings of the Leipzig Academy of Science 100, 4, Akademie-Verlag, Berlin.

Ernle, Lord [R. E. Prothero] (1972): *English Farming Past and Present*, Benjamin Blom, New York (1st edn London, 1917).

Farmer, B. H. (ed) (1977): *Green Revolution? Technology and Change in Rice-Growing Areas of Tamil Nadu and Sri Lanka*, Macmillan, London.

—— (1981): 'The 'Green Revolution' in South Asia', *Geography* 66, 3: 202–7.

Farmer, B. H. et al. (1977): 'Setting the stage', in Farmer (1977): 7–19.

Farris, William Wayne (1985): *Population, Disease, and Land in Early Japan*, Harvard University Press, Cambridge, Mass.

Federation of Malaya (1953): *Report of the Rice Production Committee*, Kuala Lumpur.

Fei, Hsiao-t'ung (1939): *Peasant Life in China: A Field Study of Country Life in the Yangtze Valley*, Routledge, London.

Fei, Hsiao-t'ung & Chang Chih-i (1948): *Earthbound China: A Study of Rural Economy in Yunnan*, Routledge & Kegan Paul, London.

Feldman, M. and E. R. Sears (1981): 'The wild gene resources of wheat', *Scientific American* 1: 98–109.

Feyssal, P. de (1934): *L'endettement agraire en Cochinchine*, Hanoi.

Fforde, Adam (1983): 'The historical background to agricultural collectivisation in North Vietnam: the changing role of 'corporate' economic power', Birkbeck Discussion Paper no. 148, University of London.

—— (1984): 'Specific aspects of the collectivisation of wet-rice cultivation – reflections on Vietnamese experience', Birkbeck Discussion Paper no. 159, University of London.

Fischer, R. A. (1981): 'Development in wheat agronomy', in L. T. Evans and W. J. Peacock (eds), *Wheat Science – Today and Tomorrow*, Cambridge University Press, Cambridge: 249–70.

Fogg, Wayne (1983): 'The domestication of *Setaria italica* (L.) Beauv., a study of the process and origin of cereal agriculture in China', in D. Keightley (ed.), *The Origins of Chinese Civilisation*, University of California Press, Berkeley: 95–115.

Food and Fertiliser Technology Centre (1974): *Multiple Cropping Systems in Taiwan*, Taipei.

Forest, Alain (1980): *Le Cambodge et la colonisation française: histoire d'une colonisation sans heurts*, L'Harmattan, Paris.

Fortune, Robert (1857): *A Residence among the Chinese*, John Murray, London.

Francks, Penelope (1983): *Technology and Agricultural Development in Pre-War Japan*, Yale University Press, New Haven, Conn.

Fream, W. (1977): *Elements of Agriculture*, 15th edn, ed. D. H. Robinson, revised and metricated by N. F. McCann, John Murray, London.

Freedman, Maurice (1958): *Lineage Organisation in Southeastern China*, University of London, Athlone Press (repr. 1970).

—— (1966): *Chinese Lineage and Society: Fukien and Kwangtung*, University of London, Athlone Press (repr. 1971).

Freeman, C. (1977): 'Economics of research and development', in Spiegel-Rösing and Price (1977): 223–76.

Freeman, D. (1970): *Report on the Iban*, University of London, Athlone Press (1st edn Sarawak, 1955).

Fujimoto, Akimi (1976a): 'Rice operation and labour input among Malay peasants in Kelantan', *Japanese J. of Tropical Agriculture* 20, 1: 35–44.

—— (1976b): 'An economic analysis of peasant rice farming in Kelantan, Malaysia', *South East Asian Studies* 14, 2: 159–76.

—— (1977: 'The effects of farming techniques on rice yields: a case study in Kelantan Malaysia', *Kajian Ekonomi Malaysia* XIV, 1: 51–8.

—— (1983): *Income Sharing among Malay Peasants: A Study of Land Tenure and Rice Production*, Singapore University Press, Singapore.

Furushima Toshio (1954): 'Suiri shihai to nōgyō nōson shakai kenkei' [Control of irrigation and relations of agriculture and farming villages], in Ōtani Seizō (ed.), *Nōchi kaikaku*: I, 175–204.

—— (1956): *Nihon nōgyōshi* [A history of Japanese agriculture], Iwanami Zensho, Tokyo.

—— (1963): *Kinsei Nihon nōgyō no tenkai* [Agricultural development in the Tokugawa period], University of Tokyo Press, Tokyo.

Fussell, G. E. (1952): *The Farmer's Tools: 1500–1900*, Andrew Melrose, London.

Gaitskell, Arthur (1959): *Gezira: A Study of Development in the Sudan*, Faber and Faber, London.

Gallin, Bernard and Rita S. Gallin (1982): 'Socioeconomic life in rural Taiwan: twenty years of development and change', *Modern China* 8, 2: 205–46.

Gamble, Sidney D. (1954): *Ting Hsien: A North China Rural Community*, Stanford University Press, Stanford, Calif.

Geddes, W. R. (1976): *Migrants of the Mountains: The Cultural Ecology of the Blue Miao (Hmong Njua) of Thailand*, Clarendon Press, Oxford.

Geertz, C. (1963): *Agricultural Involution: The Processes of Ecological Change in Indonesia*, University of California Press, Berkeley.

Geertz, H. and C. Geertz (1975): *Kinship in Bali*, University of Chicago Press, Chicago.

Gehlen, Arnold (1965): 'Anthropologische Ansicht der Technik', in Hans Freyer et al. (ed.), *Technik im technischen Zeitalter*, Düsseldorf.

Gerdin, Ingela (1982): *The Unknown Balinese: Land, Labour and Inequality in Lombok*, Gothenburg Studies in Social Anthropology 4, Gothenburg.

Gibbons, David S., Rodolphe de Koninck and Ibrahim Hasan (1980): *Agricultural Modernisation, Poverty and Inequality: The Distributional Impact of the Green Revolution on Areas of Malaysia and Indonesia*, Gower Publ. Co., Westmead, Hampshire.

Goblot, Henri (1979): *Les qanats: une technique d'acquisition de l'eau*, Mouton, Paris.

Golas, Peter J. (1980): 'Rural China in the Song', *J. of Asian Studies* 39, 2: 291–325.

Gorman, C. (1977): 'A priori models and Thai prehistory: beginnings of agriculture', in C. A. Reed (ed.), *Origins of Agriculture*, Mouton, The Hague: 321–55.

Gourou, Pierre (1936): *Les paysans du delta tonkinois: étude de géographie humaine*, Mémoires de l'Ecole Française d'Extrême-Orient, Paris.

—— (1984): *Riz et civilisation*, Fayard, Paris.

Graham, W. A., H.S.M.'s Resident and Adviser (Siamese and Malay States) (1904): *Report on the State of Kelantan for the Year August 1903 to August 1904*, Bangkok.

Gray, Jack and Maisie (1983): 'China's new agricultural revolution', in Stephan Feuchtwang and Athar Hussain (eds), *The Chinese Economic Reforms*, Croom Helm, London: 151–84.

Grigg, D. B. (1980): *Population Growth and Agrarian Change: An Historical Perspective*, Cambridge University Press, Cambridge.

Grist, D. H. (1975): *Rice*, Longman, London (5th edn).

Groslier, B. P. (1974): 'Agriculture et religion dans l'Empire angkorien', *Etudes rurales* 53–6: *Agriculture et sociétés en Asie du Sud-Est*: 95–117.

—— (1979): 'La cité hydraulique angkorienne: exploitation ou surexploitation du sol', *Bull. de l'Ecole Française d'Extrême-Orient* LVXI: 161–202.

Grove, Linda and Joseph W. Esherick (1980): 'From feudalism to capitalism: Japanese scholarship on the transformation of Chinese rural society', *Modern China* 6, 4: 397–438.

Guangdong xinyu [New descriptions of Guangdong Province], by Qu Dajun, 1st ed. late seventeenth century, repr. Zhonghua, Hong Kong, 1974.

Gustafsson, J. E. (1984): *Water Resources Development in the People's Republic of China*, Royal Inst. of Technology, Dept of Land Improvement and Drainage, Stockholm.

Habermas, Jürgen (1971): *Towards a Rational Society*, Heinemann, London.

Hamashima, Atsutoshi (1980): 'The organisation of water control in the Kiangnan Delta in the Ming period', *Acta Asiatica* 38: 69–92.

Hanks, Lucien M. (1972): *Rice and Man: Agricultural Ecology in Southeast Asia*, Aldine Atherton, Chicago and New York.

Hanley, Susan B. and Kozo Yamamura (1977): *Economic and Demographic Change in Preindustrial Japan, 1600–1868*, Princeton University Press, Princeton, NJ.

Hansen, Gary E. (ed.) (1981): *Agriculture and Rural Development in Indonesia*, Westview Press, Boulder, Colo.

Hanson, Arthur J. (1981): 'Transmigration and regional land development', in Hansen (1981): 219–35.

Harlan, Jack R. (1980): 'Plant breeding and genetics', in Leo A. Orleans (ed.), *Science in Contemporary China*, Stanford University Press, Stanford, Calif.: 295–312.

Harriss, John (1977): 'Pahalagama: a case study of agricultural change in a frontier community', in Farmer (1977): 143–54.

—— (ed.) (1982): *Rural Development: Theories of Peasant Economy and Agrarian Change*, Hutchinson University Library, London.

Hart, Gillian and Saiful Huq (1982): 'Labour and agrarian change in Java and Bangladesh', preliminary report for the ILO, Dept of Economics, Boston University.

Hasan, P. (1976): *Korea: Problems and Issues in a Rapidly Growing Economy*, Johns Hopkins Press, Baltimore, Md.

Hauser, William B. (1974): *Economic Institutional Change in Tokugawa Japan: Ōsaka and the Kinai Cotton Trade*, Cambridge University Press, Cambridge.

Havens, Thomas R. H. (1974): *Farm and Nation in Modern Japan: Agrarian Nationalism, 1870–1940*, Princeton University Press, Princeton, NJ.

Hayami, Yujiro and Vernon W. Ruttan (1979): 'Agricultural growth in four countries', in Y.Hayami, V. W. Ruttan and H. M. Southworth (eds), *Agricultural Growth in Japan, Taiwan, Korea and the Philippines*, University Press of Hawaii, Honolulu: 3–26.

Haynes, A. S., MCS, British Adviser, Kelantan (1932): *Kelantan Administrative Report for the Year 1931*, Al-Asasiyah Press, Kelantan.

—— (1933): *Annual Report on the Social and Economic Progress of the People of Kelantan for the Year 1932*, Al-Asasiyah Press, Kelantan.

Henry, Yves (1932): *Economie agricole de l'Indochine*, Gouvernement Général de l'Indochine, Hanoi.

Henry, Yves and Maurice de Visme (1928): *Documents de démographie et riziculture en Indochine*, 2 vols, Gouvernement Général de l'Indochine, publ. by the *Bull. économique d'Indochine*, Hanoi.

Higham, C. F. W. (1984): 'Prehistoric rice cultivation in Southeast Asia', *Scientific American* 250, 4: 100–07.

Hill, A. H. (1951): 'Kelantan padi planting', *J. of the Malay Branch of the Royal Asiatic Society* 24, 1: 56–76.

Hill, R. D. (1977): *Rice in Malaya: A Study in Historical Geography*, Oxford University Press, Kuala Lumpur.

Ho, Ping-ti (1959): *Studies on the Population of China, 1368–1953*, Harvard University Press, Cambridge, Mass.

Hobsbawm, E. and G. Rudé (1968): *Captain Swing*, Pantheon, New York.

Hommel, R. P. (1937): *China at Work*, Bucks County Historical Society, Doylestown, Pa; repr. MIT Press, Cambridge, Mass., 1969.

Hong Pi-feng (1979): 'An outline of group farming experience in Taiwan', in Wong (1979a): 51–65.

Horii, Kenzo (1981): *Rice Economy and Land Tenure in West Malaysia: A Comparative Study of Eight Villages*, IDE Occasional Papers no. 18, Institute of Developing Economies, Tokyo.

Hou, Chi-ming and Tzong-shian Yu (eds) (1982): *Agricultural Development in China, Japan and Korea*, Academia Sinica, Taipei.

Huang, R. (1974): *Taxation and Government Finance in Sixteenth Century Ming China*, Cambridge University Press, Cambridge.

Huang, Shu-min (1981): *Agricultural Degradation: Changing Community Systems in Rural Taiwan*, University Press of America, Washington, DC.

ILO (1977): *Poverty and Landlessness in Rural Asia*, Geneva.

IRRI (1975): *Changes in Rice Farming in Selected Areas of Asia*, Vol. 1, Los Baños.

—— (1978): *Changes in Rice Farming in Selected Areas of Asia*, Vol. 2, Los Baños.

Ishii, Yoneo (ed.) (1978a): *Thailand: A Rice-Growing Society*, University Press of Hawaii, Honolulu.

—— (1978b): 'History and rice-growing', in Ishii (1978a): 15–39.

Ishikawa, Shigeru (1967): *Economic Development in Asian Perspective*, Kinokuniya Bookstore, Tokyo.

—— (1981): *Essays on Technology, Employment and Institutions in Economic Development: Comparative Asian Experience*, Kinokuniya Bookstore, Tokyo.

Japanese Academy (1980): *Meiji mae Nihon nōgyō gijutsu shi* [A history of Japanese agricultural technology before the Meiji Restoration], Noma Scientific and Medical Research Materials, Tokyo (1st edn 1964).

Jegatheesan, S. (1980): *Progress and Problems of Rice Mechanisation in Peninsular Malaysia*, MADA, Alor Setar.

Jones, E. L. (1981): *The European Miracle: Environment, Economies and Geopolitics in the History of Europe and Asia*, Cambridge University Press, Cambridge.

Jones, L. J. (1979): 'The early history of mechanical harvesting', *History of Technology* 4: 101–48.

Kahn, J. S. (1980): *Minangkabau Social Formations: Indonesian Peasants in the World Economy*, Cambridge University Press, Cambridge.

Kaida, Yoshihiro (1978): 'Irrigation and drainage: present and future', in Ishii (1978a): 205–45.

Kanazawa Natsuki (1971): *Inasaku nōgyō no ronri* [The logic of rice cultivation], Tokyo University Press, Tokyo.

Kano Tadao (1946): 'Cereals cultivated in Indonesia' [in Japanese], *Ethnology and Prehistoric Studies of Southeast Asia* 1: 278–95.

Keesing, Felix M. (1962): *The Ethnohistory of Northern Luzon*, Stanford University Press, Stanford, Calif.

Kelly, William W. (1982a): *Irrigation Management in Japan: A Critical Review of Japanese Social Science Research*, Cornell University East Asian Papers no. 30, Ithaca, NY.

—— (1982b): *Water Control in Tokugawa Japan: Irrigation Organisation in a Japanese River Basin, 1600–1870*, Cornell University East Asian Papers no. 31, Ithaca, NY.

Kerblay, Basile (1980): 'Peasant family economy in the USSR today', in E. J. Hobsbawm, Witold Kula, Ashok Mitra, K. N. Raj and Ignacy Sachs (eds), *Peasants in History: Essays in Honour of Daniel Thorner*, Sameeksha Trust, Oxford University Press, Calcutta: 69–82.

Kitamura Toshio (1950): *Nihon kangai suiri kanko no shiteki kenkyū – sōron hen* [Historical research on Japanese irrigation customs: general volume], Iwanami shoten, Tokyo.

de Koninck, Rodolphe (1978): 'A quoi sert la révolution verte? Notes sur la Malaysia et l'Indonésie', in Gordon P. Means (ed.), *The Past in Southeast Asia's Present*, Canadian Council for Southeast Asian Studies, Ottowa: 87–101.

—— (1981): 'Of rice, men, women and machines', paper presented at the Universiti Kebangsaan, Bangi, Selangor, Malaysia, 16–18 March.

Kubo, Yoshiharu (1979): 'The cooperative farming system in the mixed farming areas of Hokkaido, Japan', in Wong (1979a): 3–13.

Kula, Witold (1970): *Théorie économique du système féodal: pour un modèle de l'économie polonaise 16e-18e siècles*, Mouton, Paris (1st Polish edn 1962).

Kuroda Hideo (1983): 'Chūsei nōgyō gijutsu no yōsō' [Aspects of medieval agricultural technology], in Nagahara and Yamaguchi (1983): 43–76.

Kyuma, Kazutake (1978): 'Climate and rice-growing', in Ishii (1978a): 164–70.

Lardy, Nicholas R. (1984a): *Agriculture in China's Modern Economic Development*, Cambridge University Press, Cambridge.

—— (1984b): 'Consumption and living standards in China, 1978–83', *China Quarterly* 100: 849–65.

Layton, E. (1977): 'Conditions of technological development', in Spiegel-Rösing and Price (1977): 197–222.

Lê Thành Khôi (1955): *Le Viêt-nam, histoire et civilisation*, Edns de Minuit, Paris.

Leach, E. R. (1954): *Political Systems of Highland Burma: A Study of Kachin Social Structures*, LSE Monographs on Soc. Anth. no. 44, Athlone Press, London.

—— (1961): *Pul Eliya, a Village in Ceylon: A Study of Land Tenure and Kinship*, Cambridge University Press, Cambridge.

Lee, Eddy (1979): 'Egalitarian peasant farming and rural development: the case of South Korea', in Dharam Ghai, Azizur Rahman Khan, Eddy Lee and Samir Radwani (eds), *Agrarian Systems and Rural Development*, ILO/WEP Study, Macmillan, London: 24–71.

Lee, Ki-baik (1984): *A New History of Korea*, Ilchokak, Seoul.

Leonard, W. H. and J. H. Martin (1963): *Cereal Crops*, Macmillan, New York.

Levine, Gilbert (1980): 'The relationship of design, operation and management', in Coward (1980): 51–62.

Lewin, Günter (1973): *Die erste fünfzig Jahre der Song-Dynastie in China*, Akademie-Verlag, Berlin.

Lewis, Henry T. (1971): *Ilocano Rice Farmers: A Comparative Study of Two Philippine Barrios*, University of Hawaii Press, Honolulu.

Li Jiannong (1957): *Song Yuan Ming jingji shigao* [A draft economic history of the Song, Yuan and Ming dynasties], Sanlian Press, Beijing.

Liefrinck, F. A. (1886): 'Rice cultivation in Northern Bali', in J. van Baal (ed.) (1969), *Bali, Further Studies in Life, Thought and Ritual, Selected Studies on Indonesia* Vol. 8, W. van der Hoeve, The Hague: 1–74.

Lim Teck Ghee (1977): *Peasants and their Agricultural Economy in Colonial Malaya 1874–1941*, Oxford University Press, Kuala Lumpur.

Lim Teck Ghee, D. S. Gibbons, G. R. Elliston and Shukur Kassim (1981): *Land Tenure in the Muda Irrigation Area: Final Report*, part 1: *Methodology*; part 2: *Findings*, Centre for Policy Research, Universiti Sains Malaysia, Penang.

Lim Teck Ghee, D. S. Gibbons and Shukur Kassim (1980): 'Accumulation of padi land in the Muda region: some findings and thoughts on their implications for the peasantry and development', paper presented at the Universiti Kebangsaan, Bangi, Selangor, Malaysia, 26–9 May.

Lin Zili (1983): 'On the contract system of responsibility linked to production – a new form of cooperative economy in China's socialist agriculture', *Social Sciences in China* 1: 53–104.

Loekman Soetrisno (1982): 'The consequences of agricultural modernisation in

Java: experiences from below', paper presented at the conference on *Village-Level Modernisation: Livelihoods, Resources and Cultural Continuity*, ISEAS, Singapore, 21–4 June.

MADA (1980): 'Progress and present status of mechanisation in Muda', paper presented at the MARDI National Rice Conference, Selangor, Malaysia.

Mangahas, Mahar, Virginia A. Miralao and Romana P. de los Reyes, with the assistance of Normando de Leon (1976): *Tenants, Lessees, Owners: Welfare Implications of Tenure Change*, Ateneo de Manila University Press, Quezon City.

Mantra, Ida Bagus (1981): *Population Movement in Wet Rice Communities*, Gadjah Mada University Press, Yogyakarta, Indonesia.

Mao, Yu-kang (1982): 'Land reform and agricultural development in Taiwan', in Hou and Yu (1982): 723–58.

Maruyama, Eizo (1975): 'Rice cultivation and water balance in South-East Asia', in Assoc. Japanese Ag. Sci. Socs (1975): 225–47.

Marx, Karl (1976): *Capital*, Penguin, Harmondsworth.

Matsuda, Toshiro (1982): 'Recent developments of rice technology in Japan: an economic analysis', in Nōdai Research Institute (1982): 440–62.

McDermott, J. P. (1978): 'Land tenure and rural control in the Liangche region during the Southern Sung', PhD thesis, University of Cambridge.

Mendis, M. W. J. G. (1977): 'Spatial considerations in the economic development of the Mahaweli region', in S. W. R. de A. Samarasinghe (ed.), *Agriculture in the Peasant Sector of Sri Lanka*, Ceylon Studies Seminar, Peradeniya, Colombo: 13–20.

Meskill, Joanna Menzel (1979): *A Chinese Pioneer Family: The Lins of Wu-feng, Taiwan, 1729–1895*, Princeton University Press, Princeton, NJ.

Miao Qiyu (1960): 'Wu Yueh Qian Shi zai Taihu diju di yutian zhidu he shuili xitong' [The poldered fields regulation of Master Qian of Wu and Yueh in the Taihu Lake area and the classification of water control], *Agricultural History Research Anuual*, Beijing, 2: 139–58.

Mingay, G. E. (1977): *The Agricultural Revolution: Changes in Agriculture 1650–1880*, A. and C. Black, London.

Ministry of Finance, Malaysia (1980): *Economic Report 1980/81*, National Printing Dept, Kuala Lumpur.

Mitcham, Carl (1978): 'Types of Technology', *Research in Philosophy and Technology* 1.

Mitchell, B. R. (1974): 'Statistical Appendix', in C. Cipolla (ed.) (1976), *The Fontana Economic History of Europe, Contemporary Economies*, volume 2, Collins, London: 625–755.

Mizuno, Koichi (1978): 'The social organisation of rice-growing villages', in Ishii (1978a): 83–115.

Mizuno, Masami (1985): *Population Pressure and Peasant Occupations in Rural Central Java*, Occasional Papers no. 4, Centre of Southeast Asian Studies, University of Kent at Canterbury.

Moerman, M. (1968): *Agricultural Change and Peasant Choice in a Thai Village*, University of California Press, Berkeley.

Moise, Edwin E. (1983): *Land Reform in China and Vietnam,* University of North Carolina Press, Chapel Hill.

Mokhtar Tamin (1978): 'Rice self-sufficiency in West Malaysia: microeconomic implications', PhD thesis, Stanford University, Stanford, Calif.

Montgomery, Roger (1981): 'Employment generation within the agricultural sector', in Hansen (1981): 99–114.

Moon, Pal Yong (1982): 'Problems of organising joint utilisation of farm machinery in Korea's smallholding system', in Hou and Yu (1982): 195–228.

Moore, Barrington (1967): *Social Origins of Dictatorship and Democracy,* Penguin, Harmondsworth.

Morio, Mese (1982): 'Joint rice farming in Japan', in Nōdai Research Inst. (1982): 464–83.

Morita Akira (1974): *Shindai suirishi kenkyū* [Research on the history of water management in the Qing period], Aki shobo, Tokyo.

Motooka, Takeshi (1978): 'Rice exports and the expansion of cultivation', in Ishii (1978a): 272–334.

Mottura, G. and E. Pugliese (1980): 'Capitalism in agriculture and capitalistic agriculture', in F. H. Buttel and H. Newby (eds), *The Rural Sociology of the Advanced Societies,* Croom Helm, London: 171–99.

Moubray, G. A. de C., MCS, British Adviser, Kelantan (1937): *Annual Report on the Social and Economic Progress of the People of Kelantan for the Year 1936,* Cheong Fatt Press, Kelantan.

Muhammad Ikmal Said (1985): *The Evolution of Large Paddy Farms in the Muda Area, Kedah,* Siri Monograph no. 8, Centre for Policies Research, Universiti Sains Malaysia, Penang.

Muhly, J. D. (1981): 'The origins of agriculture and technology – West or East Asia? Summary of a conference on *The Origin of Agriculture and Technology,* Aarhus, Denmark, Nov. 21–25, 1978', *Technology and Culture* 22, 1: 125–45.

Mukhia, Harbans (1981): 'Was there feudalism in Indian history?' *Journal of Peasant Studies* 8, 3: 273–310.

Myers, Ramon H. (1982): 'Land property rights and agricultural development in modern China', in Barker et al. (1982): 37–47.

Nagahara Keiji and Yamaguchi Keiji (eds) (1983): *Nōgyō, nosankako* [Agriculture and agricultural processing], *Social History of Japanese Technology* I, Nihon Hyoronsha, Tokyo.

Nakamura, Hisashi (1972): 'Village community and paddy agriculture in South India', *Developing Economies* 10, 2: 141–65.

—— (1982): *Studies in Socio-Cultural Change in Rural Villages in Tiruchirapalli District, Tamilnadu, India,* no. 5, Institute for the Study of Languages and Cultures of Asia and Africa, Tokyo.

Nakamura, James I. (1966): *Agricultural Production and the Economic Development of Japan 1873–1922,* Princeton University Press, Princeton, NJ.

Nakamura Satoru (1959, 1960): 'Bakumatsuki Senshū ni okeru nōminsō no bunkai – Nihon shihonshugi seiritsu no kiso katei no kyūmei' [The disintegration of the peasantry in late Tokugawa Izumi: search for underlying processes of the rise of Japanese capitalism], *Rekishigaku kenkyū* 236 (Dec.

1959): 13–28; 237 (Jan. 1960): 29–34 [Abstract in Sumiya and Taira (1979: 100)].

Needham, Joseph (1974): 'The nature of Chinese society: a technical interpretation', University of Hong Kong Gazette XXIII, 5 part 2.

Needham, Joseph and Wang Ling (1965): *Science and Civilisation in China*, Vol. IV, part 2: *Mechanical Engineering*, Cambridge University Press, Cambridge.

Needham, Joseph, Lu Gwei-Djen and Wang Ling (1971): *Science and Civilisation in China*, Vol. IV, part 3: *Civil Engineering and Nautics*, Cambridge University Press, Cambridge.

Neveux, H. (1975): 'Déclin et reprise: la fluctuation biséculaire 1330–1560', in E. Le Roy Ladurie (ed.), *L'âge classique des paysans, Histoire de la France rurale* Vol. II, Seuil, Paris.

Nickum, James E. (1980): 'Local water management in the People's Republic of China', in Coward (1980): 289–98.

—— (1981): *Water Management Organisation in the People's Republic of China*, Sharpe, New York.

Nishioka Hiroaki (1981): 'Sōdai Sushū ni okeru urato kanri to kakoda kōchiku' [The management of creeks and construction of dyked fields in Suzhou in the Song dynasty], in Chūgoku Suirishi (1981): 121–54.

Nishiyama Buichi (1959): 'Chūgoku ni okeru suito nōgyō no hattatsu' [The development of wet-rice cultivation in China], *Nōgyō Sōgo Kenkyū* 3, 1: 135–9.

Nōdai Research Institute (1982): *Proceedings of a Seminar on Agricultural Research and Education in Asia, 26–31 October 1981*, Tokyo University of Agriculture.

Nōgu benri ron [Treatise on useful farm tools], by Ōgura Nagatsune, 1st edn 1822.

Nōgyō zensho [Collected writings on agriculture], by Miyazaki Yasusada, 1st edn 1697.

Nongzheng quanshu [Complete treatise on agricultural administration], by Xu Guangqi, 1st edn 1639; re-ed. with commentaries by Shi Shenghan, 2 vols, Guji Press, Shanghai, 1979.

OECD (1985): *Agriculture in China: Prospects for Production and Trade*, Paris.

Ofreneo, Réné E. (1980): *Capitalism in Philippine Agriculture*, Foundation for Nationalist Studies, Quezon City.

Ogura, Takekazu (ed.) (1967): *Agricultural Development in Modern Japan*, Fuji Publishing Co., Tokyo.

—— (1980): *Can Japanese Agriculture Survive?*, Agricultural Policy Research Centre, Tokyo.

Ohkawa, Kazushi and Henry Rosovsky (1960): 'The role of agriculture in modern Japanese economic development', *Economic Development and Cultural Change* 9, 1 part 2: 43–67.

Oka, Hiko-ichi (1975a): 'The origins of cultivated rice and its adaptive evolution', in Assoc. Japanese Ag. Sci. Socs. (1975): 21–34.

—— (1975b) 'Floating rice, an ecotype adapted to deep-water paddies – a review from the viewpoint of breeding', in Assoc. Japanese Ag. Sci. Socs. (1975): 277–87.

242 *References*

Ooi Jin-bee (1966): 'Some aspects of peasant farming in Malaya', *Tijdschrift voor economische en sociale geographie*, The Hague, 56, 5: 170–85.

Palmer, Ingrid (1977): *The New Rice in Indonesia*, UNRISD, Geneva.

Pasternak, Burton (1969): 'The role of the frontier in Chinese lineage development', *Journal of Asian Studies* 28: 551–61.

—— (1972a): 'The sociology of irrigation: two Taiwanese villages', in W. E. Willmott (ed.), *Economic Organisation in Chinese Society*, Stanford University Press, Stanford, Calif.: 193–214.

—— (1972b): *Kinship and Community in Two Chinese Villages*, Stanford University Press, Stanford, Calif.

Peletz, Michael G. (1983): 'Moral and political economies in rural Southeast Asia', *Journal of Comparative Studies in Society and History* 25, 4: 731–9.

Perkins, Dwight H. (1969): *Agricultural Development in China, 1368–1968*, Edinburgh University Press, Edinburgh.

Popkin, Samuel L. (1979): *The Rational Peasant: The Political Economy of Rural Society in Vietnam*, University of California Press, Berkeley.

Potter, Jack M. (1970): 'Land and lineage in traditional China', in M. Freedman (ed.), *Family and Kinship in Chinese Society*, Stanford University Press, Stanford, Calif.: 121–38.

—— (1976): *Thai Peasant Social Structure*, University of Chicago Press, Chicago.

Purcal, J.T.(1972): *Rice Economy: Employment and Income in Malaysia*, East-West Centre Press, Honolulu.

Purseglove, J. W. (1972): *Tropical Crops: Monocotyledons*, Longman, London.

RID (Royal Irrigation Dept of Thailand) (1957): *The Greater Chao Phraya Project*, Bangkok.

Raffles, Thomas Stamford (1817): *The History of Java*, 2 vols, London; repr. Oxford University Press, Kuala Lumpur, 1978.

Raikes, R. (1967): *Water, Weather and Prehistory*, London.

Rapp, Friedrich (1985): 'The philosophy of technology: a review', *Interdisciplinary Science Reviews* 10, 2: 126–39.

Ravenstone, Piercy (1824): *Thoughts on the Funding System and its Effects*, London.

Rawski, Evelyn Sakakida (1972): *Agricultural Change and the Peasant Economy of South China*, Harvard University Press, Cambridge, Mass.

—— (1979): *Education and Popular Literacy in Ch'ing China*, University of Michigan Press, Ann Arbor.

Rawski, Thomas G. (1979): *Economic Growth and Employment in China*, World Bank/Oxford University Press, London.

Reed, C. A. (1977): 'Origins of agriculture: discussion and some conclusions', in C. A. Reed (ed.), *Origins of Agriculture*, Mouton, The Hague: 879–956.

Reed, Edward (1979): 'Two approaches to cooperation in rice production in South Korea', in Wong (1979a): 14–36.

de Reinach, Lucien (1952): *Le Laos*, 2nd edn, Guilmoto, Paris.

Robequain, Charles (1939): *L'évolution économique de l'Indochine française*, Centre d'Etudes de Politique Etrangère, P. Hartmann, Paris.

Sahai, Sachchidanand (1970): *Les institutions politiques et l'organisation adminis-trative du Cambodge ancien (VIe – XIIIe siècles)*, Publn de l'Ecole Française d'Extrême-Orient vol. LXXV, Adrien-Maisonneuve, Paris.

Sahara Makoto (forthcoming): 'Recent research on the Yayoi culture'.

Salomon, Jean-Jacques (1984): 'What is technology? The issue of its origins and definitions', *History and Technology* 1, 2: 113–56.

Sasaki Komei (1971): *Inasaku izen* [Before rice cultivation], NHK Books, Tokyo.

Scott, James C. (1976): *The Moral Economy of the Peasant: Rebellion and Subsistence in Southeast Asia*, Yale University Press, New Haven, Conn.

Sen, Amartya (1975): *Employment, Technology and Development*, Clarendon Press, Oxford.

Shand, R. T. and Mohd Ariff Hussein (1983): *A Socio-Economic Analysis of the Kemubu Project*, Part II, Universiti Pertanian Malaysia, Serdang.

Shanin, Teodor (1972): *The Awkward Class: Political Sociology of Peasantry in a Developing Society, Russia 1910–1925*, Clarendon Press, Oxford.

Shaw, G. E., Acting British Adviser (1926); *Kelantan Administrative Report for the Year 1925*, Government Printing Office, Singapore.

Shen Baixian, Zhang Guangcai et al. (1979): *Zhonghua shuili shi* [A history of water control in China], Commercial Press, Taipei.

Shen, T. H. (1951): *Agricultural Resources of China*, Cornell University Press, Ithaca, NY.

Shenshi nongshu [Treatise on agriculture by Master Shen], mid-seventeenth century, repr. in Chhen Hengli and Wang Dacan, *Bunongshu yanjiu* [Researches on the Agricultural treatise by Master Shen and its expanded (eighteenth-century) version], Zhonghua Press, Peking, 1958.

Shiba Yoshinobu (tr. and ed. Mark Elvin) (1970): *Commerce and Society in Sung China*, Michigan University Press, Ann Arbor.

Shimpo, Mitsuro (1976): *Three Decades in Shiwa: Economic Development and Social Change in a Japanese Farming Community*, University of British Columbia Press, Vancouver.

Shue, Vivienne (1980): *Peasant China in Transition: The Dynamics of Development towards Socialism*, University of California Press, Berkeley.

Slicher van Bath, B. H. (1963): *The Agrarian History of Western Europe AD 500–1850*, Edward Arnold, London.

Smith, Thomas C. (1959): *The Agrarian Origins of Modern Japan*, Stanford University Press, Stanford, Calif.

Smith, Thomas C. (with Robert Y. Eng and Robert T. Lundy) (1977): *Nakahara: Family Farming and Population in a Japanese Village, 1717–1830*, Stanford University Press, Stanford, Calif.

Song Yingxing (tr. E.-T. Z. Sun and S.-C. Sun) (1966): *T'ien-kung k'ai-wu: Chinese Technology in the Seventeenth Century*, Pennsylvania State University Press, University Park and London (1st Chinese edn 1637).

Speare, Alden (1981): 'Rural and urban migration: a national overview', in Hansen (1981): 202–18.

Spencer, J. E. (1974): 'La maîtrise de l'eau en Asie du Sud-Est', *Etudes rurales* 53–6: *Agriculture et societe en Asie du Sud-Est*: 73–94.

Spiegel-Rösing, Ina and Derek de Solla Price (eds) (1977): *Science, Technology and Society: A Cross-Disciplinary Perspective*, Sage Publications, London.

Stargardt, Janice (1983): *Satingpra I: The Environmental and Economic Archaeology of South Thailand*, Studies in Southeast Asian Archaeology I, Inst. of Southeast Asian Studies (Singapore), BAR International Series 158, Oxford.

Stavis, Benedict (1978): *The Politics of Agricultural Mechanisation in China*, Cornell University Press, Ithaca, NY.

Steward, Julian H. (1980): 'Initiation of a research trend: Wittfogel's irrigation hypothesis', in G. L. Ulman (ed.) (1980), *Society and History: Essays in Honor of K. A. Wittfogel*, Morton, New York.

Stewart, Frances (1977): *Technology and Underdevelopment*, Macmillan, London.

Stoler, Anne L. (1981): 'Garden use and household economy in Java', in Hansen (1981): 242–54.

Stone, Bruce (1982): 'The use of agricultural statistics: some national aggregate examples and current state of the art', in Barker et al. (1982): 205–46.

Sumiya, Mikio and Koji Taira (eds) (1979): *An Outline of Japanese Economic History 1603–1940: Major Works and Research Findings*, University of Tokyo Press, Tokyo.

Suo shan nongpu [A survey of the agriculture of Shuttle Mountain] by Liu Yingtang, 1st edn 1717, repr. Agriculture Press, Beijing, 1960.

Swaminathan, M. S. (1984): 'Rice', *Scientific American* 250, 1: 62–71.

Tada, Hirokazu (forthcoming): 'British engineers' apprenticeship in irrigation technology: the restoration of old canals in North India, 1810–1840s'.

Tadem, Eduardo (1978): 'Peasant land rights and the Philippine corporate farming program', *Philippine Social Sciences and Humanities Revue* 42, 1–4: 56–76.

Taillard, Christian (1972): 'Introduction à l'étude des berges de la Nan Ngum et du Mekong', *Asie du Sud-Est et Monde Insulindien* 3, 2: 195–233.

Takahashi, Akira (1970); *Land and Peasants in Central Luzon*, East-West Center Press, Honolulu.

Takaya, Yoshikazu (1978): 'Landform and rice-growing', in Ishii (1978a): 171–91.

Tamaki, Akira (1977): *The Development Theory of Irrigation Agriculture*, Special Papers no.7, Institute of Developing Economies, Tokyo.

—— (1979): *Mizu no shisō* [The philosophy of water], Ronso, Tokyo.

Tamaki Akira and Hatade Isao (1974): *Fūdo: daichi to ningen no rekishi* [Climate: the earth and human history], Heibonsha, Tokyo.

Tanabe, Shigeharu (1978): 'Land reclamation in the Chao Phraya Delta', in Ishii (1978a): 40–83.

Tanaka Yoshiaki (1983): 'Kodai nōgyō no gijutsu to tenkai' [The techniques and development of ancient agriculture], in Nagahara and Yamaguchi (1983): 7–42.

Tang, Anthony M. (1979): 'China's agricultural legacy', *Economic Development and Cultural Change* 28, 1: 1–22.

Tangshuang pu [Monograph on sugar], by Wang Shao; 1st edn 1154, repr. Beijing, 1956.

Tani, Tatsuo (1975): 'General status of rice storage in Southeast Asia', in Assoc. of Japanese Ag. Sci. Socs. (1975): 514–22.

Taylor, Donald C. (1981): *The Economics of Malaysian Paddy Production and Irrigation*, The Agriculture Development Council, Bangkok.

Thorp, James (1937): 'Soils', in Buck (1937): 130–61.

Toya Toshiyuki (1949): *Kinsei nōgyō keiei shi ron* [The history of farm management in the Tokugawa period], Tokyo (see Smith 1959: 81).

Tsuchiya, Keizo (1976): *Productivity and Technological Progress in Japanese Agriculture*, University of Tokyo Press, Tokyo.

Tsukuba Hisaharu (1980): 'Inasaku' [Rice cultivation], in Japanese Academy (1980): 29–126.

Twitchett, D. C. (1960): 'Documents on clan administration I: The rules of administration of the charitable estate of the Fan Clan', *Asia Major* 8, 1: 1–35.

—— (1970): *Financial Administration under the T'ang Dynasty*, 2nd edn, Cambridge University Press, Cambridge.

UN (ECAFE) (1950): *Flood Damage and Flood Control Activities in Asia and the Far East*, Flood Control Series no. 1, Bangkok.

Umemura, Mataji (1970): 'Agriculture and labour supply in the Meiji era', in Kazushi Ohkawa, Bruce F. Johnston and Hiromitsu Kaneda (eds), *Agriculture and Economic Growth*, Princeton University Press, Princeton, NJ: 21–6.

Vaidyanathan, A. (1983): *Water Control Institutions and Agriculture: A Comparative Perspective*, Working Paper no. 178, Centre for Development Studies, Trivandra, Kerala.

VanderMeer, Canute (1980): 'Changing local patterns in a Taiwanese irrigation system', in Coward (1980): 225–62.

Vander Velde, Edward J, (1980): 'Local consequences of a large-scale irrigation system in India', in Coward (1980): 299–328.

van Setten van der Meer, N. C. (1979): *Sawah Cultivation in Ancient Java*, Oriental Monographs no. 22, ANU Press, Canberra.

Vavilov, N. I. (1949): *The Origin, Variety, Immunity and Breeding of Cultivated Plants*, tr. K. Starr Chester, *Chronica Botanica* vol. 13, Waltham, Mass.

Venkayya, V. (1906): 'Irrigation in Southern India in ancient times', *Archaeological Survey of India, Annual Report 1903–4*, Calcutta: 205–11.

Vermeer, E. B. (1977): *Water Conservancy and Irrigation in China: Social, Economic and Agro-Technical Aspects*, Leiden University Press, Leiden.

Vishnu-Mittre (1974): 'The beginnings of agriculture: palaeobotanical evidence from India', in J. Hutchinson (ed.), *Evolutionary Studies on World Crops: Diversity and Change in the Indian Subcontinent*, Cambridge University Press, Cambridge: 3–33.

—— (1977) 'Changing economy in ancient India', in C. A. Reed (ed.), *The Origins of Agriculture*, Mouton, The Hague: 569–88.

Wade, Robert (1982): *Irrigation and Agricultural Politics in South Korea*, Westview Press, Boulder, Colo.

Wädekin, Karl-Eugen (1975): 'The Soviet *kolkhoz*: vehicle of cooperative farming or of control and transfer of capital resources', in Peter Dorner (ed.),

Cooperative and Commune: Group Farming in the Economic Development of Agriculture, University of Wisconsin Press, Madison: 95–116.

Walker, Kenneth R. (1984): 'Chinese agriculture during the period of readjustment, 1978–83', *China Quarterly* 100: 783–812.

Wang, S. H. and R. Apthorpe (1974): *Rice Farming in Taiwan: Three Village Studies*, Institute of Ethnology, Academia Sinica, Taipei.

Wang Zhen nongshu [Treatise on agriculture], by Wang Zhen, 1st edn 1313, Imperial edition 1783, Beijing (also modern repr. Nongye Press, Beijing, 1981).

Waswo, A. (1977): *Japanese Landlords: The Decline of a Rural Elite*, University of California Press, Berkeley.

Watabe, Tadayo (1967): *Glutinous Rice in Northern Thailand*, Monograph of the Centre of Southeast Asian Studies, Kyoto University, University Press of Hawaii, Honolulu.

—— (1977): *Ine no rōdo* [Rice road], NHK, Tokyo.

—— (1978): 'The development of rice cultivation', in Ishii (1978a): 3–14.

Watson, Andrew (1984): 'Agriculture looks for 'shoes that fit'', in Neville Maxwell and Bruce Macfarlane (eds), *China's Changed Road to Development*, Pergamon, Oxford: 83–108.

Watson, J. L. (1975): *Emigration and the Chinese Lineage: The Mans in Hong Kong and London*, University of California Press, Berkeley.

Wertheim, W. F. and M. Stiefel (1982): *Production, Equality and Participation in Rural China*, UNRISD, Geneva.

Whang, In-Joung (1981): *Management of Rural Change in Korea: the Saemaul Undong*, Seoul National University Press, Seoul.

Wheatley, Paul (1965): 'Agricultural terracing', *Pacific Viewpoint* 6: 123–44.

White, Benjamin (1976): 'Population, involution and employment in rural Java', *Development and Change* 7: 267–90.

Whyte, R. O. (1974): *Rural Nutrition in Monsoon Asia*, Oxford University Press, Kuala Lumpur.

Wiens, Thomas (1980): 'Agricultural statistics in the People's Republic of China', in A. Eckstein (ed.), *Quantitative Measures of China's Economic Output*, University of Michigan Press, Ann Arbor.

Wijeyewardene, Gehan (1973): 'Hydraulic society in contemporary Thailand', in Robert Ho and E. C. Chapman (eds), *Studies of Contemporary Thailand*, ANU Press, Canberra: 89–110.

Will, Pierre-Etienne (1980): *Bureaucratie et famine en Chine au 18e siècle*, Mouton/EHESS, Paris.

Wittfogel, Karl (1931): *Wirtschaft und Gesellschaft Chinas: Versuch der wissenschaft-lischen Analyse einer grossen asiatischen Agrargesellschaft*, Hirschfeld, Leipzig.

—— (1957): *Oriental Despotism: A Study in Total Power*, Yale University Press, New Haven, Conn.

Wong, John (1971): 'Peasant economic behaviour: the case of traditional agricultural cooperation in China', *Developing Economies* 9, 3.

—— (1973): *Land Reform in the People's Republic of China: Institutional Transformations in Agriculture*, Praeger, New York.

—— (ed.) (1979a): *Group Farming in Asia*, Singapore University Press, Singapore.

—— (1979b): 'The group farming system in China: ideology versus pragmatism', in Wong (1979a): 89–103.

—— (1982): *Labour Mobilisation in the Chinese Commune System: A Perspective from Guangdong*, ILO-ARTEP, Bangkok.

Woodard, David (1805): *The Narrative of Captain David Woodard and Four Seamen, who lost their ship while in a boat at sea, and surrendered themselves up to the Malays in the Island of Celebes*, 2nd edn, Johnson, London.

Wuhan Hydroelectric Institute (1979): *Zhongguo shuili shigao* [A brief history of water control in China], 2 vols, Hydroelectric Press, Beijing.

Wurfel, David (1977): 'Philippine agrarian policy today: implementation and political impact', ISEAS Occasional Paper no. 46, Singapore.

Yamada, Noboru (1975): 'Technical problems of rice production in tropical Asia', in Assoc. Japanese Ag. Sci. Socs. (1975): 170–201.

Yamamura, Kozo (1979): 'Pre-industrial landholding patterns in Japan and England', in Albert M. Craig (ed.), *Japan: a Comparative View*, Princeton University Press, Princeton, NJ.

Yamazaki, Mitsuru (1980): *Japan's Community-Based Industries: A Case-Study of Small Industry*, Asian Productivity Organisation, Tokyo.

Yamazaki Ryūzō (1961): 'Settsu mensaku nōson ni okeru ichi funō keiei no bunseki' [Farm management in cotton-growing villages of Settsu: the case of a rich peasant household], in idem, *Jinushisei seiritsuki no nōgyō kōzō* [Early landlordism and the structure of agriculture], Aoki Shoten, Tokyo: 130–238 (abstract in Sumiya and Taira 1979: 102).

Yang Shiting (1978): 'On the remains of cultivated rice discovered at Shixia, Guangdong' [in Chinese], *Wenwu* 7: 23–8.

Yangzi Region Planning Commission (1979): *Changjiang shuili shilüe* [A brief history of water control in the Yangzi], Irrigation and Hydroelectricity Press, Beijing.

You Xiuling (1979): 'A preliminary discussion of the origins, diversification and dissemination of rice cultivation in China, based on the archaeological rice remains from Hemudu' [in Chinese], *Acta Agronomica Sinica* 5, 3: 1–10.

Zangheri, R. (1969): 'The historical relationship between agricultural and economic development in Italy', in E. L. Jones & S. J. Woolf (eds), *Agrarian Change and Economic Development: The Historical Problems*, Methuen, London: 23–39.

Zeng Xiangxu (1902): *Nongxue zuanyao* [The essentials of agronomy], Sichuan, China.

Zhejiang CPAM (1976): 'Reconnaissance of the neolithic site at Hemudu in Yuyao County, Zhejiang Province' [in Chinese], *Wenwu* 8: 6–27.

—— (1978): 'First season excavations at Hemudu, Yuyao County, Zhejiang Province' [in Chinese], *Kaogu xuebao* 1: 39–94.

Zhejiang Provincial Museum (1978): 'A study and identification of the animal and plant remains unearthed at Hemudu' [in Chinese], *Kaogu xuebao* 1: 95–107.

Glossary

bendang: wet-rice field (Malay, used in Northern Malay States)

bund: low earthen dyke around a wet-rice field

conduit: a channel through which water is conveyed

corvée labour: free labour services owed by the individual to his feudal superior or to the state

cusec: cubic metres per second (measure of water-flow)

dibble: to sow seeds individually in pockets in the soil

extension: technical instruction given to farmers by officers directly or indirectly involved in R & D

flume: an inclined channel for conveying water

GMP: 'guaranteed minimum price'

gabion: a bamboo basket filled with stones, used in the construction of dams, weirs, etc.

Green Revolution: technological 'package' of agricultural improvements first introduced to Asian countries in the 1960s

HYV: high-yielding variety

hard-pan or clay-pan: the hard, impervious layer of ferrous soil which forms under the top layer of mud in a wet-rice field and prevents seepage

IRRI: International Rice Research Institute (Los Banos, Philippines)

KADA: Kemubu Agricultural Development Authority (Kemubu Irrigation Scheme, Kelantan, Malaysia)

kampong: village, or the dry land upon which a village stands (Malay)

krah: corvée labour (Malay)

kumiai: Japanese cooperative groups, especially *suiri kumiai*, irrigation associations

lodge: to bend and fall, of cereals with weak or over-long stems

MADA: Muda Agricultural Development Authority (Muda Irrigation Scheme, Kedah, Malaysia)

New Technology: the 'package' associated with the Green Revolution, including HYVs, chemical fertilisers, etc.

night-soil: human faeces, widely used as manure in East Asia

nōkai: Japanese farmers' associations

noria or 'Persian wheel': a large wheel with buckets around the rim used to raise water

padi/paddy: general term for growing or unhusked rice (Malay in origin)

panicle: a multiple-branching inflorescence, or seed-head, as in rice, millet

pericarp: the tough membrane surrounding the inner grain

polder: large earthen dyke used to encircle land and so to reclaim it from marshes or lakes

square-pallet chain-pump: a small wooden water-pump, often portable, operated with the feet

R & D: Research and Development

reaping-knife: small shafted knife used for cutting individual panicles of rice

sawah: wet-rice field (Malay, used in peninsula and archipelago)

sluice: a device for letting water in or out

subak: Balinese irrigation society

swape: a well-sweep, a bucket on a pivoted pole used for raising water

swidden: shifting cultivation, slash-and-burn agriculture

tank: a small reservoir

tillering: the growth of multiple shoots around the main stem of a plant

Index